FINANCIAL
SUPPLY CHAIN

FINANCIAL SUPPLY CHAIN

Sanjay Dalmia
CEO, CashTech
Pune

Best Compliments

Sanjay Dalmia

Tata McGraw-Hill Publishing Company Limited
NEW DELHI

McGraw-Hill Offices

New Delhi New York St Louis San Francisco Auckland Bogotá Caracas
Kuala Lumpur Lisbon London Madrid Mexico City Milan Montreal
San Juan Santiago Singapore Sydney Tokyo Toronto

Tata McGraw-Hill

Published by Tata McGraw-Hill Publishing Company Limited,
7 West Patel Nagar, New Delhi 110 008.

ISBN (13): 978-0-07-065666-6
ISBN (10): 0-07-065666-5

Head—Professional and Healthcare: *Roystan La'Porte*
Publishing Manager: *R Chandra Sekhar*
Manager—Sales & Marketing: *Girish Srinivasan*

Controller—Production: *Rajender P Ghansela*
Asst. General Manager—Production: *B L Dogra*

Typeset at Bukprint India, B-180A, Guru Nanak Pura, Laxmi Nagar, Delhi-110 092 and printed at Ram Book Binding House, C-114, Okhla Industrial Area, Phase-I, New Delhi 110 020

Cover Design: Kapil Gupta, Delhi

Cover Printer: SDR

RZXYCRBYRYXBD

To
My tireless spirit—gifted to me by my parents.

Reena, Vidhi and Koyna—your care, support and love which I must proclaim.

Preface

Currently, there is a considerable excitement around advancements in Financial Supply Chain, as the monies estimated to be locked up in working capital due to inefficient operations are of gargantuan proportions—in hundreds of billion dollars—and the benefits of achieving efficiencies, through fine tuning these operations, is estimated to be proportionately vast. The substantial growth in the power of computing and maturity of the Information Technology (IT) sector provide the impetus for achieving these benefits. Not surprisingly, the trickle of activities—which started in early nineties—has now gathered momentum and promises to reach a crescendo in the coming decade. This is evident from the presence of a large number and a variety of early pioneers, working together and independently, attempting to make a mark in the space!

However, while there are early indications that successful advancements and automation in financial supply chain would be experienced in the coming decade and that it will lead to higher efficiencies in the physical and the financial supply chain, the path to the peak is yet to be cleared and laid out. There are many queries around this new subject—*what* is Financial Supply Chain, *why* is it required, *how* will it be implemented, *who* will benefit from these services, *who* are the participants in the process, *where* will this service be useful, *how* does it map to what is already being practiced, etc.

This book attempts to explain some of these questions surrounding financial supply chain. Banks have much at stake and have a large role to play in advancements in the financial supply chain. They can extend their existing strengths and value proposition to benefit from the changes that are imminent and which threaten their present revenue streams. So while the book builds the corporate perspective on supply chain—it delves deeper into how the banks could structure their approach to participate in the new domain.

Chapter 1: Introduction

Advancements in financial supply chain are significant evolutionary steps—and not a revolution—organized banking as we know today has been in practice for quite some time now. It is useful to understand the historical background and existing practices surrounding money and banking, which are leading to the development of new financial supply chain offerings. Starting from the origin of money, leading to the development of banks and banking practices, the chapter trails the origins of cheques and then clearing houses for cheques, memberships of clearing houses by banks today form one of the key services offered by the banks—that of clearing and settlement.

The chapter then explains in detail the offerings that were developed by the banks starting from seventeenth century, to support and finance the trading of merchandise. These offerings became more and more sophisticated in the late nineteenth and early twentieth century with introduction of tools such as Letters of Credit and DA/DP documents, etc. While being complex these offerings have been substantially standardized during the course of the twentieth century through the support of United Nations and International Chamber of Commerce (ICC). These are generally housed in the Trade Finance division of the banks. These current set of offerings are expected to set the basis and evolve into new financial supply chain services.

Chapter 2: The Revolutionary Changes

Traditional trade finance instruments, designed to support trade practices in the nineteenth and early twentieth century, cannot be used to support trade practices of the twenty first century and are less relevant in the current context. Trade has grown by over 1,000 times in the last fifty years. This coupled with change in manufacturing practices such as Just in Time (JIT) manufacturing and outsourcing, has accelerated the speed and volumes of transactions.

There has been significant improvement in infrastructure facilities such as ports, roads, ships, trucks, airplanes, etc. New services have been introduced by transportation companies as containers, parceling, courier, etc. Goods now travel much faster to the destination than the paper documents such as invoices, etc. Most of the corporations have now automated their internal processes and have also started extending automation with their trading partners. This presents a substantial opportunity, as this automation can be extended to include banks and financial partners in this chain, to make the process more efficient.

From a banking standpoint, cash management has become big business and this has reaped two benefits: (a) Corporations have tasted success in outsourcing some of their treasury operations to banks and are now ready to do more; (b) Corporations and banks have established linkages between ERP and cash management systems and this integration is expected to be extended for providing financial supply chain services. This is leading to the merger of cash and trade services within banks, which represent a key in evolution of financial supply chain services.

Further realizing the challenges of providing integration across such cross platform transactions, there are many new collaborative initiatives in the marketplace to define and promote standards for information exchange. All these changes are large and will propel advancement in financial supply chain services.

Chapter 3: eFinancial Supply Chain—Banks, Perspective

Banks have everything to gain—revenue and relevance—by embracing the changes and providing new services around financial supply chain. Banks can enhance their support to physical supply chain by integrating with the corporate financial processes and creating linkages with the physical supply chain as well. Banks have to construct and offer such services from various aspects like market segments, delivery channels, key values of the offering and positioning these services with respect to their existing offerings. The key value that the banks provide through these services can also be multi-faceted as supply chain financing, trade settlement, risk mitigation and trade facilitation, etc.

However, as these are new services, new structures need to be built and people need to be trained in handling these, at the same time pioneering banks will march on new roads, discovering risks and rewards. The challenges come from outside and within. The corporations that are able to integrate these services, need to work out better coordination between their treasuries and the sales/purchase sections, even as banks start to engage with them. The legal position of these transactions will be tested in courts and case studies will be made available for practice, as and when these services become more prevalent. Also the collaborative standards will be developed only as the practices get more prevalent. The organization structure of the banks will need to be overhauled to adopt these new services, particularly the divisions related to cash management, trade services, credit and operations risk and the legal cell. And beyond this, all banks will need trained people, who can manage these cross section of skills, ranging from banking, IT and legal.

Chapter 4: Early Players in e-Financial Supply Chain

If one were to examine the background of early participants one would find participants as varied as banks, corporations, IT companies, courier companies, clearing companies, market infrastructure companies, collaborators, etc. Banks buying logistics companies, courier companies buying banks, companies joining together forming collaborations—each with a view of enhancing their position in the field of e-financial supply chain.

Broadly the players can be divided along two dimensions. Dimension one—whether these participants are banks or not. Dimension two is obscure. There are collaborators—who are trying to get group of companies together to create standards along which companies can interact. Standards will substantially increase efficiencies and facilitate the growth of the e-financial supply chain services. Then there are the players—who are launching competitive offerings—which offer point solutions for immediate problems and provide immediate benefit to recipients. Whereas standards will make inter-company integration more efficient—the development of competitive offerings is important as these set the context for development of the collaborative standards in the first place.

The excitement and application of so many ingenuous minds to the problem are a great platform for the success and advancement of the e-financial supply chain services.

Chapter 5: Case Studies on e-Financial Supply Chain

From the days of epics such as Bible and Mahabharata—to the current day MBA type case studies—stories have always been told to disseminate knowledge and motivate and seduce people into adoption. Case studies presented here have been drawn from real-life experiences and requirements. These highlight the direction of changes and the emerging requirements for e-financial supply chain services. These case studies will also aid banks and corporations in understanding the model of services that can be offered and consumed in their context—and set an effective template for implementing and integrating financial supply chain services in their organizations.

Chapter 6: Legal Aspects of e-Financial Supply Chain

All discussions on the e-financial supply chain do touch upon the legal validity of such transactions especially as banks finance transactions based on requests received via internet and electronic medium. While internet and phone banking are now fairly popular and IT Act is well accepted—financing commercial instruments such as invoices, bill of exchange, etc. is challenging. Banks would be generally covered under the contract act, however they will need to ensure that other legal provisions such as negotiable instruments act, stamp duty act, etc. are also adhered to. However, many of these laws vary from country to country and like in the paper world—there is no other alternative but to examine these in the context of the situation. The laws and practices would also evolve as the transactions and practice grow. As of now there are practically no case studies from the courts on disputes related to business-to-business (B2B) internet banking—which is a good news for the early adopters.

To address some of the bafflement surrounding the space and present a full picture to the reader, the book arranges the various pieces of the emerging financial supply chain jigsaw alongside the existing banking practices—while also providing the background to the development of such practices. Business managers in corporate and transaction banking should find this useful in creating and implementing their plans and offerings around financial supply chain. It will also help in defining and targeting offerings with defined value to their customers. For practitioners—who are not familiar with the traditional trade services business or cash management business of the bank—the background explanation on these would aid them in understanding the context of the new services.

The book would also be useful for managers associated with the treasuries of large corporates as well as managers associated with the physical supply chain—on both the procurement and the distribution legs—to comprehend the type of services that could be useful for them and that can be implemented by them along with their partner banks. It would also be useful by managers of entities supporting and intending to support the growth in e-financial supply chain services—IT companies, consultants and standards companies, etc.—through putting a context to such services and helping in creation of offerings.

There are significant changes that are being witnessed around the practice surrounding the financial supply chain services. The landscape ten years from now will be very different from what we know and see today.

SANJAY DALMIA

Acknowledgements

Much of the experience I gathered around the subject has been accumulated over my long working association with HSBC, ABN AMRO Bank and CashTech. I must acknowledge the help I received from my customers, corporations and banks, in further conceptualizing and refining my concepts on the financial supply chain. During my various discussions with banks such as HDFC Bank, IDBI Bank, Maybank, Kasikorn Bank, Robinson Bank, Yes Bank, etc. the requirements that these banks were receiving from their customers helped me in further consolidating my thoughts on the financial supply chain.

It must readily be conceded that all materials and knowledge necessary to compile a book of this kind are not in command of any one individual or institution. I consequently consulted many internet sites to elucidate some of the new technological solutions and business models being proposed in this new world of financial supply chain. I have also assimilated information of the legal frame-work—for providing such new services through my ramblings on the net. Then I also consulted some of the erstwhile authors on banking—for the evolution of banking history and services.

I would like to thank International Chamber of Commerce for providing me with permission for including excerpts from their publications as under.

- ICC Uniform Customs and Practice for Documentary Credits—1993 Revision
  ICC Publication No. 500 (E)—ISBN 92.842.1155.7
  Copyright © 1993—International Chamber of Commerce (ICC), Paris
  Published in its official English version by the International Chamber of Commerce.
- Supplement to UCP 500 for Electronic Presentation—version 1.0 (eUCP)
  ICC Publication No. 500/3—ISBN 92.842.1307.X (E)
  Copyright © 2002—International Chamber of Commerce (ICC), Paris
  Published in its official English version by the International Chamber of Commerce.

- ICC Uniform Rules for Collections—1995 Revision
  ICC Publication No. 522 (E)—ISBN 92.842.1184.0
  Copyright © 1995—International Chamber of Commerce (ICC),
  Paris.
  Published in its official English version by the International Chamber
  of Commerce.
- International Standby Practices—ISP 98
  ICC Publication N°590 (E)—ISBN 92.842.1247.2
  Copyright © 1998—The Institute of International Banking Law &
  Practice, Inc.
  Published in its official English version by the International Chamber
  of Commerce.*

I would also like to thank A T Kearney and ISO for responding positively to my request for including material from their publications. I would also like to acknowledge contribution from the multiple websites included under reference—which substantially helped me in creating the structure and material for this book.

I also acknowledge support from McGraw-Hill and R. Chandra Sekhar, Publishing Manager—in working with me on this project.

The key merit I claim from this book is that this is an extensive collection of facts—connected with the financial supply chain and the laws and business customs—and also a motley of case studies from my personal experience and also from my discussions with other friends in this line of activity—which define these new services. Though much information is available publicly—a lot of it is scattered and not available to a general reader. By analyzing the environment, the case-studies and the development, I have attempted to provide a conceptual structure to roles and involvement of the banks within the financial supply chain—an industry which is yet evolving. Yet notwithstanding all my endeavors to make the work as correct and comprehensive, I trust the readers will pardon me for errors and omissions on the work compiled from such a large variety of sources and provide valuable feedback in making this book more useful.

SANJAY DALMIA

---

* All available from: ICC Services, 38 Cours Albert 1er, 75008 Paris, France; and www.iccbooks.com

Contents

1

Introduction

BACKGROUND

Banks have been providing financial services to corporates for a long time. The key services that banks provide in order to facilitate the trade business of corporates include:

- Payment and clearing services
- Financing services and Forex and risk management services

In addition, banks also provide value added services for example, letters of credit.

With the passage of time business processes have evolved, thus resulting in new and modified needs. Technology for supporting solutions that address such needs is now available and is leading to the development of new services to facilitate corporate trade practices.

To comprehend the changes on such a large scale and to introduce the readers to the financial supply chain the following topics are discussed hereunder:

- Introduction to financial supply chain
- Historical developments in money and banking
- Traditional trade business at banks
- Standardization and progress in trade services

INTRODUCTION TO FINANCIAL SUPPLY CHAIN

The supply chain represents the processes involved in Trade – which can be categorized into two different parts : the physical and the financial supply chain. The physical supply chain comprises of processes involved in the physical movement of goods e.g. inventory management, shipment tracking etc . The financial supply chain includes the movements of funds resulting from the physical supply chain.

To help understand the financial supply chain it will help to place the physical supply chain alongside the financial supply chain in order to envision how and where the two are connected.

The physical supply chain starts with a buyer and a seller. Let us assume these to be a large departmental store like, for example, Wal-Mart and a toy supplier such as Toy Station. To start the physical supply chain Wal-Mart will place an order with Toy Station for buying scooters with agreed terms and conditions on quality, delivery date, delivery place and price, etc. In trade language this is called a purchase order. Refer Fig. 1.1.

Fig. 1.1 *Purchase order or PO is given by the buyer to the seller and contains the goods that the seller desires to buy along with the agreed terms and conditions*

The focus now shifts to Toy Station and its manufacturing set-up where the order is processed and the number of scooters required is manufactured. Toy Station then requisitions the service of a transportation company to deliver the goods to Wal-Mart. See Fig. 1.2.

Besides the above rudimentary supply chain, other parties too will be involved in the process. Generally, in such a commercial transaction the two parties who will be involved are:
- Independent quality inspectors
- Insurance companies

Other regulatory agencies may also be involved in the transaction and may include:
- Custom authorities
- Other regulatory bodies such as Food and Drug Administration etc.

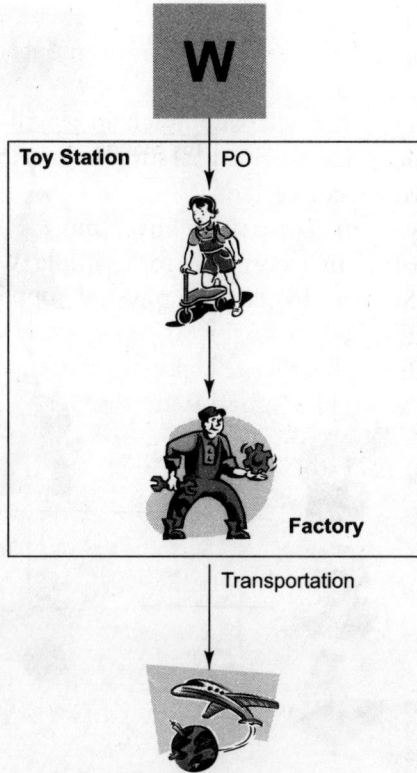

Fig. 1.2 *After receiving the PO the seller prepares the goods in his factory and then dispatches them to the buyer through a transportation company*

The modified physical supply chain would then look as shown in Fig. 1.3.

The transportation company in itself can either be very simple or very complex. It may involve couriers, packagers, lorry transport, shipping companies, airlines, freight forwarders, etc. Further, the sales model may involve dealers, distributors, depots, etc. thus adding to the variety in the supply chain process.

At this point in time it will be sufficient to understand that the physical supply chain can be very complex and there are many interactions between the various parties involved in completing one successful transaction. Though it would appear tremendously intricate and complex to an uninitiated person, human ingenuity has over a period created a high amount of repeatability in this process through sustained improvement in processes and practices.

It is now opportune to turn our attention to the financial supply chain and understand its linkages with the physical supply chain.

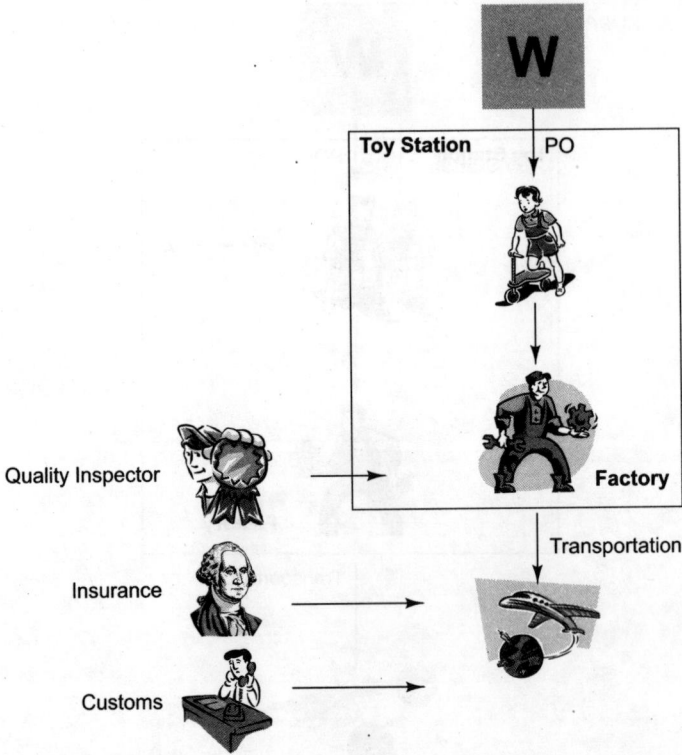

Fig. 1.3 *There are many parties involved in the satisfactory completion of a trade transaction*

As can be seen in Figure 1.4, the financial supply chain integrates with the physical supply chain in multiple places with activities largely revolving around payments and loans. While it is generally the banks that provide these services, sometimes other players within the chain may also provide them, for example:

- Wal-Mart may give a loan to Toy Station for producing the goods.
- Payment could be done through cards or other agencies like Western Union.

While providing the financial supply chain services the banks may at times extend their role, for example:

- Bank acts as a seller by selling gold to the jewelry manufacturers.
- Bank acts as a distributor for mutual funds and insurances.

The focus of our book is to explore this interaction between the physical and the financial supply chain and examine the new developments in this realm.

Though many of the examples and discussions in this book revolve around the type of physical supply chain described earlier, the concepts are relevant

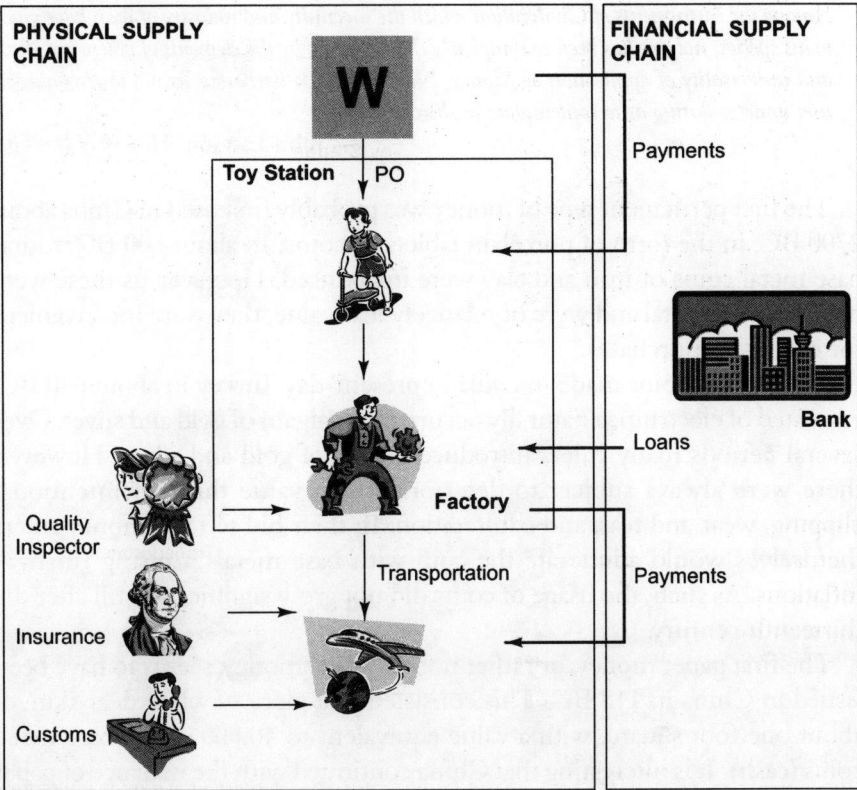

Fig. 1.4 *The physical and the financial supply chain integrate in many places in the life cycle of the transaction*

to other types of physical supply chains as well. The interested reader can find a brief discussion on these in Exhibit 3.

HISTORICAL DEVELOPMENTS IN MONEY AND BANKING

Over the years, the growth of trade worldwide—both international and domestic—or what we refer to as the physical supply chain, has been linked closely to the growth and progress of the financial supply chain. A brief history on money and banking will place in context the new developments that are occurring in the financial supply chain.

Trade in goods, commodities and services happened long before the origin of money and the earliest form of value exchange was through barter.

'Among the instruments of Civilization which the ingenuity and industry of man have given to his species, not one has been so completely characterized by the elements of potency of effects and universality of application as Money. No people is so barbarous as not to recognize its use: none so daring as to contemplate its discontinuance'

— John Lawson, *History of Banking*

The first permanent type of money was probably first used in China about 2700 BC, in the form of porcelain tablets or coins. In about 600 BC, round base metal coins of iron and clay were introduced. However, as these were made of base metal and were of relatively low value, they were inconvenient for expensive purchases.

The earliest coins made in Lydia in present-day Turkey in about 640 BC, consisted of electrum, a naturally occurring amalgam of gold and silver. Over several periods many rulers introduced coins of gold and silver. However, these were always subject to deterioration in value through intentional clipping, wear and tear, and adulteration. In their bid to raise money rulers themselves would adulterate the coin with base metals, causing runaway inflations. As such, the usage of coins did not grow significantly till after the thirteenth century.

The first paper money, or rather non-metallic money, seems to have been issued in China in 118 BC. This consisted of a piece of white deer skin, of about one foot square, with a value equivalent to 40,000 of the base metal coins (cash). It is interesting that China continued with the issuance of paper money for a long period of time, much before it became popular in Western Europe. In about 960 AD, the issuance of paper money became regular in China; but by 1032 AD, there were almost 16 note-issuing houses and the excessive supply of notes caused inflation. In 1455 AD, China abandoned the use of paper money and it was re-introduced only in the early twentieth century.

The origin of the present day bank notes can be traced back to the Bank of England in the late seventeenth century. Cheques were also introduced in the middle of the seventeenth century although it was not until the late eighteenth century that these became a popular medium for trade payments.

The first regular institution, resembling a present day bank was founded in the early 14th century in Venice, now a part of Italy. The early banks were founded to support fund raising for kings and rulers in order to help them wage wars on neighboring kingdoms. However, these were soon found to be useful for supporting merchant trade. Initially banking progressed slowly but it then spread quickly during the late eighteenth and early nineteenth century. The growth has been so rapid that in modern times the banking industry contributes about 1–3% towards the national GDP through services, employment and activities.

The early banks took deposits and lent money and then, as their promise to pay was found effective for exchanging value for trade rather than carrying sacks of coins, they started issuing bills of exchange and promissory notes and subsequently, cheques. The first clearing-house for cheques came into existence only in the late eighteenth century. It is interesting to note that in the early days when bills of exchange were issued, the issuer had to be present at the bank in order to honor the promise to pay!

The growth of banking did not come about without its associated anguish. There were several run on the banks and over-issuance of notes often led to acute inflation. Banks have now, long held the responsibility as guardians of the money and to further perpetuate and create money!

It is indeed very tempting as well as astonishing that banks can create money! There have been many historical incidents of ferocious consequences challenging such money creation. However, over a period of time it has been well accepted that money creation does add to the well-being of the economy and society at large—both emotionally and physically—and this function has been largely taken over by the Central Banks in most countries.

For readers who may not be very familiar with banking and may be grappling with questions such as 'what is money', 'how can it be created or shrunk' and 'what do the bankers really do', there can be no better resource than the story titled 'Recollections of Pine Gulch' set in the background of the gold discovery in the middle of 1800 in a small town in the Americas. The story is included in Exhibit 1 so that readers familiar with banking can progress without obstruction.

For readers interested in the origin of coins, notes, banking and clearing, more information is available in Exhibit 2.

In conclusion, it will be sufficient here to summarize that growth in usage of money and banking has had a significant salutary impact on the growth of business and trade.

TRADITIONAL TRADE BUSINESS IN BANKS

Background

Specialized trade departments in banks service the physical supply chain with very highly specialized and specific products. The Hong Kong and Shanghai Banking Corporation now HSBC, was established in 1865 to finance trade in the Asia Pacific region and has since been a leading bank in providing trade finance services for local and international business. Most other banks like ABN AMRO, J P Morgan, Citibank, etc. also provide dedicated and specialized trade services.

The trade finance business for banks started with finance of the buyer and supplier. The bank finance for trade is extended to both the buyers and suppliers in various circumstances and under various names, some of which are described in Figure 1.5.

Sl. No	Party	Type of Loan	Purpose
1	Seller	Packing credit/ Pre-shipment credit	Required by seller to procure raw material for production and packaging
2	Seller	Post-shipment	Finance to seller after shipment of goods and before sales realization is received by the seller
3	Buyer	Warehouse finance	Temporary finance to buyer for making payment to the seller

Fig. 1.5   *Key types of loans extended by the banks for financing trade*

Over a period of time the financing business of banks was supplemented with new trade products, which facilitated the physical supply chain. Most such new products were introduced in the late nineteenth and early twentieth century.

To understand the basis of such new trade finance products it is necessary to discuss the need that led to the innovation of such products.

The business of buying and selling frequently referred to as trade, happens between two parties namely, a buyer and a seller. The financial standing and the market reputation of the buyer and that of the seller may be vastly different. This gives rise to risks which the buyer and seller are exposed to. Let us consider the following examples to illustrate the point.

In the first example we will consider the trade partners to be Shell Oil and Sassaparilla Traders. Presumably most readers have heard about Shell Oil. Although it is an embarrassing admission, I must confess to not knowing about Sassaparilla Traders. Sassaparilla Traders wish to buy oil from Shell Oil and raise a purchase order on Shell Oil through a fax. The sales people are enthused at such a ready business opportunity but no one has ever heard of this company before. The finance department then insists that any shipment can only be made on receipt of 100% advance payment as they are not sure that they will receive the money after they have delivered the required goods to Sassaparilla.

In the second example, Wal-Mart raises a purchase order on Toy Station who is extremely glad to receive the order and also agrees to receive money 90 days after making the shipment of the goods to Wal-Mart. This will give Wal-Mart ample time to make a quality assessment and then process the payment. Such payment terms are referred to as open account payment terms in trade parlance.

From this, it is evident to the discerning reader that the key distinction between the first example and the second example, leading to substantially different payment terms, is the relative financial strength and reputation between the buyer and the supplier. If Wal-Mart were to buy oil from Shell, surely the finance department of Shell would have considered the payment terms more leniently or at least differently.

In many situations the relative strength of the buyer and seller may not be as extreme as suggested in these two examples, but many-a-times it would be in-between. This was precisely the type of opportunity and need that was addressed through innovation in trade finance instruments by the banks in the late nineteenth and early twentieth century. The trade finance products that were introduced by banks to meet this spectrum of demand are illustrated in Figure 1.6.

	Payment Terms	Description	
Increasing Buyer Strength	Advance payment	Advance payment	Increasing Seller Strength
	LC - DP	Letter of credit - Document against payment	
	LC - DA	Letter of credit - Document against acceptance	
	DP	Document against payment	
	DA	Documents against acceptance	
	Open account	Open account	

Fig. 1.6 *The payment terms reflect the relative strength between the buyer and the seller*

Letter of Credit (LC), also known as documentary credit has been one of the key innovations in trade finance. To understand what is LC and the above structure it is necessary to understand some of the key trade practices, which in turn will help to comprehend the new trade products that the banks introduced.

Trade Documents

Under a letter of credit or documentary credit, the banks depend upon the underlying trade documents to verify the performance of the seller before making the required payment. Therefore, an understanding of trade documents is a very essential part of trade finance operations.

When a seller sells goods to a buyer:
- The goods will generally be transported either by ship, lorry or airplane.
- The sale of goods will be accompanied by some documentation such as:

  ❏ Invoice
  ❏ Transport documentation e.g. lorry receipt or bill of lading, etc. wherever there is a sale of physical goods.

The transport document is a very important and interesting document-ation. It is the receipt given by the transport company to the seller providing evidence that they have taken possession of the goods, for transport. In many cases the transport document has the following properties:
- The holder of the document is also considered to be the owner of the goods.
- It is a title document i.e., it can be passed on to the beneficiary by endorsing it in their favor.

The holder of the transport documents can present these to the transportation company and seek release of the goods.

The transport document is a key document used by banks to create such new products as the letter of credit. In essence, the bank takes the transport document and becomes the owner of the goods. It then releases this document to the buyer on receipt of payment!

There are many other trade documents that also find usage in a letter of credit. A list of few such common documents is as follows:

Sl. No	Name of Document	Issued By	Purpose of Document
1	Invoice	Seller	Evidences sale of goods
2	Packing list	Seller	Description of the goods sold
3	Transport document	Transporter	As above
4	Insurance	Insurer	Insurance for goods under transit
5	Quality certificate	Surveyor	Quality of goods being sold
6	Certificate of origin	Chamber of Commerce	Country of origin of goods

Fig. 1.7   *Some common documents used in trade of goods*

Seller Credit Terms

The buyer and seller agree on a variety of payment terms and depending on their mutual standing and requirements they may agree on credit terms as follows:

- Buyer will pay on receipt of goods.
- Buyer will pay 30 days after receipt of goods.
- Buyer will pay 30 days from the invoice date.
- Buyer will pay 10 days after accepting the invoice.
- Buyer will make advance payment before shipment of goods.
- etc.

The agreement on the payment terms is reached, based on the mutual understanding between the buyer and the seller.

Letter of Credit or Documentary Credit

Generally, the seller perceives a risk that if they have completed the manufacturing and delivered the goods to the buyer and the buyer does not pay then they run a payment risk. In such a case of non-payment by the buyer, the seller may not be able to repossess the goods or, even if that is possible they may have to spend money on transportation and packaging to get the goods back in their possession. If the goods are perishable then repossession may not be a viable option at all.

The buyer on the other hand runs a risk of making the payment and then finding that the delivery has not been made at all or the quality of the delivery is not as per their expectations.

So, the bank acts as an intermediary between the buyer and the seller to mitigate the risks for both. In a hypothetical sense, the bank takes the goods from the seller and the money from the buyer. Once it has both the goods and the money, it then releases the goods to the buyer and the money to the seller. However, as the bank cannot take physical possession of goods, since it is physically impossible to take possession of items such as crude oil, wheat, soya meal, etc. the bank deals only in documents, which are generated as a result of the trade process.

The letter of credit is a guarantee issued by the buyer's bank to the seller, guaranteeing payment to the seller if he presents trade documents as specified in the letter of credit.

So the letter of credit document, which is issued by the buyer's bank, contains the terms and conditions that the seller has to fulfill in order to receive the payment. The bank can only examine the trade documents to verify if the conditions have been fulfilled. Therefore, the bank specifies conditions for all the documents that it expects to receive from the seller in order to verify that the seller has met their obligations.

When the buyer's bank receives the documents it verifies the documents against the specifications mentioned in the letter of credit. If the documents are satisfactory it will make payment to the seller on the due date. The buyer's bank will have to make the payment irrespective of whether or not it receives payment from the buyer!

In turn, the buyer's bank may have various arrangements with the buyer for payment, for example:

- The transport documents will not be released till such time as the payment is received.
- The buyer will provide a fixed deposit or land as security for the facility.

This explains in brief, one of the key innovations in trade finance. In practice some more parties are involved in the process, the main one being the seller's bank, which receives the documents from the seller and forwards them to the buyer's bank. This is required as the buyer's bank will not be in a position to know the authenticity of the seller directly especially if they are in a different geographical area or country.

However, Banks are generally large and reputed organizations and have established bi-lateral arrangements to verify the documents and signatures that they exchange between themselves. The buyer bank therefore, makes an arrangement with the seller bank and then relies on it to verify the antecedents of the seller and ensure that the documents that are being presented are from a genuine party and therefore likely to be genuine.

The workflow of the LC transaction would appear as illustrated in Figure 1.8.

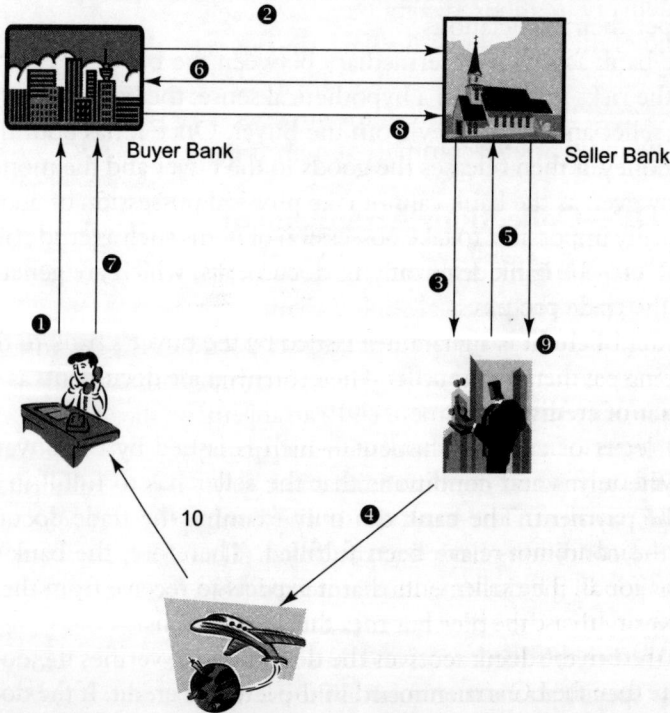

Fig. 1.8 *The steps in the life cycle of a letter of credit*

❶	Buyer	Requests his bank for issuing LC
❷	Buyer's bank	Issues LC and informs seller's bank
❸	Seller's bank	Advises LC to the seller
❹	Seller	Ships the goods
❺	Seller	Gives documents to his bank with the LC
❻	Seller's bank	Forwards the documents to the buyer's bank
❼	Buyer	Gives acceptance to pay later or pays immediately
❽	Buyer's bank	Verifies documents against the LC and conveys acceptance/ payment to seller's bank
❾	Seller's bank	Conveys acceptance/ payment to the seller
10	Buyer	Collects documents from the bank and then takes the goods

Fig. 1.9 *The steps in the life cycle of a letter of credit*

In summary, the key issue is that in certain situations especially when the transaction value is large and the transaction is further complicated by complex delivery methods, distant buyers and sellers, unequal standing and background of the buyer and seller, etc., the buyer and the seller do not trust each other sufficiently and need the bank as an intermediary to ensure that both parties meet their respective commitments. This issue can be even more profound in an internet/e-commerce environment.

DA and DP—Collections Arrangement

Apart from providing the letter of credit banks also provide additional trade services to support the physical supply chain.

As was highlighted earlier, the transport documents play an important role for releasing the goods and are therefore important to the buyer.

In a Document Against Payment (DP) arrangement, the seller forwards the trade documents to the buyer's bank with instructions to release the documents to the buyer only when the buyer has made payments for the goods. The goods thus remain in the custody of the bank—through the transport document—and are not released to the buyer till such time as the buyer has paid for the goods. The seller is thus protected from the risk of non-payment from the buyer. In case the buyer does not make payment, the seller can request the bank to return the documents and thus repossess the goods. However, this is less secure than the LC arrangement as the buyer may not take the documents and therefore not pay, and the seller will have wasted some of the expenses of manufacturing, transportation, insurance, etc.

In the Document Against Acceptance (DA) arrangement the seller forwards the trade documents to the buyer's bank with instructions to release the documents to the buyer only when the buyer agrees to make payments for the goods at a future date. The acceptance is generally obtained on a bill of exchange and the buyer is liable to pay based on this acceptance. However, this is less secure compared to the DP arrangement as the buyer would have taken the goods and may not make payment. The resulting court proceedings may then take a long time.

Similarly, the LC can also be a DP type of LC (also referred to as Sight LC), or a DA type LC (also referred to as the Usance LC). However in the case of an LC, when compliant documents are presented, the primary responsibility for payment rests with the LC issuing bank.

Figure 1.10 explains the workflow of the DA and DP document collection services offered by banks.

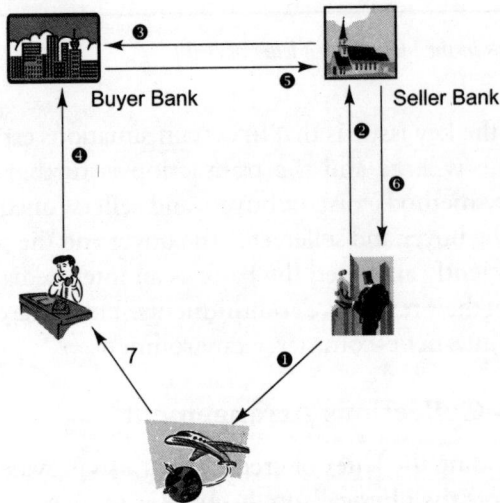

Fig. 1.10 *The steps in the life cycle of a Documents Against Payment (DP) or Documents Against Acceptance (DA) transaction*

❶	Seller	Ships the goods
❷	Seller	Gives documents to his bank
❸	Seller's bank	Forwards the documents to the buyer's bank
❹	Buyer	Gives acceptance to pay later or pays immediately
❺	Buyer's bank	Conveys acceptance/payment to seller's bank
❻	Seller's bank	Conveys acceptance/payment to the seller
7	Buyer	Collects documents from the bank and then takes the goods

Fig. 1.11 *The steps in the life cycle of a Documents Against Payment (DP) or Documents Against Acceptance (DA) transaction*

Trade Finance

Apart from the above services banks also provide trade finance, which fall in the following categories.

- *Pre-shipment Credit*—also known as packing credit, this type of finance is provided to the seller for financing the procurement and manufacturing cycle before the goods are transported to the buyer.
- *Post-shipment Credit*—also provided as bill discounting or bill finance, this type of loan is given to the seller to finance the receivables from the buyer, i.e. before the money is received from the buyer.
- *Import Loans*—also known as buyer's credit, this loan is extended to the buyer for making payment to the seller and in-turn financing the inventory from purchase.

These types of loans are made available on both types of payment terms, i.e. an LC may secure the trade, or it may be on an open account or collections basis; the banks extend the pre-shipment and post-shipment facilities for all such payment terms.

STANDARDIZATION AND PROGRESS IN TRADE SERVICES

It is thus evident that these new services offered by the banks in early twentieth century were fairly complex and subject to individual interpretation. This would lead to disputes since for example, if the bank did not make payment against an LC because of a difference in opinion with the seller on the documents presented, there was no standard mechanism of addressing such a situation. Similarly, if the bank requested for a bill of lading drawn by XYZ Shipping Company to be drawn in its favor in the letter of credit and although the seller presented this document but the bank did not find it acceptable, how would such a dispute be managed? This was not clear.

To remedy this situation, the International Chamber of Commerce (ICC), which was founded in 1919 with an aim to promote and harmonize international trade, came out with the first Uniform Customs and Practices for Documentary Credit (UCP) in 1933. This guiding document laid down in great detail:

- Model conditions that could be used in establishing letters of credit.
- The interpretation and guidelines for verifying the documents versus the documentary conditions set out in the letters of credit.
- Some model practices for handling the uncertainties around the courier and receipt of documents.

The UCP document is very detailed on the operations aspect of the letter of credit and this is the reason why it is presently incorporated in the laws of over 140 countries. It would not be out of turn to mention that over the years the UCP has led to substantial growth in trade finance services. In turn it has also been revised based on feedback and evolving trade practices leading to UCP 500, which came into effect in 1994.

The ICC subsequently also introduced Uniform Rules and Practices for Collections (URC 522) for handling collections processes related to DA and DP business.

Exhibit 9 contains the structure of these two documents with some key conditions highlighted for readers who would like to get a gist of them. For those who would like to go through the full text of the document, a visit to www.iccwbo.org is recommended.

CONCLUSION

The growth and improvements in money, banking, transportation and trade standards have resulted in significant growth in trade business worldwide. The present improvements in information technology coupled with the evolution of other business processes, challenges human ingenuity to further the improvements and growth seen over the last many centuries. That is the brave new world of our straight through integrated financial supply chain.

2

The Revolutionary Changes

INTRODUCTION

It is believed that the change and pace of change experienced and achieved during the twentieth century are immense and iconic, and that such monumental changes have not occurred within such a short time period during the entire history of mankind. The physical and the financial supply chain are definitely witnessing some rapid transformations and in this section we will attempt to understand this revolution under the following themes:

- Changing nature of trade.
- Transformation of the physical supply chain.
- Automation within and amongst corporates.
- Evolving financial services.
- Emerging consensus for new standards.

CHANGING NATURE OF TRADE

In recent times, trade—generally understood as exchange of goods and services—has almost doubled every five years. This means that the exchange of goods and services is now almost 1,000 times what it was about 50 years ago!

One way to comprehend such a large change is to understand what people purchased about fifty years ago as opposed to the things we purchase now.

Of course there are many more items purchased now than what was purchased fifty years ago, such as processed foods, toiletries, clothes, electronics, entertainment, children's merchandise, pharmaceuticals, etc. Apart from such purchases the delivery of these goods and services to end-users requires a large network of suppliers, manufacturers and dealers. Each of these would be involved in the exchange chain, thus providing a multiplication factor on the number of incremental goods and services procured by individuals. This, coupled with the population growth factor would make us believe that the number 1000 may not be wayward!

Alternatively from a viewpoint of theoretical economics, considering an average GDP growth of 5% per annum for economies and assuming a money velocity of 3 times, the exchange growth appears to be around 15% per annum. Based on this 15%, a year-on-year growth for 50 years would provide similar results.

Such tremendous growth in trade and services has been facilitated by:
- Substantial advancement in transportation technology.
- Improvements in manufacturing techniques.
- Use of, and advancements in information technology.

Improvements in aircrafts, ships, trucks, roads, air and sea ports, etc., have amongst other things, resulted in one big benefit for trade, namely reduction in shipment time. With larger availability of means of transport, better infrastructure and more efficient interchanges and linkages between two carriers, average shipment times have been reduced by almost 10 times in the last 50 years. So, what used to take 50 days earlier is now generally achieved in 5 days!

Improvements in transportation, growth in trade and advancements in communication channels have resulted in the widening of trade networks. Most of the larger corporations cover greater geographical areas—both domestic and international—in their bid to increase sales. Most of the smaller corporate also look to large geographical distribution through partner networks, as well as on their own. Similarly, at the procurement end too, large as well as small corporates consider all locations, both near and distant, in order to achieve the best possible deals. Corporations do take a certain amount of risk when dealing with new vendors and dealers. However, they do have assistance in the form of better information on these counter-parties through availability of better information from banks, local traders and companies such as Dun and Bradstreet, and are also supported by an improving and uniform legal framework.

The Japanese introduced the Just-in-Time (JIT) manufacturing technique with all the surrounding processes, to support such manufacturing processes and thus substantially cut down the procurement and holding costs. One significant outcome of such a change was the reduction in size of an average shipment. In a recent Celent report, it was estimated that the average US dollar size of a shipment in 2001 was 42% of what it was in the 1970s!

From a trade operations point of view this is a noteworthy change as it means that there were many more transactions of a smaller value compared to a few large transactions in the earlier process, resulting in a larger number of items to be reconciled.

These fundamental changes in trade have an important bearing on the new financial supply chain services discussed in this book, as we will see later.

TRANSFORMATION OF THE PHYSICAL SUPPLY CHAIN

The trend towards global organization of both manufacturing and marketing highlights the critical importance of logistics and supply chain management. The complexity of the logistics task appears to be increasing exponentially as a result of the increased range of products, shorter product life cycles, marketplace growth and number of supply channels. Increase in customer service requires claims and warranty handling processes, returns, and handling of outmoded goods, to be integrated closely with the supply chain. This has resulted in focused factories, i.e. limiting the range of products manufactured in a single factory and thus improving economies of scale; and centralization of inventories, thus reducing the total inventory requirement by having regional distribution centers serving much wider geographical areas.

Another challenge faced by organizations is the need to serve the location specific differences in customer and consumer requirements, e.g. even within India there are differences in consumer taste between various regions and of course, the language also varies. One strategy that is being used to address this is the concept of postponement. Postponement, or delayed configuration is based on the principle of designing products with a common platform, where the final assembly or customization happens for the final market destination on demand.

Such requirements necessitate very sophisticated logistics management. There are several options for the management of transportation and the trade-offs are complex depending upon the different product and market channels, e.g.:

- Direct shipment from each source to the factory.
- Consolidation in the supply region for each factory.

Figure 2.1 illustrates a simple network for the transportation of goods to highlight the complex integration chain required for movement of goods:

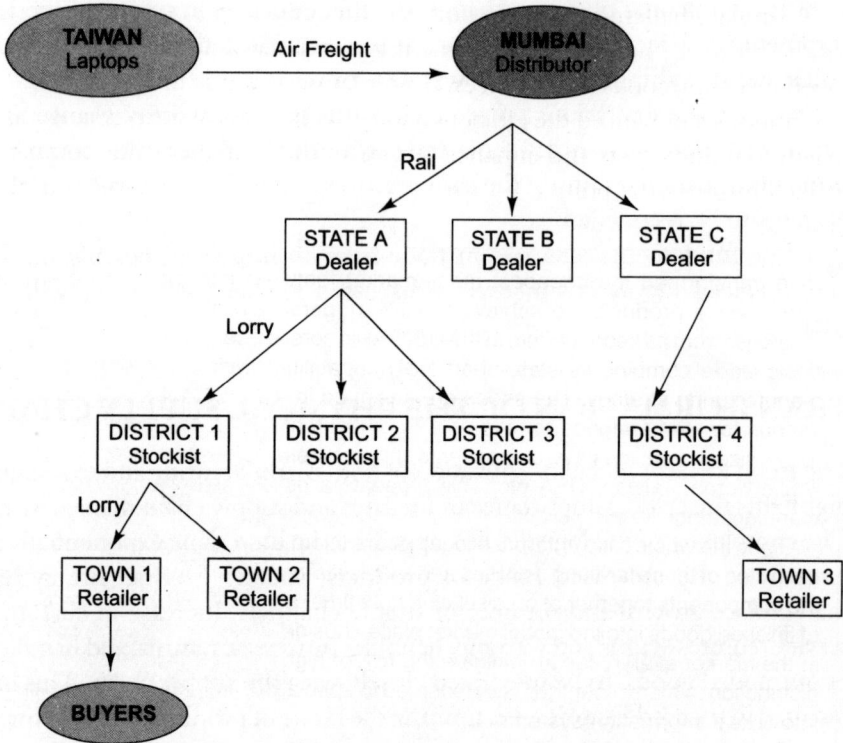

Fig. 2.1 *Example of a typical network for the physical distribution of goods*

This could be further complicated if for example, there is no direct flight from Taiwan to Mumbai and the goods have to be moved from one carrier (e.g. Singapore Airlines) to another (e.g. Air India) in order to reach Mumbai. This type of complication extends to all other parts of the distribution chain as well. Each of these legs represents the following risk and cost in the distribution chain:

- Cost due to unused inventory
- Risk of damage
- Risk of loss in transit
- Risk of losing customer demand if the goods do not reach the shelf on time

Considering that the warehousing requirements for goods such as frozen foods and packaging material can be very different, and there are numerable different types of products, the logistics chain for consolidation can be further complicated depending on the source and type of each product material. Sometimes the local regulatory tax structures will also influence the consolidation and logistics strategy.

A similar challenge exists on both the procurement and distribution legs of the business. Logistics management forms a very high proportion of the overall cost of goods and services. To remain competitive, companies have continuously enhanced the efficiency and effectiveness of the physical supply chain to reduce costs and enhance service to the customers. An example of Nike illustrates the point.

Nike transformed the cheapest mass-market footwear into high-tech and high performance products. To achieve this Nike operates a globe-spanning, virtual enterprise from its headquarters in the USA. At its core is a set of business processes, designed to combine its state-of-art R&D capabilities with a ruthlessly low-cost manufacturing strategy. The shoes are designed in the USA but manufactured in various focused factories for example South Korea (men's sizes) and Indonesia (boy's sizes), from over 100 components supplied from various countries e.g. Japan, South Korea, Taiwan, USA etc. This presents a risk of extended lead times for manufacturing!

Tying the whole Nike enterprise together are information systems that co-ordinate each step of these far-flung activities and a logistics infrastructure capable of bringing the components together at precisely the right time, as well as managing the supply of finished goods into the global market place, thus delivering over 300 new designs in the market every year! To mitigate the risk of high finished goods inventory the distribution in many countries is outsourced to specialist third parties who are linked into Nike's information systems.

Thus, the supply chain is now becoming a confederation of organizations that agree on common goals and bring specific strengths to the overall value creation and value delivery system. This process is being accelerated as the trend towards outsourcing continues.

Source: Martin, Christopher, Logistics and Supply Chain Management.

AUTOMATION WITHIN AND AMONGST CORPORATES

Information technology implementations have made rapid strides in the last two decades. Most large corporations now have sophisticated enterprise systems for various activities including procurement and distribution planning. During the first wave of automation in a corporation, many of the in-house tasks have been automated. These include tasks like accounting, inventory management, etc.

Having achieved a great degree of automation for their internal tasks, corporates are now more than prepared and are advancing towards integration with their trading partners in order to achieve higher efficiencies in the operations processes. The interaction with trading partners starts from the pre-sales quotation process and continues to the post-sales deliveries and the settlement process. A report from A.T. Kearney estimates that with effective collaboration between various partners in the supply chain, the cost of purchased raw material can be reduced by about 6%.

Underpinning the concept of extended enterprise is a common information 'highway'. It is the use of shared information that enables cross-functional management to support the responsive flow of goods and services from one end of the pipeline to the other.

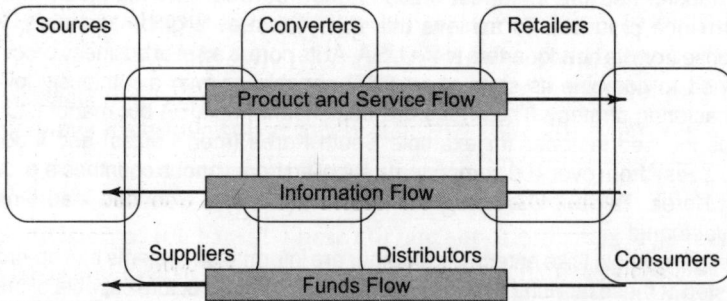

Source: A.T. Kearney

Fig. 2.2 *The concept of extended enterprise*

Various corporates are at various stages of internal automation and integration with their trading partners. However, most large corporates are ready and there clearly is a great desire to integrate with their trading partners in a manner in which maximum Straight Through Processing (STP) can be achieved. The larger corporates are pushing this along with all their trading partners, including banks. Through the payment and settlement services they offer, banks play a key role in linking the transaction together. It is no wonder therefore, that corporates want the bank to advance their services to link up and close the loop on the supply chain.

EVOLVING FINANCIAL SERVICES

Contrary to allegations, banks too have been reacting albeit a bit tardily, to the changes in the environment by offering new services to meet the demand imposed by the corporates. Three key emerging services that reflect this transformation and are discussed here are:

- Evolution of cash management
- Merger of trade services and cash management
- New trade products and services

Evolution of Cash Management

At a recent industry forum, a senior banker contended that, "customers have been doing cash management since they wrote cheques. So, what essentially we have done in cash management is nothing revolutionary."

The cash management services provided by banks are not revolutionary but definitely do form a very key evolution. A list of some of the key achievements of cash management includes the following.

- The cheque collection system focuses on clearing. Riding on top of this clearing system, the cash management services have provided for, as options, some of the following key benefits:
  - ❏ The logistics of picking up cheques directly from the distribution network of the corporate, e.g. dealers, distributors, customers, etc. thus supporting the process outsourcing of these functions.
  - ❏ Carrying the transaction information, relating to the physical supply chain e.g. dealer code, depot number, etc. and, thus supporting reconciliation for the corporate.
  - ❏ Providing linkages to the corporate ERP system for transaction upload and status downloads and thus starting the process of integration and STP.
- The benefits on the payments system have been equally significant. Again, as above, the cash management systems have made use of the standard payment methods such as cheques and electronic clearing with some startling benefits:
  - ❏ Corporates have been able to outsource their entire payments to banks, resulting in creation of virtual payment factories at the banks. The banks print cheques, pay orders, electronic transactions, etc. based on customers' instructions and virtually outsource all of the customer's payment processes.
  - ❏ While processing the payment information, the transaction information relating to the physical supply chain e.g. invoice number, goods etc. is carried along with the transaction and also passed on to the vendors, thus facilitating reconciliation.
  - ❏ The payment instructions and the status of the payment instructions are linked to the corporate ERP system.

All the above aspects are extremely critical for the ongoing progress on linking the corporate's systems to the bank's systems and becoming more tightly integrated with the supply chain of the corporate.

There are two other important developments in cash management that are worthy of mention here.

Networking Amongst Banks Leading to Highly Efficient Clearing

As has been discussed in the previous chapter under 'Historical developments in money and banking', in the late eighteenth century banks got together to form clearing houses in order to facilitate easy transfer of funds from one bank to another for cheques drawn on each other. While this solved many problems initially, by the 1950s, as more and more traders ventured to increase their procurement and distribution network, the growth in domestic and international trade presented a new set of challenges to the banks.

So, while a bank in India was a member of the clearinghouses in India, it was not a member of the clearing houses in the USA. To overcome such difficult situations the bank in India forged a partnership with a bank in USA. They took the cheques and payment instructions from the Indian bank and settled them in the USA, much like a corporate customer gives instructions to its banks.

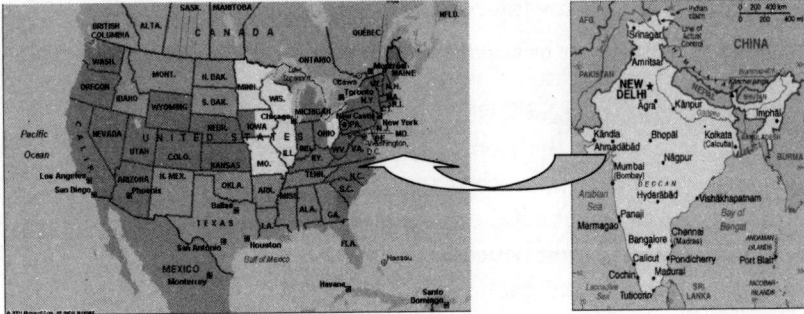

Fig. 2.3   *Example of flow of money from India to USA*

So for example, cheques and payment instructions for money to be paid to an American seller would flow from State Bank of India, Mumbai (where the buyer holds an account) to Citibank, New York, where SBI holds an account with Citibank. Thus Citibank, which participates in New York clearing, could then clear such instruments and the account of the seller could be credited to his account with for example, JP Morgan Chase.

This example of moving money from India to USA will be more complicated when we try to further understand the following two aspects of clearing:

1. How SBI transfers money into its account with Citibank, USA.
2. The way Citibank maintains its account with the clearing-house Fedwire, and the way it transfers money into its account with the clearing-house.

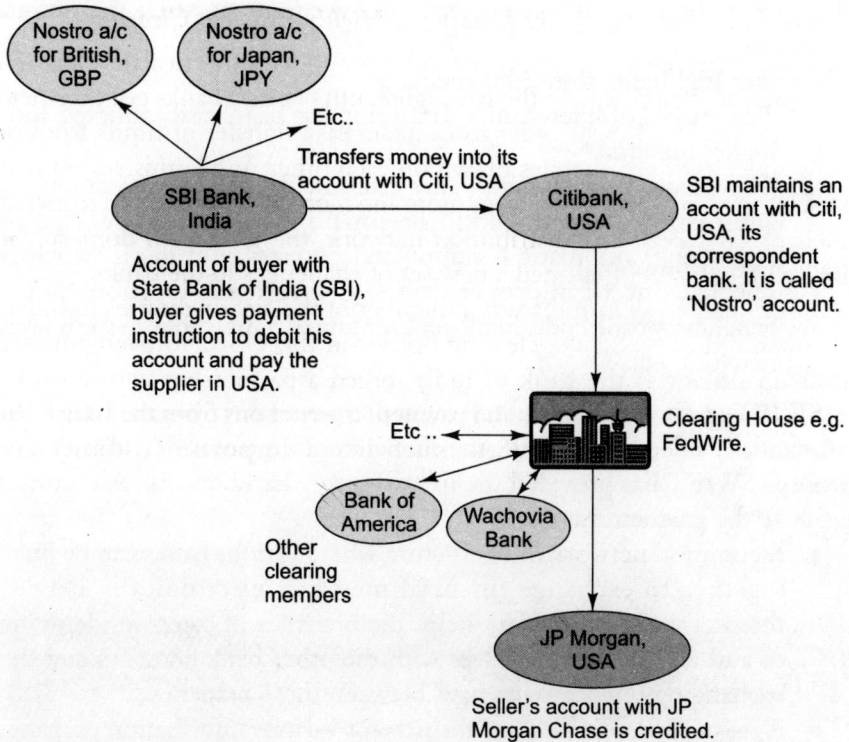

Fig. 2.4 *Example of a simple payment network*

Further, both these transfers are a small network themselves and use principles similar to those explained earlier.

The network can be further substantially complicated when the seller bank is not a direct member of the clearing, or when SBI does not have a direct relationship with any bank in the USA and has to go through another bank in India who has such a relationship with another correspondent bank in the USA. The network for receiving money is very similar and mirrors the previous method for paying money into the USA.

The same difficult situation can also manifest itself domestically, if for example, Citibank in India had only a handful of branches in say, four Indian cities, but while handling collections for a large pharmaceutical company like Glaxo, received checks from many other locations within India. There are about 10,000 clearing locations in India and Glaxo could be selling in many of these locations! In such a situation, Citibank would establish an arrangement with for example, State Bank of India in order to facilitate settlement in locations where SBI had branches.

Similar to the movement of goods from port to port, and their bulking and de-bulking in the physical supply chain, the flow of money for settlement also moves through various branches and accounts to reach the ultimate beneficiary.

The key highlights about this model are:

1. This model of inter-bank relationship has been vastly adopted and is highly matured.
2. The model has become highly efficient through a high amount of automation for transaction origination, transaction receipt and processing, automatic handling and correction of items which get rejected due to improper data, e.g. erroneous location code or beneficiary bank code, intelligent routing of transactions to the relevant network, etc.

SWIFT, a financial industry owned co-operative organization, has substantially aided in enhancing the efficiency of the payment and settlement process. SWIFT has provided the following key backbone infrastructure to facilitate the payment network:

- A common network infrastructure where various banks can be linked together to exchange financial messages electronically between themselves. This network helps the branches of banks in identifying or authenticating themselves with the other bank branches and then exchanging financial messages between these branches.
- A set of common message formats for various information exchanges such as payment message, confirmation of payment, account statement etc.

SWIFT thus provided a common platform and a common language for the various banks to exchange financial information with each other and thereby made the whole process of money exchange more efficient.

The model already operates at a very high level of efficiency in most cases and further automation is making it almost fault-proof and perfect. Such large efficiencies have laid a solid foundation for the banks to now extend their settlement services further to integrate with the physical supply chain processes of the corporate.

Corporate Connectivity to Banks through SWIFT

Corporate have more and more integrated their payment systems with those of banks through growth in cash management services. One of the popular ways of linking the corporate treasury to the banks payment systems has been through the use of payment files for vendor payments, salary payments, dividends, reimbursements, etc. The corporate ERP system generates a payment file, which is sent to the banks' system for uploading and processing in their systems.

While originally these files were being hand delivered through floppy media and subsequently, through the internet offerings of the banks, the large corporates now increasingly wish to directly connect and upload to the bank payment systems. Their requirements are driven from the following considerations:

1. Reducing the number of touch points reduces the chances of errors.
2. It provides better security as the files cannot be tampered by any one.
3. The data in files have already been adequately processed in the ERP systems of the corporate and therefore does not need any further processing manually.

This facility has been offered by the banks through host-to-host gateway connectivity, where the payment systems of the banks are exposed to the corporate for directly transmitting the file at the given address.

While the above solution works for large corporates, the issues are:

1. For each bank the gateway address is different and requires separate programming and tracking.
2. The number of failure points increase, for e.g. if one of the files could not be transmitted to the destination for some reason or was transmitted twice, then tracking and maintaining the audit trail for all such transactions becomes very essential. This increases risks for the corporate.

This is where SWIFT has introduced an offering to enable the corporate to directly access the banks, using the SWIFT network. This is being offered under the MA-CUG facility (Member Access - Corporate User Group). SWIFT acts as a single gateway to all the banks for the corporate, and thus reduces the failure points and tracking risks for it. As SWIFT is already connected to most major banks this is a considerable advantage to corporates, banks and SWIFT itself.

Given the growth in the trade business and also the capital markets activity over the last two decades, such services for integrating the ERP Systems with the Payment Systems of banks under the cash management services provided by the banks have certainly contributed by providing a robust platform to achieve this growth. They have also laid the foundation for providing higher efficiency and productivity for servicing future business.

Merger of Cash and Trade

Trade services like LCs, have been provided by the banks for over hundred years now. As such, trade services and trade departments have been fairly established in the banks for a long time. The correspondent banking business, also referred to as Financial Institution (FI) business, has also been established for a long time. The key activities of the correspondent banking business provide the following services.

(a) A network for clearing services to the partner bank as discussed earlier under the evolution of cash management, e.g. State Bank of India does not have branch presence in the US and uses Citibank as its partner bank in the USA by opening a US Dollar account with it. So, if any US Dollar payment has to be made or received from USA by State Bank of India, it does so by routing the transaction through its account with Citibank in the USA. This is very similar to what a corporate does for making or receiving domestic payments for which they open an account with a bank.

(b) Authentication arrangements for handling transactions bi-laterally. In the olden, golden era this was achieved through an exchange of signatures of all officers of the bank. So, if an LC or a demand draft was issued by State bank of India in favor of the seller in the USA, Citibank would verify the signatures to ascertain if it was genuine and indeed issued by State Bank of India. However, it would be evident that it was very difficult to maintain signatures of all officers of various banks especially as bank officers were transferred or changed jobs. In the new world, this function has been taken over by exchanging electronic passwords as most transactions are concluded electronically.

(c) Credit limits for discounting of LCs etc. where, Citibank would extend money to the seller based on the LC/guarantee provided by State Bank of India.

As is apparent from this activity (a) above pertains to the cash management business now being offered by banks to corporates. However, historically the activity of correspondent banking has been linked closely to the trade department of the bank, mainly because of activity (c), which is more oriented towards trade services.

Compared to trade services and correspondent banking, cash management is a new business for the banking industry with a history of about 3 decades. In the last decade, some banks assembled trade services, cash management and correspondent banking under the umbrella of transaction banking to achieve better integration through the similarities in these lines of business. Within these, there is an increasing trend to merge cash and trade services under a single ownership or create a new line of business under supply chain in order to address the increasing need of better integration from the corporates.

To get an understanding of the thought process behind such a change, we will try to realize the elements and the linkages within the supply chain, which are driving this trend. For a corporate, the supply chain process generally proceeds as under:

Step 1	Buyer places a purchase order on the corporate
Step 2	Seller procures raw material, produces the finished products and delivers
Step 3	Seller raises invoice on the buyer
Step 4	The buyer accepts the invoice
Step 5	The buyer pays to seller as per agreed terms

Fig. 2.5 *Key steps in the supply chain process of a corporate*

From a bank's perspective the cash management team of the bank gets involved during Step 5.

The trade services team of the bank will get involved in Step 1 if an LC has to be issued and will be further involved in Step 3, 4 and 5 when the documents are submitted and payments made. Alternatively, if it is a DA/DP collections arrangement, the trade services department of the bank will be involved in Step 3, 4 and 5.

It is evident from this, that if the payment terms for the trade are open account, then the cash management team of the bank is involved. On the other hand, if the payment terms are through an LC or through DA/DP collections, then the trade services team of the bank gets involved! However, there are many good reasons within the banks that cause this strict boundary between cash management and trade services to blur.

While there has been tremendous growth and transformation in the physical supply chain, the basic need of buyer and seller for mitigation of payment and delivery risk based on their mutual standings, which led to the introduction of trade services by banks over hundred years ago, has not changed. The benefits provided by all the various trade products e.g. LC, DA/ DP collections, pre and post shipment finance, etc. are all very relevant in the current environment as well.

However, the methods of delivering the traditional trade services are far less relevant to the realities of the modern physical supply chain. This has restrained the growth and use of traditional trade services in many of the new situations today, where the benefits of these trade services could still be relevant.

As an example, consider the case where edible palm oil has to be imported into Chennai, the Eastern coast of India from Malaysia. The buyer from India issues an LC in favor of the Malaysian seller in the traditional way. The dispatch department of the seller loads the edible oil on the ship, say on July 1, 2006, which is a Saturday. The dispatch department, in a very efficient case, presents the document to their finance department who are processing the LC and interfacing with the bank on Monday morning, since Saturday and Sunday are holidays. The finance department after compiling from various places, documents such as the insurance policy, invoice, certificate of origin, transport document etc., provides these to the bank by end of day on Monday. In the best case, the seller's bank does not find any discrepancy with the documents and couriers them on Tuesday. The courier takes at least 2 days to deliver the documents to the buyer's bank, i.e. on Thursday afternoon. The buyer's bank processes the documents on Friday and calls the buyer to accept these documents if there are no discrepancies with them. The fact that there were no discrepancies in the document would itself be a miracle, in most cases. The acceptance or payment of the buyer can be processed only on Monday, while the paper work can be completed with the bank, and also payments made for customs duty etc. The buyer can then collect the documents on Monday for release of the oil on Monday or Tuesday, which is July 10, 2006 or on July 11. Meanwhile the ship will already have arrived at the port on July 5, 2006 and the demurrage for these extra days can be very large! Refer to Figure 2.6 for a linear view of the timelines and the activities and linkages involved therein.

Further points to be highlighted from this example are as follows.

- In the case shown, many of the operations regarding handling of the paper documents such as handling of papers by the delivery team of the seller, finance team of the seller, seller's bank, courier and the buyer's bank, could take substantially more time than that estimated in Figure 2.6. Further it is estimated that 60%–80% of the documents received under LCs by banks are discrepant—resulting in substantial delays in document processing between buyer, seller and banks! However, in spite of all the effort put in by various parties in discovering discrepancies in the documents, it is further estimated that only 1 in 1000 document is really rejected. In most cases the buyer and the seller agree on the discrepancy and pay under the LC. However, discrepancies add to substantial delays in the process.
- If the shipment is by air the demurrage and costs for storage of goods in the warehouse could be even higher.
- Sometimes the transport documents are used for trading, e.g. for trading of crude oil. In such a case the transport documents may pass through many more parties and therefore, take much longer.

Other than the significantly higher transportation efficiencies, the other striking diversity of the present day supply chain lies in the large number of participants in both the procurement and the distribution chain. It is not unusual for companies to source from tens and hundreds of specialized vendors and then again distribute through an even larger number of distributors and retailers. The processes set out for traditional trade services were much before the introduction of such monumental changes and therefore do not cater to many of the situations arising in modern trade.

Sl. No.	Date	Activity	Who	Risk of Delay
1	July 1 Sat	Dispatch department loads oil and gets bill of lading	Seller	
2	July 3 Mon	Dispatch department prepares documents and hands over to Finance department	Seller	If the port/dispatch is in different location from finance office, transport of documents will take time
3	July 3 Mon	Finance department verifies the document	Seller	Usually to and from between finance and dispatch department on perfecting document could lead to delays
4	July 3 Mon	Finance department gives documents to their bank	Seller	
5	July 4 Tue	Bank verifies the documents and couriers these to the buyer's bank	Seller Bank	Usually to and from between finance department and bank on removing discrepancies in document could lead to delays
6	July 6 Thu	Courier delivers the documents to the buyer bank	Buyer Bank	
7	July 7 Fri	Buyer bank examines the documents and presents them to buyer for acceptance	Buyer Bank	Discrepancies, if any, found in the documents could lead to large delays
8	July 7 Fri	The finance and procurement department of the buyer examine the document versus the order terms and the LC	Buyer	This co-ordination and verification could take longer
8	July 8 Sat	Buyer accepts the documents and makes payment for the goods	Buyer	Transfer of money from some other bank through clearing could take time
9	July 10 Mon	Buyer collects documents and initiates the release of goods	Buyer	

Fig. 2.6 *Comparison of the timelines of the physical movement of goods versus the movement of documents and the potential points of delays in movement of documents*

As a result of such changes many transactions of the modern physical supply chain do not get processed in the trade services department and get settled in the cash management departments of the banks. Despite that, some of these transactions may need the support of some of the trade services offered by banks. Though no published figures are available, it is estimated that more than 90% of international trade, by volume, is settled on open account basis and therefore through the cash management departments of banks. However, this figure is estimated to be a little lower—at about 80%—by value, for settlement of trade under open account basis, especially as the trade instruments like letter of credit have been used for larger value transactions such as import of crude oil. It is estimated that about 90% of the international trade used to be settled under letter of credit in the 1950s, indicating that the use of LCs has not kept pace with the growth in international trade. For domestic trade, it is estimated that over 95% of the transactions are settled on an open account basis.

However, this has led to one advantageous situation. The adaptation of cash management services by the corporate has increased and kick-started the following processes:

- Corporates have outsourced some of their operations activities to the banks. Both the banks and corporates now have working relationship, experience and linkages at the operations level. Such corporates are now open to outsourcing more of their processes to the bank and such processes generally tend to further integrate the supply chain processes of the corporate with the payment and settlement services provided by the banks.
- Through cash management, linkages are being established between the corporate ERP systems and the bank systems. Such integration platforms can and are being extended to further integrate the corporate supply chain with the trade services of the bank.

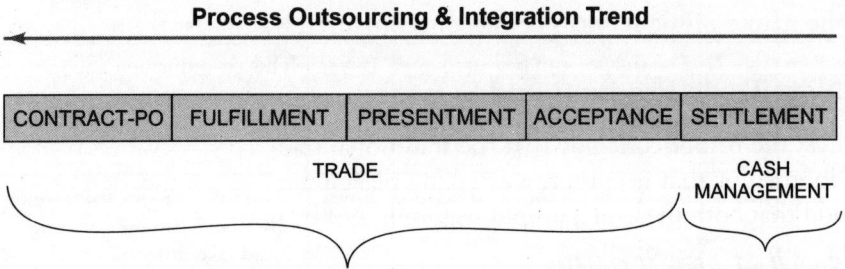

Process Outsourcing & Integration Trend

CONTRACT-PO	FULFILLMENT	PRESENTMENT	ACCEPTANCE	SETTLEMENT

TRADE   CASH
                                                        MANAGEMENT

Fig. 2.7 *Traditional boundaries of trade and cash management business within banks and the process outsourcing and ERP integration trend by corporates*

From a corporate treasurer's point of view the cash management and trade services are departments of the bank. For corporate treasury operations all trades need to be settled and reconciled, irrespective of the payment mode. The corporate treasurer would like to freely organize loans against his physical supply chain, settle the payments through various payment methods and have a single interface within the bank for all such payments. Some of the banks, realizing this need and linkages have further closely linked trade and cash management services and have put them under one head or have created new departments to service this emerging need.

In a recent conference, on the topic of Financial Supply Chain, the representative of a large multi-national pharmaceutical company—posed the following teaser to fellow bankers. "The payment operations are still some way away from complete integration and STP. How does one reasonably expect the banks to support automation along the financial supply chain—which is much more complex." He then went on to explain the workflow complexity of their international trade operations—largely centered around LC and with high degree of regulating complexity. The point was very well received. However, as was explained that the—complexities of a payment method can be broadly classified in the following levels of ascending order:

- Advance Payment or Open Payments
- Document Against Payment
- Document Against Acceptance
- Letters of Credits

The attempts on early solutions around the Financial Supply Chain are tuned more towards simple transactions—and drawing on simple cases—possibly around each of the above 4 mentioned payment types. The most complex cases on Supply Chain—which center around the existing LC or trade business—will continue to be done as they are done today and it will take a while before—advancements in technology adaptation and collaboration—make the automation of complex cases feasible.

We will subsequently examine in a little more detail in chapters 3, 4 and 5, the nature of the services being conceptualized by such specialized units.

New Trade Products and Services

Lest the reader conclude that the traditional trade services of the banks are doomed or that no progress is taking place therein, I would like to hastily add that both these presumptions would not be true.

Standby Letters of Credit

Traditional trade services continue to satisfy the need of specific market segments where:

- Some companies like Dow chemicals have centralized all their LC and documentation processing for their sales in order to achieve much higher processing accuracy and efficiencies through economies to counter some of the inefficiencies in the paper process. The fact that Dow is a very reputed company helps them to keep the documentation simple by enforcing their terms on the buyers so that there are not too many discrepancies against the LC when documents are presented. The LC thus provides them mitigation for payment risk.
- Large transactions for trade in crude oil are generally covered under LCs. Again as previously, the LCs require very simple documentation so that the risk of dispute and returns is very low. This is done, as crude oil is a commodity and if the buyer does not take delivery for

any reason, then although the seller may be able to take back the consignment, any fluctuations in the price of crude or the return shipment cost, would more than erode any profit margin of the sellers.

It is therefore, apparent that under specific situations some of the traditional services are still relevant. Albeit from earlier days of the LC, there is one noticeable change in the way that some LCs are now drawn. Many of the new LC documentation require a very minimal set of documents, unlike the comprehensive set of documents required by some other LCs, which makes them easy to verify and the chances of discrepancy and dispute is therefore, minimum.

In line with these market practices, the *International Chamber of Commerce* (ICC) introduced the first set of rules and practices governing Standby Letters of Credit (*SBLC*), called *ISP98*. ICC states that, 'the rules will make it possible to draft a standby letter of credit correctly, without being an expert'. The structure and key conditions of ISP98 are included in Exhibit 9.

Unlike LCs, which require expertise in handling at various stages by all parties involved, SBLCs are much simpler. Under an SBLC the seller can generally request for payment by just submitting a request for payment, in the format specified in the SBLC, to the buyer's bank that has issued the SBLC. First associated with the US market, the standby is now a truly international product. The number of standbys outstanding in value terms is estimated to exceed those of commercial credits by a ratio of more than 5:1!

A high level workflow on operation of an SBLC is shown below:

Sl.No.	Activity	Who
1	Buyer requests bank to issue SBLC in favor of seller	Buyer
2	Buyer bank issues the SBLC and sends the SBLC to the seller bank	Buyer bank
3	The seller bank advises the SBLC to the seller	Seller bank
	The steps below are repeated many times as required by the seller and buyer	
	(a) Buyer raises purchase order on the seller	Buyer
	(b) Seller supplies as per purchase order and raises an invoice on buyer	Seller
	(c) Buyer pays to the seller	Buyer
	The step below is executed only in case of an exception	
	Buyer fails to pay the seller as per agreed terms	
4	Seller raises a demand for payment through his bank as per specifications in the SBLC	Seller
5	Seller bank verifies the request and forwards the request to buyer bank	Seller Bank
6	Buyer bank verifies the payment request and pays as per the terms of SBLC	Buyer Bank
	Buyer bank recovers money from buyer as per agreement between them	

Fig. 2.8   *Key workflow steps in the life cycle of standby letter of credit*

As against an LC, a SBLC puts the buyer at a higher risk—as a unilateral demand for payment by the seller—could jeopardize the interest of the buyer. However, in many cases—where the seller is of a relatively higher standing—this model works just fine.

Building Efficiencies in the Existing Models

Banks have furthered the services under trade finance and services by enhancing the efficiency of the existing models through:

- Scanning the documents and making available trade documents electronically.
- Multinational banks like ABN AMRO have created special structures for some of their customers in Europe who source goods from Asia so that the LCs are issued from the same branch at which the seller in Asia, subsequently submits the documents. This helps in cutting down verification from two places and also ensures a faster turnaround time for the documents. This particular case is discussed in more detail in a subsequent section.

Of course many banks have now made access to their trade services available electronically, over the Internet. This allows customers to establish LCs, view the document status and make payments over the Internet.

Apart from introduction of the standby letter of credit to support the growth in electronic commerce, a supplement to UCP 500 called the e-UCP was proposed in 2002 to deal with the presentation of all electronic or part electronic documents. The first version of e-UCP was released in April 2002 but is yet to gain usage and acceptance. Some of the key considerations of e-UCP are included in Exhibit 10. The e-UCP was developed as a supplement to UCP due to the strong sense of feeling at the time that banks and corporates together with the transport and insurance industries were ready to make that 'leap' into the electronic world of document and data delivery. The hope and expectation that surrounded the development of e-UCP has failed to materialize into day-to-day transactions and its usage has been, to put it mildly, minimal.

Emerging Consensus for New Standards

With the growth in business and transaction volumes there is a recognized need for more efficient processing of trade transactions. With advancements in information technology, one method being proposed is to connect the various parties involved in the trade transaction through electronic messages. However, if the IT systems of the various parties involved in the trade transaction are to exchange information in a straight through manner, there has to be consensus on standards for the message formats and the medium. A great amount of effort and resources are being spent on this area to facilitate more efficient processing of trade transactions.

The general consensus around XML (eXtensible Mark-up Language) as a medium has provided an opportunity to create flexible but standardized data transfer formats over the Internet. In the payments and commercial sphere, a number of groups grasped this opportunity with a view to setting standards for straight through processing, including the automated processing of collections and receipts. This is estimated to substantially increase inter-connectivity and STP processes between corporate and bank, corporate and corporate, and bank and bank!

As described, there are many workflow steps for the conclusion of a trade transaction. Each of these workflow steps is further composed of smaller activity steps or exchange of messages, which lead to the conclusion of the workflow steps. These steps and the activities may also differ based on the business requirements of the industry and the corporate and their counter-party. To illustrate the sample workflow steps for concluding a trade transaction consider the following in a traditional paper world:

1. Buyer issues purchase order.
   (a) Buyer types purchase order.
   (b) Sends the purchase order to seller by courier.
   (c) Seller confirms receipt of purchase order.
   (d) Seller confirms acceptance of purchase order.
2. Seller ships the goods and presents invoice.
3. Buyer accepts the goods and invoice.
4. Buyer makes payment.

The above illustration of workflows and activities could be much more complex in real life, demanding for example amendment, cancellation, etc.

Further illustration of the steps and various interactions that could be followed for a simple payment transaction are shown in Figure 2.9.

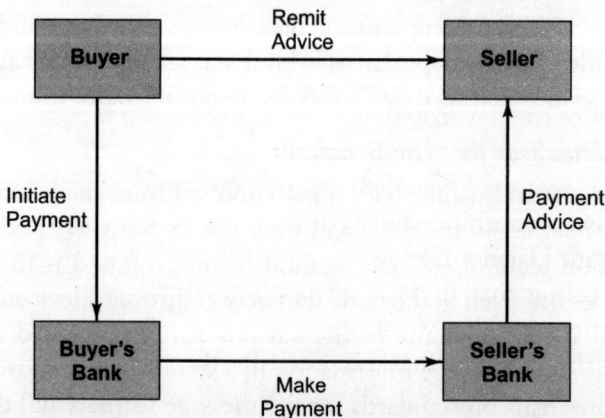

Fig. 2.9   *Illustration of steps that would be followed by various parties for a simple payment transaction*

As can be seen from this, if all these messages for various workflows and scenarios are to be exchanged electronically in a standard manner between various organizations, there is considerable amount of work that needs to be done in order to:

- Define the standards that can be adopted by the various trade participants.
- Get the various trade participants to agree on the standards.
- Aid the implementation and change the 'standard' definitions from learning's of the implementation.
- Additionally each of the messages are further broken down into receipt acknowledgements, acceptance and rejections, handling of duplicate messages, handling of lost messages, etc.

Nearly 70 organizations are involved in developing financial or financially related XML messaging, including but not limited to:

- SWIFT
- CIDX (Chemical industry)
- IFX (Banking Industry sponsored)
- Open Applications Group (ERP and Oracle sponsored)
- PapiNet (Paper and pulp industry)
- RosettaNet (Electronic component, technology and telecommunications industry)
- TWIST
- UN/CEFACT TBG5
- X12 XML

Several participants from the banking community support many of these initiatives. Many companies including Shell (TWIST), Nokia, Intel, Cisco, Texas Instrument and National Semiconductor, the RosettaNet Payment Milestone Program pilot leaders have led corporate participation in these developments.

The results of their analyses and pilot projects have been used for the improvement of the new payment messages proposed herein.

As it became clear that these separate message development initiatives would not lead to a single standard, major banks encouraged several of these organizations to combine their efforts. The result is the International Standards Team Harmonization.

It is interesting that there is tremendous enthusiasm among various sections of the corporate world for arriving at standards. This is natural considering the large savings potential by the implementation of such standards.

So far, many of the integration efforts between various counter-parties involved in trade have been bi-lateral. This has led to say, General Motors integrating its ERP systems with all its dealers and vendors. However, this model is not extensible. If Ford has to integrate its ERP systems with the same dealer or vendor the integration would have to be carried all over again by Ford and the counter-parties. Considering the large number of organizations involved in trade the theoretical number for which is say, N; then for complete integration each of these N organizations would need to integrate with each of the other N organizations. This works out to N^2 integrations, which will have to be executed. However, if a standard interchange medium can be specified, the number of integrations need to be only N, as once an interface has been created it can be used with every other counter-party. This is a substantial economic saving! Thus, if we consider that there are about 100,000 organizations in a country, the problem of integration reduces from 10,000,000,000 (100,000 x 100,000) to 100,000 when standards are implemented and accepted in the country economy. It could be argued that not all organizations will need to be integrated with each other. One could therefore, make an assumption that each organization would need to be integrated with say, 30 other organizations. Even then the number of integrations required after standardization i.e: 100,000 would be much less than 3,000,000 i.e. less by 30 times and this is indeed a large saving for an economy.

While the work on standards is yet to progress to a meaningful proportion, the thought that it would happen at sometime in the future is certain and exciting. The magnitude of this change is akin to establishment of common law for all citizens, which substantially enhances order and progress of a society. Such standards once formed, accepted and implemented at large, have the potential to create a similar progress and efficiency in the world of commerce. That would be substantial e-commerce! More details on what some of these organizations are trying to achieve in the space of standards are discussed in subsequent chapters.

3

e-Financial Supply Chain—Banks Perspective

WHAT IS AT STAKE FOR THE BANKS?

"The new economy barbarians are at the gate and the authorities have started to dismantle the walls". This was the concern of a very senior banker in a multinational bank, in 2000. Although, with the dot com melt-down such fears proved to be premature, many of the service offerings from new age service providers do threaten sources of revenues for the banks.

Credit and float income have traditionally dominated over two-thirds of the revenues for wholesale banking activities; the rest is contributed by treasury and fee income. However, the income from traditional credit products in banks have declined due to:

- Rise in use of market instruments like commercial papers and debentures, which have been used to finance the trade business, instead of traditional instruments such as bill discounting, loans and overdraft facilities. This has been facilitated by an increasing number of corporates getting their debt instruments rated by agencies like Standard and Poor and Moody's.
- The operations costs associated with the use of typical trade finance facilities is high for both banks and the corporate and this has resulted in a decline of such instruments.

While the investors in the earlier trade finance and other loan instruments were largely banks, the investors in the treasury instruments are very often corporate and mutual funds with surplus cash.

There is pressure in payments space as well since payment products have now become more like commodities, and revenues and margins from traditional products have been squeezed. This is as a result of:

- Improving efficiencies in the clearing networks through greater use of electronic and straight through clearing processes, inter-bank clearing houses and automated linkages between correspondent banks, thus leading to reduction in float opportunity for the banks.
- Non-bank companies such as Pay-Pal, Western Union, Remit2India, etc. are encroaching on to the territories of banks in the regular payment space. While this trend is at present seen more in the retail and small remittances space, with a larger spread and ease of automation iBos style payment clubs of corporates cannot be ruled out.
- A large non-bank, technology company, Oracle announced a partnership with MasterCard to provide transaction data integration programs for purchasing cards. There are many other companies like TradeCard and others mentioned earlier, who have their sights on financial supply chain automation.
- Some big multinational corporates with large subsidiary and branch networks have set up in-house treasuries and follow a practice of netting payments, resulting in payments transactions through the bank networks being greatly reduced. With better automation such practices will increase.
- Increasing competition in payments space is forcing players to cut prices.

By providing efficiency in working capital management and financial supply chain optimization, the banks have an opportunity to regain some of the lost territory and also enhance their position in the payments space.

However, increasingly the banks and corporates realize that working capital optimization is closely linked to the automation and integration with the supply chain; and, it is not just linked to the last leg i.e. the settlement or payment leg, of the supply chain. Large efficiencies can be achieved in many steps in the supply chain, by closely linking the financial processes with the physical processes.

Although the ERP companies appear to hold an advantage on the issue of 'integration of the financial supply chain', the banks too are in a strong position. Presently, a large number of companies rely on banks to provide or receive remittance information. Most companies rely and trust the banks very highly and have demanded the following key services to increase their use of electronic payment services through the banks:

- Integration with the accounting payment systems
- Standard interface formats for remittances and payments
- Improved fraud control
- Reconciliation services from banks

The inefficiencies in the financial supply chain is a ripe area for banks to provide a solution, especially with the tremendous growing interest and awareness surrounding the space within the corporates. There is a huge amount of working capital and operations efficiency to be achieved in the supply chain. Banks can play the perfect role of an intermediary since the interests of the buyer and seller are typically diverse on the payment date, where the buyer wants to increase his days payable and the seller wants to reduce his days payable and collect as soon as possible. The bank can allow the buyer and the seller to select an appropriate funding option through a mix of payment–credit structure so that both can manage their working capital most efficiently.

SERVICE POSITIONING OF BANKS

Banks have traditionally been:
  (a) Facilitating clearing, and
  (b) Providing Loans and Risk Management Services

For services in the e-financial supply chain domain, the banks would have to anchor their services around the above two key value propositions in order to support the other elements of the physical supply chain of the corporate. Banks cannot and should not aspire to be logistics providers or freight-forwarders. However, if some of the processes within the supply chain can be facilitated by better integration with these two key value propositions, banks would then need to examine such a proposition. A pictorial of the space that the banks could operate in is shown in Figure 3.1.

From the above positioning map, it is evident that banks can add value to the corporate processes in the following space as marked out:
  A. In the area marked 'A' the bank can add value to the corporate by integrating the banking proposition along with the financial processes of the corporate e.g. payments, collections, etc.
  B. Integrating the banking proposition with the financial processes of the corporate and also the physical supply chain of the corporate. A few such cases are described in a later section in this book as cases for the financial supply chain.
  C. There is no role for the bank unless it wishes to follow the example of JPMorgan Chase Vastera. This case is discussed in a subsequent section.
  D. Integrating the banking proposition with the physical supply chain of the corporate. Some of such cases are described in a later section in this book as cases for the financial supply chain.

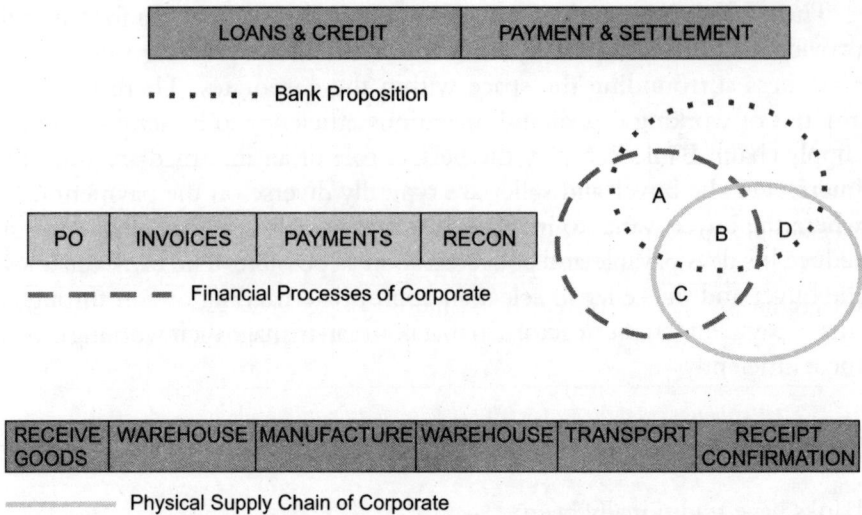

Fig. 3.1 *Integration of the physical and the financial supply chain and the value map for services*

Such positioning would allow the banks to grow their offerings by anchoring around their core competencies.

One key challenge faced by banks is the gargantuan variety in the processes and information carried in the supply chain of the various corporates. Amazingly, it differs within an industry between two corporates as well. However, organizations like TWIST and RosettaNet are examples of increasing co-operation and standardization within the corporate sector to achieve uniformity in their processes for better integration between themselves. Banks will therefore, need to create targeted offerings by identifying the market segments where specific offerings can be targeted.

Further, integration holds the key to the success of the financial supply chain services. To start with, the banks will need to internally integrate their services around trade and cash to facilitate smoother delivery and supply chain efficiencies to the corporate.

The banks would like to place their existing offerings and delivery channels alongside the new offerings that they intend to provide for the supply chain.

The positioning and the various dimensions of e-financial supply chain services within the overall product and channel portfolio at the bank would be as depicted in Fig. 3.2.

For any commercial offering, the banks will need to define the value proposition that the corporate will enjoy out of the offerings and will also simultaneously need to examine the sources of revenues that they can expect by offering such facilities to their corporate customers.

Market Segment	By Industry	By Need	By Client Base e.g. Dealers, Vendors, Client	
Delivery Channels	Web	SMS	Branches	Cards
Core Products	Trade	Cash		
e-Financial Supply Chain	Supply Chain Financing	Trade Settlement	Trade Facilitation	Risk Mitigation
Integration	Cash	Treasury	Supply Chain e.g. Dealers, Vendors, Client	Partners e.g. Insurance, Logistics

Fig. 3.2 *Positioning and the various dimensions of e-financial supply chain services that can be offered by banks*

A more detailed break-up of the type of e-financial supply chain services, the value proposition of each of the services and the income that the bank can expect to be earned from each of the initiatives is shown in Fig. 3.3.

e-Financial Supply Chain		Value Proposition	Revenue Type
Supply Chain Financing			
1	Manufacturing Centric	Dealer, Vendor, Client Finance	Interest
2	Buying House Centric	Pre-shipment and Post-shipment	Commission
3	Wholesale Distribution	Dealer/Vendor Support	Fee
4	Fast Moving Consumer Goods	Working Capital Efficiency	
		STP and End-to-end Integration	
		Reconciliation	
		Operations Efficiency	
		MIS—Invoices outstanding, Tracking, Credit outstanding etc.	
Trade Settlement Models			
5	Assured Settlement	Working Capital Efficiency	Commission
6	Conditional Settlement	STP and End-to-end Integration	Fee
7	Structured Payments	Reconciliation	
8	Open Payment	Operations Efficiency	
9	Exchange Settlement	MIS—Invoices outstanding, Tracking, Credit outstanding etc.	

Trade Facilitation Models			
10	Document Preparation	Outsourcing, Document Accuracy	Fee
11	Partner Validation	Security/Deal Validation	
12	Logistics Integration	Operations Efficiency	
13	Buyer Credit Limit Processing	MIS	
14	Expense Budgets Tracking		
Risk Mitigation			
15	Supplier Credit Insurance	Credit Insurance	Fee
16	Supplier Credit Re-Insurance	Packaged with above services— Operations Efficiency	Re-distribution Fee
			Commission

Fig. 3.3   *Value offering to clients and possible sources of revenue for services under e-financial supply chain*

As can be seen, banks can offer multiple types of services under the e-financial supply chain umbrella to the different type of entities involved in trade and more can be added as one goes along. Considering that each of these can be further combined with one or more of the offerings, e.g. one of the supply chain financing models can be offered along with one of the trade settlement models, the number and variety of offerings can be very large. There lies the challenge and the opportunities in the e-financial supply chain. Successful banks will be able to create offerings where these services can be constructed in small blocks and the bank can then combine these blocks to offer the full range of e-financial supply chain services.

To further elucidate these models, Figure 3.4 associates them with some of the case studies listed in Chapter 5.

Though some of the models here do not have a corresponding case study, this figure will provide readers with a fair idea of the possibilities and nature of e-financial supply chain services.

While offering e-financial services some of the key objectives of the bank would be:

- To be able to participate in the entire transaction flow, end-to-end.
- Establish a relationship with key anchor tenants in the supply chain.
- Create an environment that works for everyone and where it can facilitate the participation of other banks and vendors.

e-Financial Supply Chain		Chapter 3, Case Study	Case No.
Supply Chain Financing			
1	Manufacturing Centric	Technolux, Kea Furniture	10,12
2	Buying House Centric	Duke Mart	9
3	Wholesale Distribution	Lube Oil	8
4	Fast Moving Consumer Goods		
Trade Settlement Models			
6	Assured Settlement	Orion Plastics	2
7	Conditional Settlement	FMCG Co	3
8	Structured Payments	Oyster Petroleum, Rose Mall, Rio Dev Agency	1,5,6
9	Open Payment	Rose Mall, Rio Development Agency	5,6
10	Exchange Settlement	e-Payment Exchange	7
Trade Facilitation Models			
10	Document Preparation		
11	Partner Validation		
12	Logistics Integration	Argyll Co	4
13	Buyer Credit Limit Processing		
14	Expense Budgets Tracking		
Risk Mitigation			
15	Supplier Credit Insurance		
16	Supplier Credit Re-Insurance	Organic Chemicals	11

Fig. 3.4 *Elucidation of e-financial supply chain models by associating these to the cases mentioned under Chapter 5*

The bank would not want to:
- Offer credit facilities to everyone, as it cannot practically or alternatively, establish an account relationship with everyone; although, like any commercial organization the banks would like to maximize their revenue and profits by providing services to possibly all the vendors, dealers and supply chain partners of a corporate. However, there are limitations in any enterprise and a single bank cannot lend to or service everyone or monopolize the entire business.
- Compete only on the basis of pricing.

From an overall objective of profit enhancement, the e-financial supply chain model is attractive as it enables the banks to tap the large procurement and distribution chain of the corporate. The bank knows the corporate well and the corporate knows the partners in their supply chain well. This adds substantially to the comfort of the bank.

However, from a credit decision-making point of view, the credit structure has to be very different from the typical credit decision tools and structures used for commercial credit. As many of the transactions and credit limits will be of a low value the operating costs for credit decisions should also be low. Credit scoring engines along with the comfort that the corporate enjoys and provides for the supply chain will have to be the key decision drivers for credit in such cases.

CHALLENGES FACED BY THE BANKS

While many organizations and banks have been keen on advancing along such e-financial supply chain services, the progress has been slow. The key challenges faced by banks in advancing these services to their customers are:

- Co-ordination challenges within the corporate.
- Implementation of collaborative standards—the chicken and egg situation.
- Legal hurdles.
- Silos of organizational structure.
- Availability of trained resources.

Co-ordination Challenges within the Corporate

While there is considerable interest in improving the working capital efficiencies at a corporate, the progress has been limited. One of the big challenges faced by the banks is the way corporates are structured and the defined role of the Chief Financial Officer (CFO) with whom the banks generally interact, and his sphere of influence within the organization.

In a 2004 *GTNews* working capital survey, more than 85% of the respondents felt that their working capital processes could be made more efficient. While over 88% of the treasurers played a key role in managing the finances of the company, only a small minority was accountable for efficiency of the accounts payable and accounts receivable functions of the corporate. In most corporates this function is the domain of the procurement and sales team, respectively. However, if larger working capital efficiency has to be achieved, more integration has to be demonstrated by the corporates in their various organizational functions, viz. procurement, sales, IT and finance. This will enable a more wholesome dialog between the bank and the corporate.

The other challenge faced by the banks in dealing with corporates is that the corporates would not like to disturb their processes and would prefer the bank's offerings to be integrated into their existing processes and systems. This is both costly, time consuming and also propagates the proprietary systems.

From a corporate perspective, they are outsourcing some of their business processes to the bank. Like any other business process outsourcing transaction the corporate has to take care of the following key aspects related to outsourcing:

- Outsourcing of the process activities to the bank should not reduce the efficiency of its existing processes. This includes both the processing and also the timely availability of information.
- Outsourcing of the business process should be done with adequate security safeguards. The pipeline where the bank processes integrate with those of the corporate would be most vulnerable to a security breach.
- There should be an adequate audit trail to ensure that the outsourced process has been performed as per the mandate for process given by the corporate.
- Confidentiality issues surrounding the transaction should be maintained.

The bank processes and systems will need to be tailored to meet such requirements of the corporate.

Implementation of Collaborative Standards—the Chicken and Egg Situation

Providing solutions and services requires integration and automation across the many accounting and ERP systems at the corporate and also with their supply chain partners.

However, banks face a quandary as their proprietary middleware and legacy systems, which have historically acted as differentiators, are becoming an unsustainable modus operandi. Investing in new proprietary systems and bi-lateral interfaces with ERP systems of corporates is expensive and maintaining these is even more difficult, especially when banks would like to introduce new services rapidly in the evolving environment of financial supply chain!

By adopting standard interfaces and reducing the number of bi-lateral interfaces, and enabling straight through processing between the bank's systems and the accounting and ERP systems of the corporate and its supply chain, the banks can not only reduce their operations cost but also generate new revenue streams.

Presently however, adoption of standards is faced with a chicken and egg situation because of the following considerations:

- Standards are only as useful and strong as the number of participants who have adopted them in a chain. Banks will continue to face situations, even assuming substantial progress on standards adoption over a period of time, where there will be a good number of customers who would continue to work with proprietary interfaces. In the transition period the banks will have to invest in interfaces for standards as well as in proprietary interfaces.

  For companies where the IT resources are scarce and where the proprietary interfaces are already in place and working fine, there is very little incentive to undertake change especially if it could disrupt existing operations without substantial additional benefits.

- The standards are themselves new and yet to stabilize through usage and user acceptance over a wider spectrum of industries, customers, business situations and workflows. While the early explorers will benefit from early bird advantage they will also have to incur extra investment and cost in the learning process of the stabilization of these standards.

- For new products, services and offerings for the financial supply chain, the competitive offerings are in the nascent state of evolution. Here the pioneer banks have no choice but to develop these offerings and practices before any standards can evolve in such domains.

This is a chicken and egg situation.

- Until the standards are adopted and used these will not be good and comprehensive.

- Until the standards are good and comprehensive, there is resistance to implementation of these standards by the market participants, except from some of the missionary organizations.

Another similar dilemma lies in development of new offerings:

- Unless there are stable market offerings on the e-financial supply chain, the standards development bodies do not have sufficient facts and justification to develop standards.

- Unless there are standard methods of linking up with the various participants in the financial supply chain, there is disincentive for banks to add new services through use of proprietary interfaces.

As the chicken and egg situation did occur, as is evident from their present existence, the current state of affairs will also be overcome. Some banks and corporates are together charting new services, which can be offered in an incremental manner with justification for the investment while also pushing the whole sphere of services to the financial supply chain domain. The case studies provided under Chapter 5 are examples of where the bank and the corporate have worked together to achieve the task.

Legal Hurdles

While the base legal framework for electronic commerce has been established by the UNCITRAL, a member body of the United Nations, and has been accepted and adopted by many countries in their legal constituents, there is still much progress to be made by banks in terms of understanding and implanting legal documentation and processes for delivering financial supply chain solutions. For example, some of the legal dilemmas being faced by the banks are:

- If invoice financing services are offered, does the bank need to have a physical copy of the invoice? If yes, then should the invoice be presented before the finance or can it be made available subsequently?
  If the bank does not require the physical invoice, does it need to audit the same at the corporate premises at periodic intervals?
- In some countries e.g. Thailand, every financing over a certain amount (e.g. all financing over USD 25,000) requires a Promissory note (pronote) to be accepted by the borrower. So every invoice finance transaction over USD 25,000 has to be accompanied by a physical pronote!
  Can such a pronote be accepted electronically? Can it be accepted subsequently, after the execution of the transaction? Alternatively, can such a pronote be waived under the overall Loan agreement between the borrower and the bank, which is the underlying contract?
- In some countries, the bill of exchange, is a negotiable instrument used for trade finance, is subject to Stamp duty. Here, the physical instrument is drawn on a government-registered paper of certain value, or stamps are affixed on a bill of exchange that has been drawn by a drawer!

How is such stamp duty to be paid in the case of financial supply chain? Can the Bank collect such a stamp duty on behalf of the corporate and pay the government department with due reconciliation?

Many such issues are country and jurisdiction specific and there are no right or wrong answers with anyone—the banks, the corporate and the regulators! The pioneering banks just need to graft their way and charter a course for themselves, along with the different entities and the system, which then sets the trend for others to follow. To the early explorer, the risks and the rewards are commensurate with each other.

Silos of Organization Structure

Despite the fact that it is the technology changes that are expected to drive most of the changes and efficiency in the financial supply chain, the banks cannot hope to provide such solutions with just technological changes. Banks will also need to re-structure their organizations in order to provide the new financial supply chain services.

The successful organizations in cash management have created the following organization structure for themselves:

- Product
- Sales
- Implementation
- Operations—Back office
- Operations—CRM
- Information Technology

Although such an organization structure may seem obvious to the accomplished players in cash management, many banking organizations are yet to achieve this level of focus in their product and services sales. Also noticeable is the implementation team, which the banks have been using to create linkages with the ERP systems of their clients.

However, if the banks are to realize their vision on the e-financial supply chain, further organizational changes will be required to meet the objectives.

1. Trade and Cash

At present, most banks have separate departments for trade and cash. However, creating offerings and solutions for the e-financial supply chain requires a good understanding of the systems, processes and business fundamentals of both the trade and cash services of the banks. It is necessary for banks to realize the complicity of trade and cash in order to further their services in the e-financial supply chain space.

However, this is easier said than done. The existing trade services business continues to be a meaningful revenue source for the banks and many corporates are dependent on it as well. It will be naïve to suddenly forsake existing trade finance business and exert full energies in a yet un-chartered territory.

Like change, which is always in the state of continuum and most natural changes are evolutionary, banks will need to create a spectrum of services involving traditional trade, cash management and the e-financial supply chain. Depending upon the speed of changes in the market, the banks will need to gradually increase their efforts and resources to the e-financial supply chain.

2. The Credit Chain

An efficient e-financial supply chain also means being able to offer an efficient hybrid of payment and credit services to the supply chain of the corporate.

Very often dealers and vendors in the supply chain of a corporate have a financial standing, which is significantly smaller when compared to that of the corporate. Trying to evaluate them on the same yardsticks used to measure the multinationals and large corporates does not help, as the results are always unfavorable.

- For a large corporate, the credit committees of commercial banks would generally examine the balance sheet and profit and loss account to estimate its financial health. This could be a serious problem when financing the supply chain as many of the dealers and vendors may be small enterprises, partnership companies or individuals with very small and unstructured financial statements, or no financial statements worth their while at all!
- Credit committees may want to examine and value the security collateral for such commercial lending. However, considering the size of the supply chain of the corporate this traditional examination exercise could in itself very often, be more expensive then the value of the security itself, which also changes hand very rapidly.
- The credit chain may want to examine the credit ratings or the market position of the borrowers as reflected in the stock markets or ratings in industry associations. Again, this could become difficult for the multiples of vendors and dealers involved in the supply chain of a corporate.

Very clearly the credit products and the credit processes for the e-financial supply chain have to be structured between the structure and processes for:
- Retail banking
- Investment banking/commercial banking

The lending process and decisions have to be template driven, like they are for retail banking. Yet, in implementing these templates the bank will need to derive comfort from the following factors:
- The length of relationship in years between the corporate and his dealers or vendors.
- Annual turnover of the dealer or vendor through the corporate.
- Investment of the dealers or vendors in the business of the corporate.
- Margins or returns to the dealers or vendors on their investment as estimated by the corporate.
- Credit history of the dealer or vendor with the corporate.
- The standing of the corporate in the market.

Such factors are important considerations in deriving a comfort level when creating lending products for the e-financial supply chain. In order to consider such aspects the existing credit processes will need to be overhauled. Credit committees of the banks will realize that for many decades the fertilizer and seed companies have been selling in remote areas through dealers and distributors without the comfort of a well-stacked annual report, and most of them have done well in their business. Banks will need to take similar business decisions and restructure their business processes, as corporates intend and offer to outsource and integrate parts of their supply chain business to the banks. As in the case of their retail lending business, the banks may wish to consider loan assets provisioning for such businesses. The credit chains will need to be evolved accordingly.

3. Role of Product

The role of product—where such function exists within the banks—is very often to conceptualize new product offerings in conjunction with sales and meetings with the corporate, and writing white papers on these. In very few banks is the function extended to exert influence on:

- Operations
- Technology
- Legal
- Credit

To offer products and services for the e-financial supply chain the product team of the bank will need to be well integrated with all the above functions. As highlighted earlier, efficiencies and effectiveness in the supply chain, which is highly operations driven can only be achieved through adequate automation. The product manager needs to be able to effectively maneuver the operations processes based on the requirements of the corporate and also set the direction for the technology team.

Strong linkages and influence with the legal team cannot be understated as in this evolving stage there are no set patterns. If one tries to follow the patterns of documentation of traditional banking products such legal processes will strongly hurdle the launch of products for the e-financial supply chain.

The role of credit chains in delivering credit products for the financial supply chain has been discussed earlier. It therefore, goes without saying that the product manager needs to be able to work closely with the credit team to create credit offerings for the supply chain.

Availability of Trained Resources

While the role of the product management team of the banks as illustrated earlier, encompasses the multiple aspects of banking, it also requires the individuals managing such teams to be familiar with all these aspects.

Automating the financial supply chain implies automating the operations. When the bank is managing thousands and millions of transactions every day the operations risks can be significant. These arise from handling exceptional situations such as:

- Delays in processing due to infrastructure bottlenecks.
- Handling un-reconciled transactions.
- Operations mistakes.
- Granting of daylight or short-term excesses or over-dues.

They need to be clearly understood and prioritized by the product manager and respective safeguards must be taken to mitigate such risks.

As advancements in the financial supply chain are being driven by automation and technology, the product manager needs to understand the technology well in order to propose relevant, contemporary and scalable solutions to enable extension of the services and integration to other corporate, as required. The role of technology also needs to be understood in terms of covering operations risks, where these could be significant.

While traditional trade services evolved and standardized over a period of time, they allowed the banks to standardize their legal processes in support of trade services. They also enabled organizations like the International Chamber of Commerce (ICC) to provide support services for better understanding the legal infrastructure by providing the relevant case studies and international courts for arbitration. Much of this is yet to evolve for the new domain of financial supply chain services. The product management team will need to understand legal risks associated with these transactions and cover these through appropriate documentation or, clearly separate the business risk from the legal and documentation risk so that the bank is clear on the risk it is undertaking.

In addition, when the product manager meet their credit committees they will need to be well aware of all the above structural risks associated with the transaction and also the credit risks involved. The product manager will also be required to propose a quantification of the risk reward parameters so that the bank can create a loss provision or a sinking fund for say, a total of 3% of the total portfolio upfront, much like retail lending, so that the bank can monitor its risk and losses. The product manager will also be required to provide transaction safeguards through relevant recourse structures or exit structures based on the relative strength of the corporate for which the transaction is being structured in order to protect the interests of the bank.

In the last decade, many banks have moved away from a 'generalist' structure to a more specialized style of functioning as such banks very often have experts in the respective fields. However, with the e-financial supply chain requiring cross-functional expertise on trade and cash and with adequate exposure to other aspects to banking as already listed, along with an understanding of the corporate processes and ability to work with a cross-section of people—both within the bank and also at the corporate level, to sew together a solution—such expertise is scarce. Banks will need to find and develop such people in order to take forward their mission of the e-financial supply chain.

THE WAY AHEAD

For long, the corporate world has been investing large amounts of money to make their supply chain processes more efficient. Now, the Internet has accelerated the process by providing collaborative networks for the various parties in the trade chain to interact with each other. It is also makes it much easier and more cost-effective to roll out these services.

Traditional trade finance products permeated by merchants in the seventeenth century are not live to this change. Letters of credit, which were used for about 90% of the international trade transactions in 1950s, are now used for less than 10% of such transactions. Also, just providing an electronic medium for traditional trade finance products is not the answer since corporates look towards improving their operations efficiency through reduced paperwork and reconciliation and also to making their working capital more efficient. Some banks have sought to out-source or centralize their trade finance operations. However, while this is a cost saving move, it does not generate the value proposition that could significantly increase efficiencies at the corporate.

Banks have meanwhile, been slow to react to this trend and are now being pulled by corporates to match up to their enhanced efficiencies in the supply chain. However, the banks on the one hand can lose market share or become redundant to companies like DHL and UPS if they do not catch up with the corporate; and on the other hand, they stand to cannibalize their existing business offerings in the process:

- Efficiencies in the supply chain would free up working capital. This could mean reduce borrowings or reduced current account float to the banks.
- It could accelerate the trend for reduction in use of letters of credit.

However, the imaginative banks have not lost the point and are not worried about this potential loss. It is worth considering that over 90% of international trade by volume and over 95% of domestic trade is conducted on an open account basis. If the banks stand to lose some part of this 5–10% of volumes they have much to gain by extending their business to the balance 90–95% of the volumes. The big players have now woken up to this opportunity and there is a race amongst them to innovate services and solutions in order to dematerialize trade-related data into electronic documents and also to support the trade and make the trade-related processes more efficient for the corporate. As more and more corporates move to open account processes, the emerging solution is to integrate trade finance into cash management and deliver trade finance offerings in much the same way as cash management is offered presently.

However, not all is easy, as it never is. While the companies want efficiency in their supply chain, they do not want their existing processes, people, vendors or dealers to be disturbed in any way, and want the bank systems to snugly fit into their processes. Money is not as much an issue as is the inconvenience of disrupting the processes that are in place.

Simple First Steps

International trade can be complicated. Some types can be extremely complicated while other exclusive ones can be even more so!

Complexity has its degrees! However, not all trade or international trade is complicated with the same plurality. It is important to identify such simple supply chains where value and efficiencies can be added, as the first step towards the overall journey towards e-financial supply chain fulfillment. There is an important lesson to be learnt from the struggle of organizations like BOLERO who took the path of providing solutions for extreme complexity and are braving all odds against them. Alternatively an approach, of identifying the relatively simple supply chains and providing financial supply chain services around these makes the chances of such a change happening much higher, and also allows all other participants namely the corporate, dealers, vendors, lawmakers etc. to assimilate the change in their processes, thus laying a stable foundation for the next step—which could incorporate the next degree of complexity.

Another important aspect to be realized is that it may not be possible to automate the entire process at one go as one may ideally want to. For example, it may be best to have rich information along all legs of the transaction from all sources , say, for payments being received from a third party bank. However, this may not always be possible. It is important to realize that even in the existing situation and processes of corporate, like Banks the corporate also face the same problems today as they cannot receive all information for credits into their account! So, if the services from the bank can enhance the service offering to the corporate and reduce their pain by one step, it would still be worthwhile, considering that this improves the overall position of the corporate by that one important step.

Successful banks are benefiting from the incremental approach. Pioneering banks find that they can effectively sell and implement if they focus on one pain point and one decision-maker. The subsequent structures can be built on top of this foundation.

Although the win-win solution positioning of the financial supply chain appears to be obviously beneficial to everyone, integration and automation hold the key to success. These new services have the potential to unlock the billions of dollars tied up in the supply chains of companies.

The suggested models working presently are simple:

- They expect the buyer and supplier to be on the same platform and within the same bank in the most preferred situation. They also provide the early explorer with the benefit to forcefully get more customers, which justifies the early investment that these pioneers are making in the domain.

  However, such models once working and accepted by the industry can be easily extended to multi-platform and multi-bank models through the use of collaborative standards.

- The present problems being addressed are simple and can possibly be solved through the involvement of just one or two more departments at the corporate level, apart from the treasury. This helps in narrowly focusing on the problem for quicker implementation and more well defined benefit to the individuals in the chain.

Subsequently, these models will act as a catalyst to spur a much larger growth in variety and volume of offerings in the e-financial supply chain space.

A simultaneous approach of offering and refining competitive services along with adoption of collaborative industry standards is the way to go. Corporates have everything to gain by participating in and adopting these new services in their attempt to centralize their treasuries and achieve straight through processing and thus reducing operations costs. Banks will have to tow the line from the demand pull being created by the corporates, by re-defining their value proposition, embracing open standards and re-hauling their technology infrastructure.

So, with big spending needed to keep up with the demands of technology—is there room for only a few and is consolidation expected in banking around offerings on the e-financial supply chain? There are different views on the outcome:

- On the one hand, technology is becoming cheaper and more easily accessible.
- Also, it is unlikely that some banks can meet the financing needs for all the players in the supply chain.
- Some of the larger corporates may not want to put all their eggs in one basket by running their critical operations through only one or two banks.

It therefore, appears that there will be space for smaller and specialist banks to participate and provide services in the e-financial supply chain. Then again, the way the services are structured and offered will change with the introduction of standards.

4

Early Players in the
e-Financial Supply Chain

INTRODUCTION

There must be something exciting about the e-financial supply chain for it to attract such varied players as SWIFT, a financial messaging infrastructure provider; J P Morgan Chase, a large multinational bank; Shell, a company in hydrocarbons; DHL, a courier company; and many others, as well as a host of new players.

However, the world of financial supply chain automation has been filled with unknowns or terra incognita. In a 2004 *GTNews* working capital survey, more than 85% of company treasurers viewed their working capital processes as sub-optimal. Improvements in working capital management are pivotal upon automation and integration of the financial supply chain. In most companies this is fraught with inefficiencies that cut across multiple subsidiaries, departments and financial institutions. The order to cash position consumes significant time and resources—30 days is typically a minimum, while 120 days is common if there is a dispute. Most companies have at best, automated only fragments of the financial supply chain and presently, only the largest corporations like GM and Ford Inc. have established buyer–supplier connectivity via proprietary electronic data interchange.

Perceptibly therefore, considering the size of the problem and the commensurate rewards to the early solution providers, there is tremendous interest in untangling the knot to this problem. Broadly, the players in game at present can be divided into the following categories, as shown in Fig. 4.1.

	Banks	Non-Banks
Collaborative	IFX	TWIST SWIFT-TSU
Competitive	J P Morgan	Trade Card Visa

Fig. 4.1 *Positioning of different types of players in the financial supply chain*

Firstly, there is tremendous interest among non-banks to participate in the financial supply chain revolution. It is also interesting that many of these non-banks have started with collaborative offerings.

Collaborative offerings have been proposed by many organizations as a method of achieving end-to-end automation through co-operation and collaboration between the various partners and systems in the financial supply chain. The aim is to define and adopt common information standards for various activities, so that the integration between the various systems can be achieved in a straight-through manner. For example, if the invoice definition is standardized across all organizations then the various systems can easily exchange invoice information between themselves.

Some key challenges that the collaborative offerings have faced are (a) definition and consensus on the standard definition. Considering the wide variety of industry practices for one similar activity such as invoicing, and the multiple activities involved in a trade transaction e.g. acceptance, goods receipt, returns, etc., it has been extremely tough to arrive at common standards; (b) the standards are beneficial only if they are adopted by a wide range of market participants. However, the early birds will need to invest and also provide the required R&D and experimentation budgets without corresponding benefits. While many initiatives have been invested in and progressed, these are still quite some distance away from market adoption.

Competitive offerings on the other hand, have been launched to take advantage of the immediate market requirements. While these may not provide end-to-end automation, they certainly help in moving a few steps forward with clear benefits to the players engaged in these offerings. The innovating players benefit from an incremental approach as they can focus on one decision-maker and one pain point. The benefit of this approach is that once a few financial supply chain models have been established and accepted by the market they can be catalysts for launching a wider array of services. These offerings could also help in understanding the market requirements and further fine tuning of collaborative standards.

PLAYERS IN THE e-FINANCIAL SUPPLY CHAIN— COLLABORATIVE SPACE

BOLERO

BOLERO, originally proposed as an acronym for Bill Of Lading Electronic Registry Organization, is one of the first organizations that proposed improvements in the financial supply chain through collaborative standards on handling of bill of lading i.e. the transport documentation issued by shipping companies, electronically. .

BOLERO was incorporated in 1997, as a joint venture between SWIFT (Society for Worldwide Inter-bank Financial Transactions) and the TT Club (Through Transport Mutual Insurance Association Ltd). BOLERO was proposed as a cross-industry global initiative to facilitate paperless international trade via the internet between various parties involved in trade, namely the buyer, seller, freight forwarders, shipping agents, carriers, banks, etc.

The origin of BOLERO is said to have been inspired from the trade of crude oil in the Nordic countries where generally, the ship travels between for example, England and Scandinavia in less than 2 days. However, the bill of lading, which is the paper transport document receipt given by the shipper and required for release of the crude oil at the port of destination, would sometimes not be available for as long as over 60 days! Apart from the delays involved in the paper process, one major factor causing the delay was the fact that the crude oil on the ship was being traded on commodity exchanges. It would go through many trades on the exchange, which was normal; however the bill of lading, which had to be endorsed by the seller in favor of the buyer would take a long time to be completed as it had to physically travel from one trader to another depending upon the number of trades executed with respect to the particular shipment. Workarounds in the form of shipping guarantees were established so that the oil could be released without waiting for the original bill of lading document. However, these were costly and cumbersome. At the same time, statistics from the United Nations revealed that seven percent of the total global cost of international trade arises from the need to issue paper shipping documentation! The objective at the origin of BOLERO was to digitize the paper of bill of lading and the name BOLERO, therefore appeared an apt acronym for bill of lading electronic registry organization.

However, despite a very focused objective on improving the processes surrounding the paper bill of lading, BOLERO presumed that it would not be possible to isolate only this in the process and that they should consider in its scope, the digitizing of all trade documents in a trade transaction and not just the bill of lading.

With this objective and amongst tremendous excitement in the market surrounding this new collaborative infrastructure, BOLERO launched an Internet platform in November 1999, which provided infrastructure for:

- Exchange of all trade-related documents electronically between the various parties involved.
- Registry for bills of lading.
- Rule book incorporating the operational and legal aspects surrounding the use of the facilities proposed by BOLERO.

The excitement surrounding BOLERO could be gauged from the fact that many of the world's largest banks and corporates—from Citibank, USA; to Fuji Bank, Japan; Cargill Traders, Evergreen shipping company, and many more—joined with BOLERO in the pilots. The expectation that the solution to the financial supply chain problem could be achieved and the entire purchase order to payment process could be automated was too monumental for anyone associated with it to be left behind.

However, from then on success has been a challenge for BOLERO. It announced many pilots and one key commercial launch in 2000, when the Colombian Coffee Federation (FNC) which represents about 35% of the trade from about 500,000 Colombian coffee growers, agreed to work together with BOLERO to automate the entire trading process.

However, progress remained slow and BOLERO attempted to discover their sweet spot from where they could catalyze automation in the financial supply chain. In 2001, BOLERO launched a new service, SURF (Settlement Utility for Managing Risk and Finance), allowing all parties in the transaction to share orders and inventory information online. In its new form SURF was proposed to enable paperwork related to trade to be provided electronically and making it easier to handle funds required for payments. However, this too did not meet with much success.

In 2002, BOLERO launched two new products, BOLEROApply and BOLEROAdvise, for LC application and LC advising. The proposed services required low capital investment and could be implemented quickly. BOLERO proposed that these would provide step-by-step means for realization of the full benefits offered by BOLEROSurf. While a few banks have adopted these products in offering services to their customers, the value proposition of these versus the overall objective of BOLERO in offering a collaborative framework for automation of the financial supply chain is doubtful.

To understand the challenges faced by BOLERO in its journey, let us understand the scope of what it was attempting to address.

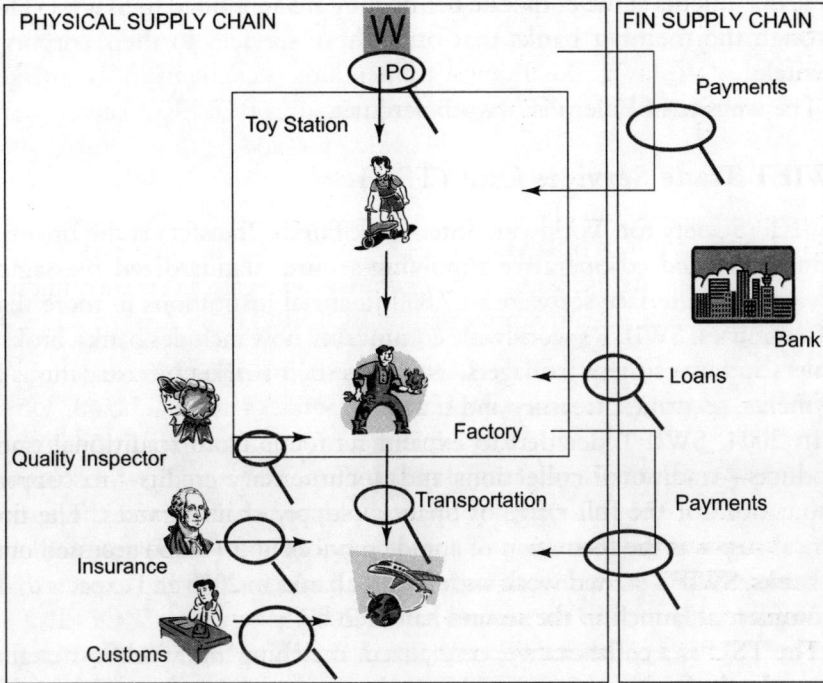

Fig. 4.2 *The circled areas represent some of the interactions that BOLERO aimed to automate*

BOLERO proposed to address all and more of the linkages highlighted in the supply chain in Fig. 4.2. In hindsight it was an extremely ambitious objective. To attempt to get together so many different organizations and systems is a Herculean task, especially when the terrain is new and the routes and practices not known to anyone clearly.

Towards the end of 2004, it was proposed to have a closer working co-operation between SWIFT and BOLERO and it was agreed that BOLERO would act as a supplier of technology to SWIFT for its new SWIFTNet TSU (Trade Services Unit) initiative, which would utilize BOLERO's Surf technology.

SWIFT has chosen BOLERO as a supplier of technology for the TSU, which is an independent, complementary and non-competitive service to BOLERO. The TSU is proposed as a bank-centric solution with no direct corporate access. BOLERO continues to operate entirely in the corporate-centric space, where one or more corporates could be a part of the BOLERO based services. Where the TSU proposes matching of sub-sets of data from trading documents submitted by one or more bank, BOLERO offers applications designed to support the full compliance process for generating these documents at the corporate before they are submitted to SIWFT-TSU through the member banks that offer these services to their corporate clientele.

The website of Bolero is: www.bolero.net.

SWIFT Trade Services Unit (TSU)

SWIFT (Society for Worldwide Inter-bank Funds Transfer) is the financial industry owned co-operative supplying secure, standardized messaging services and interface software to 7,800 financial institutions in more than 200 countries. SWIFT's worldwide community now includes banks, broker/dealers and investment managers, as well as their market infrastructures in payments, securities, treasury and trade.

In 2004, SWIFT decided to expand its focus from traditional trade products—traditional collections and documentary credits—to support automation for the full range of financial supply chain services. The first tactical step was the formation of a trade services unit (TSU) accessed only by banks. SWIFT started work with 20 pilot banks in 2005 and expects to do a commercial launch in the second half of 2007.

The TSU is a collaborative, centralized, matching and workflow engine for use by the banking community to enable it to provide competitive supply chain services. SWIFT proposes to build on its traditional strengths in providing standards and messaging services and re-use the SWIFT infrastructure already available in the back offices of banks.

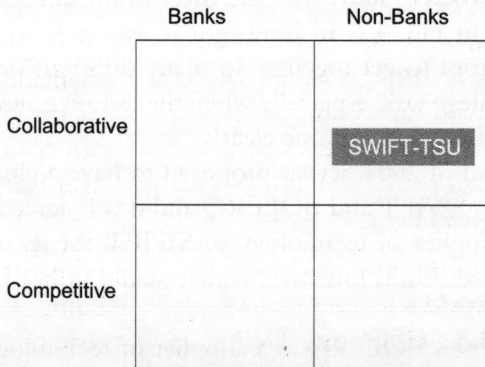

Fig. 4.3 *The positioning of SWIFT TSU services*

The SWIFT-TSU solution consists of:

- **Application**—A centralized matching and workflow engine, that compares and matches a sub-set of data from trade documents and provides transaction workflow associated with the matching process. For example, where the SWIFT-TSU is used, the sequence of steps could be as follows:

  ❏ Buyer uploads PO information to his buyer bank.
  ❏ The buyer bank passes this information to the seller bank.
  ❏ The seller bank passes this on to the seller.
  ❏ The seller gives his acceptance of the PO to the seller bank.
  ❏ The seller bank routes this information to the buyer through SWIFT and the buyer bank.
  ❏ When the seller subsequently uploads invoice information to his bank this is matched versus the original PO information at the SWIFT TSU application, and if found valid it is forwarded through to the buyers bank and the buyer.

- **SWIFTNet messaging services**—SWIFT's secure IP network and messaging services. It is expected that SWIFTNet, FileAct, InterAct and Browse will be used over a period of time. This is the existing infrastructure of SWIFT, which is widely tested and very stable.

- **Standards**—SWIFT will deliver standards for the data sub-sets, from business documents, plus instructions, notifications and reports, e.g. standards of purchase order data formats, invoice formats etc. These standards use sub-sets of data, which are extracted from existing paper or electronic documentation, e.g. an invoice, transport or insurance data set, etc.

- **Rulebook**—A legal framework defining the roles and responsibilities of TSU users in originating and accepting transactions. These rules will be applicable for the member banks and their customers utilizing the SWIFT-TSU infrastructure. This will be reflected in TSU operating rules.

- **Integration**—SWIFT will support the implementation of the solution both at the bank and corporate level by enhancing its own interfaces and operating a comprehensive partner program. SWIFT would share and make data visible to both banks—the buyer bank and the Seller bank—as agreed between parties.

The first phase of the TSU is under pilot since February 2006, involving up to 20 of the world's leading trade banks, including JPMorgan Chase Bank, Citibank N.A., HSBC etc. The pilot will prove the functionality of the following PO processing.

Stage 1

Buyers and sellers send purchase order documentation to their banks, who then send the relevant data into SWIFT standard XML PO format. The TSU matches the baseline data submitted by the buyer's and seller's banks and/or advises any discrepancies. Once baseline total data is matched successfully, the buyer and seller are assured of the trade transaction details.

With this assurance the banks can make supply chain finance decisions with greater confidence in the validity of the transaction. For example, in Case 11 related to Kea Furniture in Chapter 5, if the supplier bank and the buyer bank are both not Creative Bank, then Creative Bank can still extend finance to the vendors if it is the vendor's bank, when it is sure that the purchase order information available from Citibank through SWIFT is confirmed and the purchase order is indeed established and from the mentioned buyer!

Stage 2

Once the PO baselines have been matched, the required documents such as invoice and transport data set information can be presented. The seller provides the necessary invoice or transport information to his bank, which then imports the data and submits a standard message to the TSU, who matches the data submitted to the baseline data and identifies any discrepancies. Both bank parties are notified of the match or discrepancies. The buyer is notified in turn and can authorize or decline payment.

In Case 2 related to Orion Plastics in Chapter 5, the receipt of transport information under a previously exchanged PO by the buyer's bank, say Creative Bank, from the bank of Orion Plastics, say Citibank, through SWIFT, could cause a demand for payment on Creative Bank.

SIMPLE TSU OPEN ACCOUNT FLOW

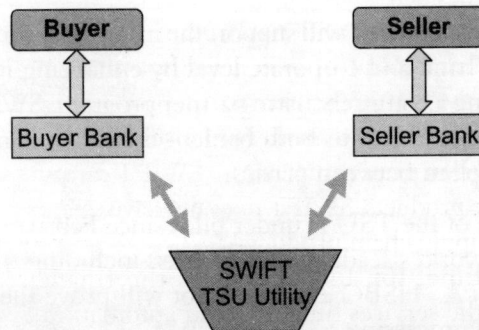

Fig. 4.4 *Interaction between the buyer and seller bank through the SWIFT-TSU utility*

By providing (a) a centralized infrastructure for exchange of information and (b) message standards, the TSU, a collaborative centralized matching utility, is expected to allow banks to potentially not only increase revenues but also share costs when providing services such as:
- Finance and risk mitigation
- Management information
- In-sourcing of payables and receivables
- In-sourcing of trade data checking

However, much of the above benefits cannot be directly achieved just by use of the SWIFT network and the existing message standards and the banks will need much more innovation to enable the relevant products and infrastructure to realize the proposed benefits.

The TSU model of SWIFT has some very clear benefits over the BOLERO model:
- It allows access only through banks, thus narrowing its scope on the parties with whom it will interact.
- It has focused on one business process surrounding the purchase order to start with. The success here could be used as a stepping-stone.
- It is already present and connected to multiple banks. Through the provision of additional message flows, growing services on this existing infrastructure would be much easier than establishing a new infrastructure and a new working paradigm.

The value chain that SWIFT proposes to address is shown in Fig. 4.5.

The linkages that are highlighted in blue are those where SWIFT would provide infrastructure for transacting. The linkages highlighted in dotted line are those where SWIFT may set standards in future.

Despite the above substantial advantages, there are some risks in the overall approach. SWIFT has mentioned that 'the market practice for bank services is not within SWIFT's responsibility, although SWIFT expects to facilitate the development of such rules'.

If one looks back to the traditional banking products such as payments or letters of credit, on account of which SWIFT came up with the standard messages such as MT 103, etc, during the last 30 years, one thing that is obviously apparent is that the market practices for both letters of credit and payments were well in place much before SWIFT came up with collaborative standards for these products. SWIFT does not have this advantage with respect to the financial supply chain products!

At the same time, for automation of the financial supply chain—considering that the services hinge around automation of the processes—it

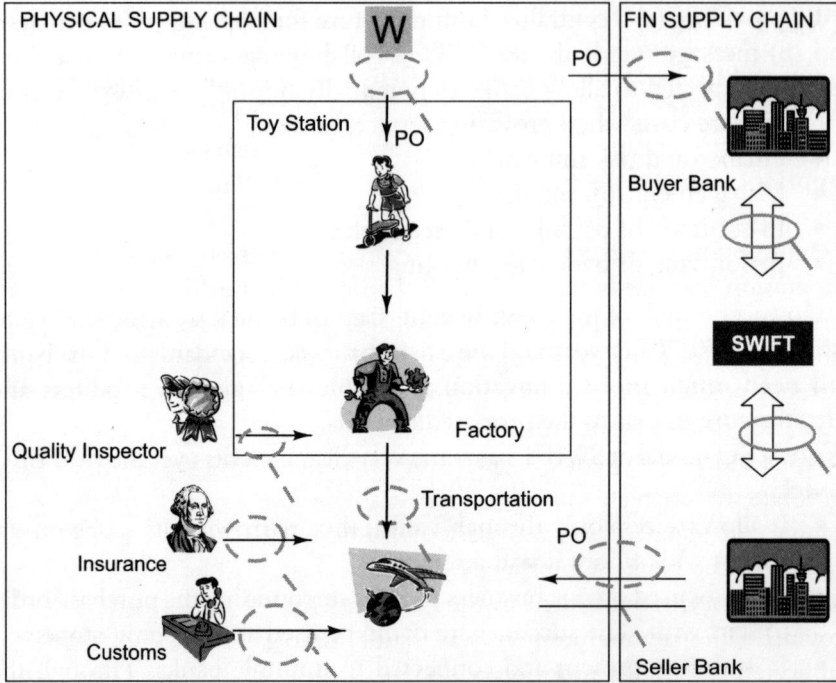

Fig. 4.5 *The circles in solid line represent the interactions directly being facilitated by SWIFT. The circles in dotted line represent the interactions where SWIFT may provide standards but will not directly participate in these*

is expected that the collaborative and the competitive offerings will develop hand-in-hand.

However, would one look to SWIFT to develop or propagate in a consultative manner, such market practices and competitive offerings, or would one expect SWIFT to walk hand-in-hand and develop standards as the market practices emerge? Considering that SWIFT's position is to provide a collaborative infrastructure, it would appear to be the latter.

For more information on SWIFT visit the site www.swift.com.

OTHER COLLABORATIVE ORGANIZATIONS FOR STANDARDS

Apart from SWIFT there are other organizations working on standards. These have been sponsored by key industry players and are in various stages of progress and adoption. We will discuss some of the main ones here.

TWIST

Conceived in 2001, the Transaction Workflow Innovation Standards Team (TWIST), led by the treasury departments of Shell, HP and GE, is a non-profit industry group of corporate treasurers, fund managers, banks, system suppliers, electronic trading platforms, market infrastructures and professional services firms.

At inception, the objective of TWIST was focused as a treasury workstation integration standards team. TWIST brought to the fore the corporate perspective. Large corporates like Shell, HP and GE have their own ERP and treasury systems to manage their money position with banks, foreign currency positions, receivables and payables, etc. As banks began to extend their cash management and subsequently treasury services, through their internet and other client offerings, the challenge being faced by the large corporate was to create integration across all these systems and also maintain a single consolidated view across all the systems.

Each of the banks was proposing their proprietary treasury workstation and integration requirement to the corporate for the various services they provided. The key requirement was the definition of 'standards' to reduce duplicated efforts on proprietary systems. Additionally, there were some activities that could be performed better at the corporate level with better standards for exchange of information.

The objectives of TWIST have evolved taking into consideration the many linkages and challenges inherent in the process. The primary aim of the TWIST organization is to close the gaps in the physical and financial supply chain to release the enormous value locked up in disjointed paper-based processes, through collaborative processes.

To achieve this, TWIST rationalizes financial industry standards by creating user-driven, non-proprietary and internally consistent XML-based standards

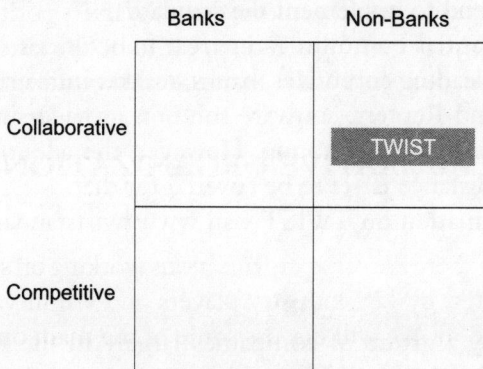

Fig 4.6   *The positioning of TWIST services*

for the financial supply chain. Where existing standards and technologies are already widely accepted, such as FIX, FpML and SWIFT messages, TWIST aims to leverage these and works with the relevant standards organizations to avoid duplication of effort and to ensure harmonization on standards. TWIST also co-operates with other standards organizations where joint efforts can accelerate the qualitative design of messages.

TWIST intends to deliver non-proprietary XML-based standards in the following areas:
- Wholesale financial market transaction processing
- Payments
- Treasury management
- Financial supply chain and working capital financing
- Identity management

The first four define standards in the area of business workflows while the fourth one defines standards in the area of security and identity management. Security and identity will be discussed in greater detail in a later section.

Some examples of message standards being proposed in each of the above business areas are shown in Figure 4.7 and illustrate the type of messages under discussion. The full list of messages and the message structures is available on www.twiststandards.org.

TWIST is running a pilot with VOCA that aims to provide automatic matching of remittances to invoices and to support reconciliation of receipts to invoices. The TWIST message standards being used in this pilot relate to invoice and invoice disputes. VOCA maintains the successful BACS payment network in the UK.

Unlike SWIFT, TWIST does not propose to provide any technology infrastructure for processing any transactions. However, it does offer advisory services on organizational and system controls and implementation support for those who intend to implement the standards.

There is substantial community interest in activities of TWIST with participants from leading corporates, banks, market infrastructure providers like Bloomberg and Reuters, software solution providers and professional services firms like Ernst and Young. However, the adoption is still to be found and lot of distance is yet to be covered for that.

For more information on TWIST visit www.twiststandards.org.

RosettaNet

Set-up in 1998 by a group of companies largely in the IT & EC sector (Information, Technology and Electronic Components), RosettaNet sought to enhance efficiency in the IT supply chain and electronic components

Sl. No	Area	Message	Party
1	Wholesale Financial Market	Request for Price	Client
2	Wholesale Financial Market	Cancel Request for Price	Client
3	Wholesale Financial Market	Respond with Price	Bank
4	Wholesale Financial Market	Accept Price	Client
5	Wholesale Financial Market	Confirm Execution	Bank
6	Payments	Request for Payment	Client
7	Payments	Request for Payment Status	Client
8	Payments	Payment Status Response	Bank
9	Payments	Remittance Advice to Beneficiary	Bank
10	Treasury Management	Request Order for say FX Txn	Client
11	Treasury Management	Acknowledge Request Order	Bank/Broker
12	Treasury Management	Reject Request	Bank/Broker
13	Treasury Management	Confirm Request Executed	Bank/Broker
14	Treasury Management	Cancel Order	Client
15	Financial Supply Chain	Request For Quotation	Buyer
16	Financial Supply Chain	Quotation	Seller
17	Financial Supply Chain	Purchase Order	Buyer
18	Financial Supply Chain	Purchase Order Acceptance	Seller
19	Financial Supply Chain	Purchase Order Rejection	Seller
20	Financial Supply Chain	PO Acceptance with Amendment	Seller
21	Financial Supply Chain	Invoice	Seller
22	Financial Supply Chain	Invoice Disputes	Buyer

Fig. 4.7 *A sample of messages for which standards are being proposed by TWIST*

industry, enabling businesses to operate more effectively and allowing the IT industry to better serve its customers.

Unlike SWIFT-TSU and TWIST, it must be noted that the initial focus of RosettaNet was to provide standards for information exchange in the corporate-to-corporate space. Realizing the tremendously large number of electronic components and their varied specifications e.g. transistors, resistors, memory, chips, etc., RosettaNet set to create standards so that this information could be exchanged easily between the various organizations.

RosettaNet proposed to adopt, promote and facilitate the deployment of open content and open transaction rules for increasing the IT supply chain and electronic commerce efficiency. Its mission is to provide common business interfaces for supply chain trading partners and their customers to exchange information and transactions.

In 1999 RosettaNet introduced:

- The first ever, technical dictionary for unified e-commerce language, which contained approximately 3,600 words describing the technical specifications for a wide range of IT products. For example, there are as many as 900 words to describe all the properties of a personal computer—everything from modems and monitors down to the amount of RAM.

  The IT industry is tremendously fragmented and every distributor and manufacturer had its own proprietary dictionary of terms resulting in redundant, overlapping efforts by individual companies as well as confusion in the procurement process due to each company's unique terminology.

  With the RosettaNet technical dictionary, these companies could now use a common platform to conduct business processes.

- Furthering one of the most ambitious standards implementation efforts in history. In late 1999, it announced the release of its first 10 XML Partner Interface Processes (PIPs). These are designed to align the electronic business processes of trading partners within the information technology (IT) supply chain.

  RosettaNet's PIPs are specialized system-to-system XML-based dialogs that define how business processes are conducted between IT manufacturers, software publishers, distributors, re-sellers and corporate end-users. RosettaNet PIPs use the standard technical dictionary and are essential to enabling the standardization of e-business processes among buyers and sellers in the supply chain. Examples of PIPs from a list of over 110 PIPs are:

  (a) Query product information
  (b) Query marketing information
  (c) Query technical information
  (d) Distribute design engineering information
  (e) Request material composition information
  (f) Request shipping order
  (g) Remittance advice, etc.

- In 2000, RosettaNet introduced The RosettaNet Implementation Framework, which is a core specification for the packaging, routing and transport of all PIP messages over a network.

RosettaNet then followed this up with many pilot programs called 'Milestone' programs. A list of some of the completed programs is:

- Automated ticketing
- Collaborative forecasting
- E-customs declaration
- Freight invoicing
- Material release
- Payment, etc.

In terms of implementation of standards, RosettaNet has been the most successful. Some of the RosettaNet implementation with PIP interfaces have been used at Intel, Arrow Electronics, Avnet, etc. More details on these case studies are available on the website of RosettaNet at www.rosettanet.org. However, wider industry acceptance is awaited.

One key reason for its success has been its initial focus and objective of improving efficiencies in supply chain for the IT and EC industry. The great detail in which the Dictionary and the PIPs are defined is a proof of this extreme focus. Figure 4.8 highlights the interactions that RosettaNet focused on.

The early focus of RosettaNet on the supply chain linkages between the buyer and supplier helped it to great purpose of action.

Like all standard organizations, RosettaNet subsequently attempted to increase the scope of its activities to propose coverage of the supply chain for

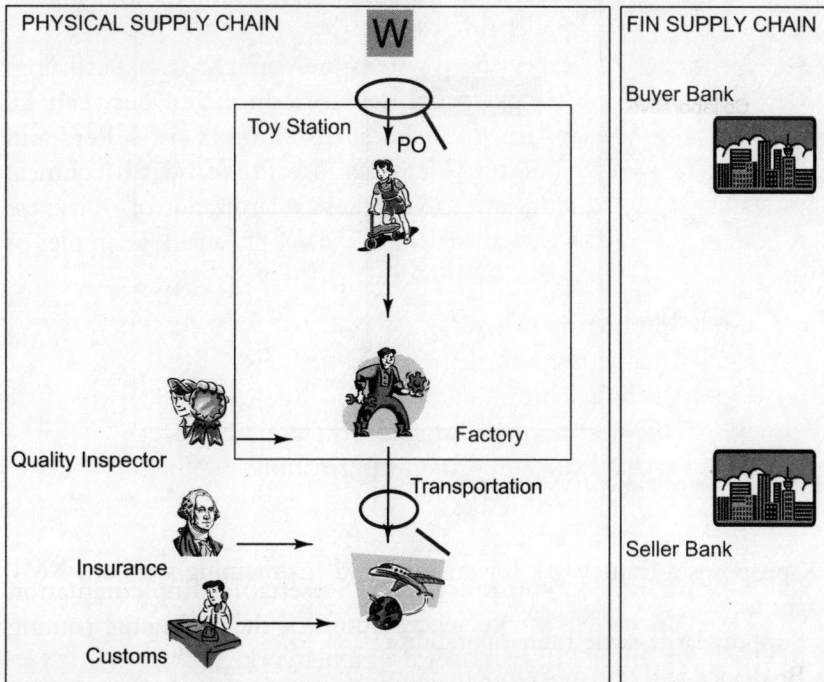

Fig. 4.8 *The circles highlight the focus area for RosettaNet*

all industries. And like all its predecessors it faces an uphill task on adoption of these standards across the industry.

More information on RosettaNet is available at www.rosettanet.org.

IFX

In 1997, The Banking Industry Technology Secretariat (BITS), a consortium of large American bankers, with keen participation from Bank of America, Microsoft, and Cheque Free, announced that it would publish the Interactive Financial Exchange (IFX) business message specification. IFX proposed XML-based standards that would enable financial transactions and integration through Web services type interfaces. The standard provides the ability to exchange financial data regardless of technology platform. IFX is a co-operative cross-industry, non-profit initiative of parties working to achieve standardization in the following areas of banking:

- Business banking
- Electronic Bill Presentment and Payment (EBPP)
- Automated Teller Machine/Point of Sale Devices (ATM/POS)

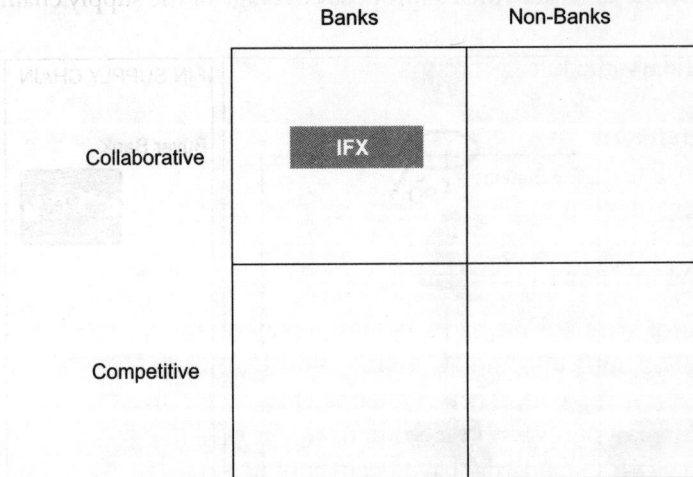

Fig. 4.9 *The positioning of IFX services*

IFX proposes a framework for creating and maintaining standard XML messages to:

- Support large-scale inter-operability.
- Be device and transport independent.
- Facilitate multi-party handling of data.

- Guarantee consistent understanding of who owns data and what it represents.
- Allow for customization and extensibility.

The IFX business message specification facilitates the exchange and sharing of financial data and instructions between banks, their customers and service providers through standard XML formatted messages. The specification may be used to provide transaction-processing services across multiple organizations and networks.

Some examples of the standard messages being proposed under the various heads are listed below:

- Business banking
  - ☐ Payment origination
  - ☐ Direct debit origination
  - ☐ Payment acknowledgement
  - ☐ Remittance details
  - ☐ Balance and transaction reporting, etc.
- EBPP
  - ☐ Customer enrolment
  - ☐ Delivery of bill summary information
  - ☐ Payment status reporting
  - ☐ Holiday schedule communication, etc.
- ATM/POS
  - ☐ Withdrawal
  - ☐ Transfer
  - ☐ Check deposit
  - ☐ PIN change
  - ☐ ATM inventory management, etc.

Such sets of standard messages would greatly increase inter-operability between the various banks and the service industry as well, e.g. where banks share their ATM networks such standards would help the banks in easily integrating their systems with each other.

Adoption of IFX standards, have been slow to date, but the standard is well-positioned to become widely used within the financial services industry. There is awareness of the general benefits of the IFX standards, however the adoption has been possibly slow for the following reasons:

- Adoption of standards generally follows 'exponential function', i.e. the growth rate is always proportional to its current size. The adoption can grow exponentially or decay exponentially. Since the current size of adotption is small, the growth rates also are small but promise to grow rapidly in future.

- Presently there is no big economic incentive or regulatory dis-incentive for non-adoption of standards. This would change as adoption increases.

The big advantage to IFX is that it is very narrowly focused on specific banking integration scenarios, which aid the implementation and verification of these standards.

More information on IFX can be obtained at www.ifxforum.org.

OAGi

The Open Applications Group (OAGi), the organization that oversees the OAGIS (Open Applications Group for Integration Standards) was formed in November 1994, in an effort to dramatically ease everywhere-to-everywhere integration (inside and outside of the enterprise, as well as across the supply chain). OAGi members include individuals, and small, medium and large companies like IBM, Oracle, Sun Microsystems, Lucent, Ford and Agilent, to name just a few.

OAGi uses XML as the common alphabet for defining business messages and for identifying business processes (scenarios) that allow businesses and business applications to communicate. OAGIS provides large set ready XML business messages and also accommodates the additional requirements of specific industries by partnering with various vertical industry groups.

One of the key differences between OAGi and other standards providers like IFX, SWIFT, TWIST is that while each of the other group focuses on a specific industry vertical or practices, OAGi provides the horizontal backbone for integration across vertical industries. In that sense, it provides a more technical framework along with XML definition for some of the verticals and also provides for linkages within its structure to accommodate the use of existing and proposed industry specific standards.

A very high-level overview of the structure proposed by OAGi is shown in Fig. 4.10:

The content of the OAGIS standard is:
- Business processes, called business scenarios.
- Business messages, called Business Object Documents (BOD).

The business scenario could, for example, be the purchase process. The BOD would be the various messages to execute the business process, e.g. raise PO, acknowledge PO, accept PO, reject PO, amend PO, etc. The business scenarios also capture the sequence in which the messages are intended to occur, the dependencies, the scope and the error handling that has to be addressed.

The ISO/UN component can be for example a standard list of country and currency code. The industry A overlay would be, for e.g. IFX defined message structures.

BOD

INDUSTRY A OVERLAY	INDUSTRY B OVERLAY	COMPANY A OVERLAY

OAGIS Business Object Document			META MODEL	NAMING & DESIGN RULES	BOD ARCHITECTURE
IST/ ISO COMPONENTS	UN/CEFACT COMPONENTS	OAGIS TYPES COMPONENTS			

XML Schema (XSD)

UML Models

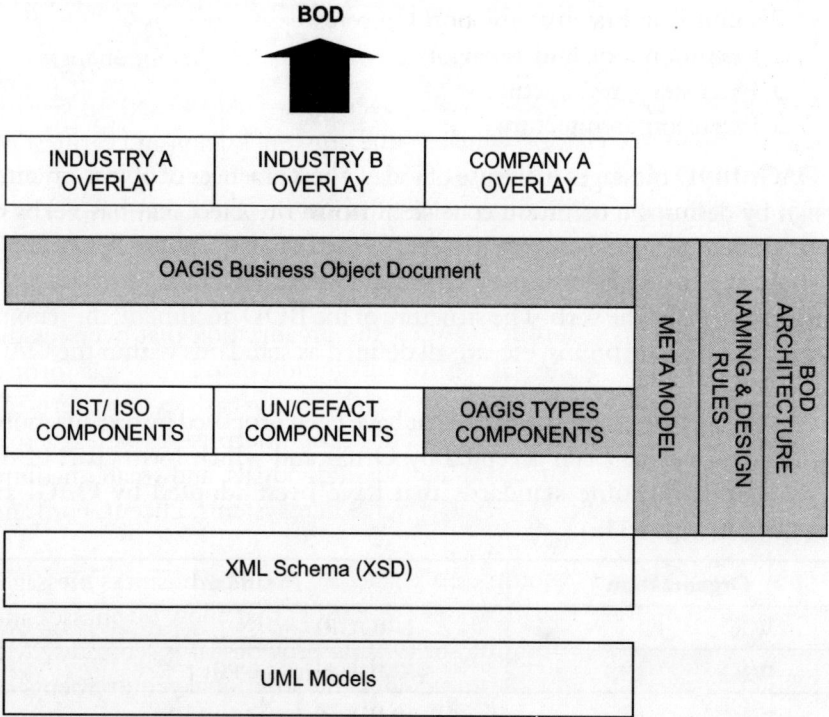

Fig. 4.10 *The framework structure proposed by OAGi*

The BODs are similar in concept to what is being done by SWIFT, TWIST, RosettaNet etc. in terms of defining a standard XML formatted document. OAGi Release 9 has specified 434 BODs or business messages covering over 70 business scenarios. Specific industry associations like Automotive Industry Association Group (AIAG), Automotive Aftermarket Industry Association (AAIA), and Standards in Technology for Automotive Retail (STAR) have defined further 85 BODs, thus providing tremendous automotive industry coverage to the initiative.

From a technical viewpoint OAGi also provides the following:

- Canonical or rule based format
  - ❏ Common object model (for noun definitions).
  - ❏ Class libraries, e.g. for currency codes.
- Naming and design rules
  - ❏ UN/CEFACT based.
- Transaction and context model
  - ❏ Use of nouns and verbs for transaction definition.
- Application architecture
  - ❏ Document typing
  - ❏ Meta-model

- Technical architecture for BOD
  - ❏ Common look and behavior
  - ❏ Extensions architecture
  - ❏ Extrusion architecture

OAGi BOD messages make use of today's best practices of object-oriented design by defining a common consistent **noun** or object that has **verbs** or methods that indicate the action to be performed upon the noun. For example, in a purchase order the buyer could be the noun and the raise purchase order message would be the verb. The structure of the BOD document, the naming conventions for the nouns, etc. are all defined as standards within the OAGi framework.

Additionally, there are standards that have been proposed by organizations, e.g. ISO, which has been accepted by OAGi and which forms part of the OAGi standard. Some standards that have been adopted by OAGi are described in Fig. 4.11.

Organization	Standard
W3C	URL/URI
W3C	XML Schema 1.0 Part 1
W3C	XML Style language
ISO	ISO 20022 (UNIFI Financial standard)
ISO	ISO 4217—Currency codes
ISO	ISO 639—Language codes
UN/CEFACT	ATG2 Naming and Design rules

Fig. 4.11   *Examples of some standards that have been adopted by OAGi*

OAGi recognizes the fact that no matter how many smart people work on a standard, all possible uses of the messages cannot be addressed. For this reason, it allows users to extend OAGIS messages by using either:

- User-area extensions which allow simple extensions of a few fields to an existing OAGi component, or
- Overlay extensions which allow users to extend an OAGi BOD, noun and component to meet their own needs, even adding new BODs, verbs, nouns and components where necessary.

The first release of OAGi was developed in 1995 to address the need for a common business language that would enable business applications to communicate. Because of this long history, OAGIS has support from application vendors and implementation providers and has been implemented in over 40 countries worldwide. Some key business scenarios that OAGi covers are:

- E-commerce
  - ❏ E-catalog
  - ❏ Price lists
  - ❏ RFQ and quote
  - ❏ Order management
  - ❏ Purchasing
  - ❏ Invoice
  - ❏ Payments
- Manufacturing
  - ❏ MES
  - ❏ Shop floor
  - ❏ Plant data collection
  - ❏ Engineering
  - ❏ Warehouse management
  - ❏ Enterprise asset management
- Logistics
  - ❏ Orders
  - ❏ Shipments
  - ❏ Routing
- CRM
  - ❏ Opportunities
  - ❏ Sales leads
  - ❏ Customers
  - ❏ Sales force automation
- ERP
  - ❏ Financials
  - ❏ Human resources
  - ❏ Manufacturing
  - ❏ Credit management
  - ❏ Sarbanes/Oxley and control

Key success of OAGi has largely been in the automobile industry vertical. Large adoption remains a challenge. From a financial supply chain integration perspective it has yet to make headway in the adoption of these standards by banks.

More details on the organization are available at www.openapplications.org.

OASIS

OASIS (Organization for the Advancement of Structured Information Standards) is a non-profit, international consortium that drives the development, convergence and adoption of e-business standards. Founded in 1993 under the name SGML, OASIS has more than 5,000 participants representing over 600 organizations and individual members in 100 countries. The consortium hosts two of the most widely respected information portals on XML and Web services standards—XML.Org and Cover Pages—both of which have technical orientation.

The consortium produces XML and Web services standards with standards for security, e-business and standardization efforts, for the public sector and for application-specific markets. Some of the specific verticals on which OASIS works are:

- E-commerce
- Law and government
- Security
- Computing management
- Supply chain
- Conservation

More information on OASIS can be obtained at www.Oasis-open.org.

As would be evident from discussions of these various organizations, the standards definition has a large range, from business oriented such as SWIFT to technical oriented such as OASIS. Each of these are relevant and are pieces of a jigsaw puzzle that need to be put together in order to make the whole thing work with high efficiency.

MDDL

A large working group of Financial Information Services Division, USA members met in 2001, to launch a formal activity designed to produce an open XML standard for market data. Tentatively labeled MDDL (Market Data Definition Language), the primary focus is the development of an open XML standard needed to describe:

- A security or a trading paper, like a government paper or shares.
- Its price.
- Messages for transacting in these securities.

In a sense, this initiative is similar to the RosettaNet initiative, which was undertaken for the information technology and the electronic component sector; while this initiative was launched to enable the banks to trade in securities.

The rationale for MDDL is threefold: (1) facilitation of straight through processing, (2) ease of mapping between market data applications, and (3) enhanced market data product functionality. The definitions cover a variety of market instruments such as:

- Equity
- Debt

- Foreign exchange
- Time series
- Index
- Accrual
- Agency ratings
- Auction date

There is significant interest and growth in membership of MDDL and with its sharp focus it promises to be successful.

Although the standards being proposed by MDDL are little removed from the topic of supply chain, it goes to highlight the different types of work and focus in the area of standards by various organizations and shows how these could help in achieving enterprise-to-enterprise connectivity.

More information on MDDL can be had from www.mddl.org.

UNIFI

ISO 20022-UNIversal Financial Industry Message scheme (UNIFI) is a new international standard published in 2004, which defines the ISO platform for the development of financial message standards. The standards allow users and developers to represent financial business processes and underlying transactions in a syntax-independent but standard notation. As XML (eXtensible Mark-up Language) is already the preferred syntax for e-communication, the first edition of UNIFI proposes a standardized XML-based syntax for messages. The standard was developed within the technical committee TC68 financial services, of ISO, the international organization for standardization.

The cornerstone of the infrastructure is the financial repository, which is maintained by the UNIFI (ISO 20022) Registration Authority (SWIFT), with the help of a series of standards evaluation groups comprising experts in specific domains of the financial industry and under the supervision of a registration management group consisting of senior experts.

It is composed of 5 parts: two international standards and three technical specifications that were published by ISO in December 2004.

Two International Standards

ISO 20022 parts 1 and 2 cover the following.
- A general explanation of the concepts that are used for the definition of UNIFI (ISO 20022) compliant messages. The explanation gives a high level description of the business-centric message design methodology and the rationale behind this methodology.

- A description of the financial repository that will contain all UNIFI (ISO 20022) message standards and their re-usable components.
- The rules that govern the maintenance of the financial repository by the UNIFI (ISO 20022) Registration Authority i.e. SWIFT, and its publication on www.iso20022.org.

Three Technical Specifications

ISO 20022 parts 3, 4 and 5 are ISO documents that give more detailed information regarding technical aspects of the standard such as:
- Modeling guidelines for development of syntax-independent business standard.
- XML design rules.
- Reverse engineering approach for existing non-compliant messages.

UNIFI is targeted at the standards initiatives outlined in Fig. 4.12, that are generally driven by communities of users looking for more cost-effective, XML-based communications to support specific financial business processes.

For more information on UNIFI and the work in progress, consult www.iso20022.org.

ISTH

Several organizations have been working in the area of standards development. All of them share a common vision of enterprise-to-enterprise connectivity for straight through integrations processes. However, as sponsors from different industries and from different geographies support these organizations, their approach and objectives in achieving the vision have naturally, been different. Also, there are overlapping efforts in certain areas such as purchase order processing, invoice processing, payment processing, etc.

As a result, the International Standards Team Harmonization Initiative (ISTH) was launched in 2003 to synchronize the efforts of the various standards organizations and also specifically, to drive a single core payment XML kernel that can be used globally by any corporate. The IST harmonization team is made up of members from four leading industry standards organizations. These are:
- IFX, creating and maintaining standards for financial business processes and services globally, including the corporate market.
- OAGi, a leading standards development in the ERP marketplace.
- SWIFT, a leading financial services standards and network, used to facilitate transaction delivery across financial providers globally.
- TWIST, a global treasury management and commercial payments standard.

Standard Body	Description	Applicable To	Business Aspect Covered
SECURITIES INDUSTRY			
MDDL	Market Data Definition Language	Broker, Dealer, Investment banks	Equities, Mutual funds, Indices, Bonds, Foreign exchange, Futures, Corporate actions
FIXML	Financial Information Exchange	Banks, Broker, Dealers, Institutional investors, Stock exchanges	Securities, Derivatives, Equities, Future & Options, Fixed income, Foreign exchange
FpML	Financial Product markup Language	All buy and sell side firms	Over the counter derivatives
INSURANCE INDUSTRY			
ACORD	Standards Definition for Insurance Industry	Agents, Brokers and other data partners in the Insurance, Re-insurance and related financial services industries.	Life & Annuity, Property & Casualty/ Surety, Re-Insurance
FINANCIAL INSTITUTIONS			
IFX	Interactive Financial Exchange Forum	Financial services companies	ATM/POS, Electronic bill presentation and payments
SWIFT	Society For Worldwide Inter-bank Financial Telecommunication	Banks, Broker & Dealers and Investment managers	Payments, Securities, Treasury and Trade
ISTH	International Standards Team Harmonization (IFX, OAGi, TWIST and SWIFT)	All Financial institutions and Corporates	Core payment XML kernel, Reconciliation, Direct debit, Bank statement
CORPORATE ORGANIZATIONS			
TWIST	Provides Standards to assist organizations in implementing straight through processing, with single points of data entry, from end to end of the relevant processes	Corporate treasuries, Banks	Wholesale financial market transaction processing, Commercial payments & collections, Working capital finance, Cash management

RosettaNet	Standards organization for inter-organization Trade	Corporate Organizations	Collaborative commerce, Global supply chain
OMG	Object Management Group. Produces and maintains computer industry specifications for interoperable enterprise applications	Computer industry	Model driven architecture that separate business and application logic from the underlying platform. Applicable for J2EE, Net and Web services
TECHNOLOGY STANDARDS			
OAGi	Open Applications Group, Inc.	All organizations	XML solution to support integration needs both outside the enterprise and inside the enterprise using Web Services
OTHER STANDARDS			
VRXML	Vendor reporting Extensible mark-up Language	NYSE and its vendors	Market data billing, reporting
RIXML	Research Information Exchange Mark-up Language	Buy and sell side firms	Investment and financial research. Standards to support easier and more efficient to categorize, aggregate, compare, sort and distribute research data
XBRL	Extensible Business reporting Language	All organizations	Standards used for reporting Financial Data e.g. Balance Sheets and Annual Reports of companies.

Fig. 4.12 *The List of standards initiatives targeted by UNIFI that are generally driven by communities of users looking for more cost-effective, XML-based communications to support specific financial business processes*

The objectives of the IST harmonization team are to:
- Resolve content differences between the messages proposed by various standards groups and agree on message content.
- Standardize the representation of the content (tags, schema structure, etc.).

- Establish a method of inter-operability to have extended or related message packaging.
- Recommend a common core payment message kernel that can be accepted into each of the XML standard bodies.

Each group is responsible for obtaining approval for the incorporation of the kernel within the organization of its own standards. SWIFT standards extends its business validation group, adding representation from the IFX, TWIST, OAGi, UN/CEFACT and RosettaNet to validate the work over the broad banking and corporate community.

The initial work definition for ISTH is development of the core payment XML kernel that provides the definition of an XML message that will be used for making a payment as indicated in three message types: payment initiation, status and advice. Reconciliation, direct debit and bank statement are addressed in future phases of work, while other types such as extended remittance advice, working capital management and card payments are currently out of its scope.

By 2004, the ISTH successfully produced an XML-based core payment kernel to be used for payment initiation and status updates. These sets of XML messages were first to be approved and registered as UNIFI (ISO20022) compliant. The business areas and the messages in the payment kernel, which have been modified in 2006, include:

- Payment initiation, which includes the following messages.
  - ❏ Customer credit transfer initiation.
  - ❏ Payment status report.
  - ❏ Payment cancellation request.
  - ❏ Customer payment reversal.
  - ❏ Customer direct debit initiation.
- Payment and clearing settlement, which includes the following messages.
  - ❏ Payment status report.
  - ❏ FI-to-FI customer direct debit.
  - ❏ Payment return.
  - ❏ Payment cancellation request.
  - ❏ FI-to-FI payment reversal.
  - ❏ FI-to-FI customer credit transfer.
  - ❏ Financial institution (FI) credit transfer.

Source: www.iso20022.org/index.cfm/item_id=59950

To give the readers a flavor of the standards message and the business scenario associated with the customer credit transfer initiation, Exhibit 5 and Exhibit 6 contain one of the standard messages and the associated business scenario proposed by ISTH.

Having succeeded with the payment kernel, the ISTH is now tackling bank advices and account statements. The payment initiation set is the first of the portfolio of payment messages that will cover the end-to-end payments transaction chain. This successful co-operation between these various standards organizations also holds promise of acceptance of other standards as they develop.

Presently, one limitation of ISTH has been their decision to keep the rich remittance advices outside their scope. While expectedly, development of a pan-industry remittance advise standard would be a Herculean task given the nuances across industries e.g. lawyers, tour payments, shipping, etc., it would be good if standards for such remittance advice can be generated for a few industries so that other industry associations could use that as a model to define standards for themselves.

BENEFITS OF COLLABORATIVE STANDARDS

The collaborative standards, with reference to a payment standard for example, are expected to provide the parties with the following benefits.

General benefits to all communities:

- Set clear direction for one single standard for core payment functionality.
- Reduce operational cost by increasing the level of straight through processing (STP).
- Improve inter-operability between market participants.
- Promote universal applicability.

Specific benefits to the corporate community:

- Facilitate straight through processing.
  - ❑ Acknowledgement of receipt of payment instruction.
  - ❑ Debit advice in respect of payment.
  - ❑ Credit advice to beneficiary and reconciliation of account receivables.
- Improve payments process.
  - ❑ Full remittance advice linked to payment.
  - ❑ Counter-party data.
- Reduce costs of a host-to-host file delivery implementation.
  - ❑ Open, harmonized XML message standards.
  - ❑ Flexible standard that can be used by any corporate irrespective of size with any bank.
  - ❑ Inter-operability with other industry verticals.
  - ❑ Potential for off-the-shelf solutions from system vendors.
  - ❑ Leverage ERP investment to automate integration with trading partners.

Specific benefits to the banking community on implementation of standards are:
- Respond to corporate demand.
- Minimize number of standards to be developed and maintained.
  - ❏ Focus effort on XML standards development.
  - ❏ Lower development and testing expense.
  - ❏ Reduced resources required to participate in multiple standards forums.
- Universal applicability of standards.
- Reduce costs of a host-to-host file delivery implementation.
- Reduce costs and improve customer service through better STP.

Specific benefits to the software community include:
- Respond to corporate demand.
- Minimize number of standards to be developed and maintained.
  - ❏ Focus effort on XML standards development.
  - ❏ Lower development and testing expense.
  - ❏ Reduced resources required to participate in multiple standards forums.
- Standard development tools can be used, reducing required investments.
- Universal applicability increasing customer value of payment related utilities.

We will now take a break from the standards organization and look at a few other types of organizations in the competitive space in the area of e-financial supply chain.

PLAYERS IN THE e-FINANCIAL SUPPLY CHAIN—COMPETITIVE SPACE

TradeCard

Founded in 1999, the mission of TradeCard has been to automate procurement through payment. TradeCard strives to offer the most effective service to connect buyers and sellers with their service providers and to automate the financial processes of global trade, so that all parties realize the greatest process and cost efficiencies. It provides this by directly making available its Internet hosted platform to the buyers and suppliers, as well as the other parties involved in the supply chain and charging a fee for doing this.

TradeCard provides support for the complex trade processes through three key processes on its Internet platform:

- Trading partner management
  - ❑ Collaborative processes for purchase order management.
  - ❑ Invoice processing, invoice verifications versus purchase order, dispute resolution.
  - ❑ Linkages to logistics partners, quality inspectors, etc.
- Accounts Payable (AP)/Accounts Receivable (AR)
  - ❑ Reconciliation of invoices versus purchase orders.
  - ❑ Reconciliation of payments versus invoices.
- Financial management
  - ❑ Linkages to banks and insurance companies.

TradeCard connects all the trading partners through the Internet and routes and stores their trade documentation electronically, from purchase orders to electronic invoices. All parties have appropriate access to view and amend documents as the transaction progresses. This provides paperless ease and efficiency.

TradeCard also supports linkages to the logistics and inspection companies and has tied-up with over 100 logistics companies. The buyer or the seller can request for proof of delivery to the logistics service provider, who can then get on to the Internet and provide proof of delivery. Similarly, the partner inspection companies can provide the inspection passed/failed status of the transaction on the Net.

TradeCard also automates the accounts payable and accounts receivables process by:

- Automatically generating payment instructions for the vendor invoices that are accepted. For accepting vendor invoices, it also supports matching of the vendor invoices with the purchase orders raised and advises discrepancies, if any.
- For sales, it matches the invoices with the monies received in order to facilitate smoother accounts receivables reconciliation.

TradeCard further provides insurance and credit, in partnership with some insurance companies and banks. The buyer or the seller can seek finance against their transactions from partner banks of TradeCard. However, this particular service ran into contention with the banking community as in the mechanics of loan disbursal and loan repayment, the service treaded on some of the activities of a bank and in its early days was seen as a competition to banks.

Contrary to the significant expectations from TradeCard in its early days, its success has been limited. In around 2002 or 2003, the company decided to focus on specific industry verticals –such as the footwear and apparel industries in order to facilitate business growth. It has had some good success stories in these industries from Northern Group Retail, which is a large apparel company in Canada with over 275 outlets and sourcing from many parts of Asia including Taiwan, China and Hong Kong.

One of the key challenges faced by TradeCard lately, is its positioning with respect to the ERP systems like SAP who for example, has substantially extended its functionality to support linkages with the physical supply chain for a corporate.

More information on TradeCard can be obtained from www.TradeCard.com.

Xign

Founded in 2000, Xign provides an Internet platform where the suppliers and buyers can interact to perform their financial settlement operations. Xign solution offers to automate the entire supply chain financial processes from purchase order, receipt of invoices, validation of invoices, routing and approval, handling of disputes, payment processing and informing the supplier of the payment information, to subsequent reconciliation of the bank accounts, for the payables organization of a corporate.

The Xign solution offers a shared, supplier directory and leverages supplier participation, eliminating one-to-one interaction for vendor set-up and maintenance. Xign integrates with popular ERP applications and leading financial services providers to offer secure, precise movement of funds via bank provided Automated Clearing House (ACH) processing and the MasterCard Corporate Purchasing Card® network.

The typical process flow for the customers of Xign would be as follows:

- The buyers can raise purchase orders on the suppliers who are pre-registered on the Xign Internet platform. The buyers may have their own workflow processes for approval, which can be set up on the system and are supported through the Xign solution.
- The purchase orders are then visible to the suppliers who can process them and then upload their invoices on the Internet offering.
- The invoices are automatically checked against the conditions laid down in the purchase order and the irregular conditions are highlighted.
- The invoices can be accepted by the buyers as per the workflow followed in their organization, which can be set up as a part of the solution.
- The accepted invoices are then available to the buyer, for payment.

In addition to reducing financial settlement processing costs and cycle time through elimination of the paper process, Xign's solution offers management discount opportunities for early payment.

In 2003, Xign tied up with JPMorgan Treasury Services to provide an e-payables solution for the financial settlement of business-to-business commerce.

In the same year, it also integrated with the MasterCard settlement option so that buyers and sellers can collaborate within a single environment, streamline respective processes, and use the MasterCard Corporate Purchasing Card® for payment. The credit card company rolled out MasterCard e-P3, a new business-to-business payment program that integrates its existing purchasing card program, which is used for small ticket purchases, with electronic invoicing programs. Buyers install an e-P3 adapter, which is based on an E-payment platform from Xign Corp., in their back-end accounts payable and purchasing systems. They can then post purchase orders on an Internet site. Suppliers can respond by either automatically reformatting the electronic order into an invoice, fill in a standard invoice offered by MasterCard, or upload a file of any format from their back-end systems. Business rules allow the MasterCard system to detect discrepancies and bounce back any unsatisfactory invoices to the supplier even before passing them on to the buyer.

Once invoices pass the automated inspection, they are available to the appropriate party on the buyer side, who authorizes the payment on a MasterCard corporate purchasing card. Online collaboration tools of Xign enable buyers to communicate regarding any disputes or clarifications on purchase orders and invoices.

However, as with TradeCard, Xign faces a challenge from the evolving ERP systems. There is also the integration required by the ERP systems, which has to be done by the buyers. Additionally, the buyer bank and the seller bank must have the incentive to sell these solutions.

More information on Xign is available at www.xign.com.

Bottomline Technologies

Based out of USA and founded in 1989, Bottomline Technologies provides payments and invoice automation software and services. The company's solutions enable banks and corporations to automate, manage and control processes involving payments and collections, invoice approval, reporting and document archives.

The solutions from Bottomline are categorized as follows.
- To banks:
  - ❑ Cash management
  - ❑ Financial supply chain automation
- To corporates:
  - ❑ Purchasing management
  - ❑ Invoice management
  - ❑ Payments management
- Legal spend management

Bottomline started by providing technology solutions for cash management to banks and is extending its scope into financial supply chain automation. Bottomline provides white-labeled service to banks for capturing invoice information for the account payables of corporates. These invoices can then, be matched with the purchase orders, validated, approved and forwarded for payment.

The purchase management solution allows employees across the enterprise to requisition for goods and services from approved suppliers using easy-to-complete templates. A standard "shopping cart" interface tracks purchases originating from product databases, CDs and intranet catalogs, or externally hosted market sites and trading exchanges. Purchases requiring approval are then automatically routed through an authorization matrix, configured to support the organization's business rules and policies. Once approved, automated budget management capabilities provide purchasing and finance decision-makers with up-to-date views of spending by cost center and cost code.

When goods and services are delivered, invoice details are recorded to facilitate purchase order matching. These invoices or others received directly are then available for approval and payment.

The legal spend management solution allows the corporate to view and approve the legal spends of their lawyers and the activities, and also to track these versus the budgets before the bills are raised, so that the legal cost can be controlled and remains transparent. Features of the solution include:

- Electronic billing—the invoices can be submitted by the lawyers, and go through a series of checks versus the budgets and the order and discrepancies, if any, are highlighted to the lawyers. Subsequently, the invoices are available to the corporate for approval.
- Budgeting—allows for general and task-based budgets and the purchase orders and invoices are tracked versus the approved budgets.
- Reporting.

Bottomline has a very large customer base, indicating that its model has been very successful. Its financial supply chain model extends their historical capabilities in cash management, well.

For more information visit www.bottomline.com.

Metavante

Headquartered in the USA, Metavante is the leading provider of banking and payments technologies to financial services firms and businesses worldwide.

The payment solution group of Metavante provides electronic funds transfer (EFT) and credit and debit card solutions, ACH processing, ATM driving and monitoring, gateway transaction processing, merchant processing, transportation payment solutions, healthcare identification card fulfillment, and flexible spending account processing.

The government payment solutions of Metavante provide payment solutions for taxes, utilities, registrations, citations and fees, child support, permits, corporate filings etc. Specific information as required for the respective payments is captured along with the transaction and validated for accuracy. Metavante runs a LINK2GOV service, through which people can pay 24/7 via the Internet, phone, debit cards, credit cards or even cheques. The solution then integrates with the respective government department to download the collections information into their system.

The health management solution is targeted towards healthcare providers like doctors and hospitals for invoice generation and collection. The solution also enables banks to act as custodians for employer sponsored medical insurance that insurance companies offer with their plan, and then support specialty claims payment distribution.

Metavante also offers technology solutions and white-labeled services for Electronic Invoice Presentment and Payment (EIPP) and Electronic Bill Presentment and Payment (EBPP). Both the above products offer solutions for accounts receivable. For the B2B EIPP, the solution offers:

- Biller service provider—The solution helps in designing the invoice for the corporate and the corporate can post the invoices on their own websites or on the websites of selected partners.
- E-bill distribution—The bills can be distributed through the network of other billing consolidators or the financial institutions. This helps in presenting the invoices to the customers through a single website, if they so prefer.
- Bill payment—This functionality supports payments for both types of consumers, those who have subscribed to receiving invoices electronically as well as for consumers who just wish to pay electronically.

The EBPP offering for the B2C business provides corporate and bill consolidators with a solution for presenting bills online and supporting payment for these bills.

Designated Vendor Financing Solutions, this white-labeled Internet based solution, allows processing, credit analysis, documentation generation and funding services to support the dealer acquisition processes for quick decisions at the point-of-sale. This solution also provides linkages with the lenders and financial institutions.

Metavante provides EFT and card services to over 1,600 financial institutions, transportation agencie, and health insurance companies in the United States. The EIPP and EBPP services are offered to over 2,800 clients!

For more information visit www.metavante.com.

CashTech

CashTech started its operations in 1994 as a technology provider to banks in the area of cash management. Over a period of time, CashTech has had substantial success in implementation of its cash management system across many multinational banks and large private and public sector banks like ABN AMRO, HSBC, HDFC, ICICI, Maybank, etc.

Cash management is the settlement leg of trade transactions and CashTech has, over a period of time, been exposed to such requirements extending into the realm of trade through closer integration of cash and trade related services from the bank. It also has the advantage of already experiencing integration with the corporate ERP systems through its cash management offering to the banks.

The e-financial supply chain offering from CashTech provides support for new age cash and trade products as a result of the merging nature of cash and trade financial processes. The building blocks of its solution are comprised of three basic sections as follows:

- The cash management collections and payment services.
- The receivables management services, which offers electronic invoice presentment and payment (EIPP) services along with reconciliation services between the invoices, and the payments and collections.
- Financial supply chain services, which include financing against invoices and purchase orders and other services such as LCs, collection and payment support type of services.

The cash management section is strongly linked to the core funds transfer services, which provide strong funds transfer and message management capability to the banks, to and from the clearing systems and also with partner banks along with sophisticated liquidity management services.

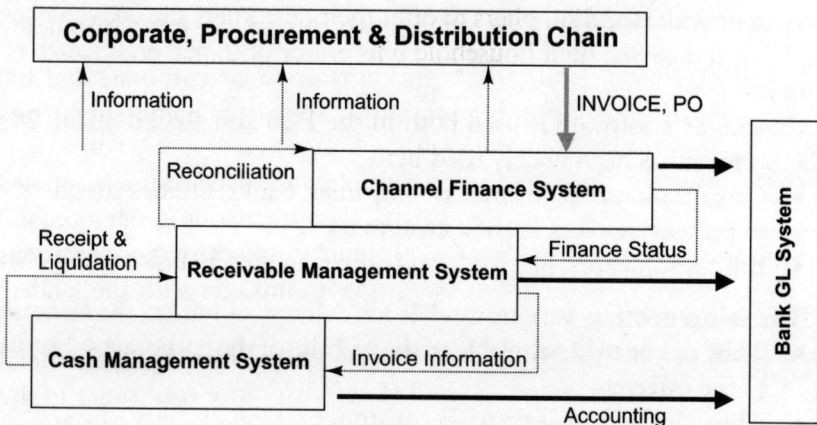

Fig. 4.13 *The supply chain services model offered by CashTech*

In providing these solutions CashTech continues with its existing model of offering a technology platform to the banks, which can in turn, sell these services to their corporate clients, just like they are selling the cash management services presently.

The services support the entire supply value chain of the corporate and can be configured to meet their specific requirements.

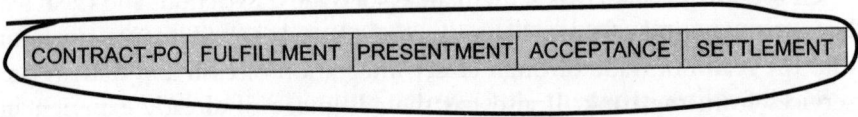

CONTRACT-PO	FULFILLMENT	PRESENTMENT	ACCEPTANCE	SETTLEMENT

Fig. 4.14 *CashTech supply chain services span across the full value chain*

The solution is extensible to support the collaborative standards as they get adopted in the market place. In the meanwhile, banks can extend these competitive offerings to their corporate clients. CashTech is a subsidiary of Fundtech. USA and more information on CashTech can be obtained at www.cash-tech.com.

CheckFree

Founded in 1981, CheckFree Corporation provides electronic financial electronic commerce services and products to organizations around the world. CheckFree started out in the domain of bank payment software solutions and has over a period of time, extended its scope in the area of providing software solutions for securities trading and investment management, electronic bills presentment and payment (EBPP) and operations risk management.

The EBPP solution of CheckFree Electronic Commerce enables financial services providers and suppliers to offer their customers the convenience of receiving and paying their household bills online or in person through retail outlets.

CheckFree's software is used both in the B2B and B2C domain. In the B2C sector it has been widely used by:
- Organizations like insurance companies, banks, utilities suppliers, etc. to present invoices to their customers.
- Bill consolidators, like banks and others, to present bills to their clients.

The solution offers various models for delivery of bills to the customers:
- They can be made available to the website of the corporate subscribing to the offering.
- They can be e-mailed to the consumer.
- They can be made available to customers through bill consolidators.

- They can be made available for payment through the infrastructure and network of CheckFree.

The service also offers multiple payment options such as:
- Pay by phone—offers an Interactive Voice Rresponse (IVR) service that lets customers pay bills on the phone through use of debit and credit cards and other ACH networks as supported.
- Walk-in bill payments—CheckFree provides outsourced service and maintains managed retail locations where bill payments can be accepted in person.
- CheckFree payment—the system supports the debit of consumer accounts through direct debit instructions for credit into the corporate account.

The CheckFree solution is also available for banks and financial institutions to integrate along with their web offerings, so that their customers can view all the bills on the bank's website and then give payment instructions appropriately.

In the B2B domain, the company allows for dynamic invoice presentment, e-mail notification, action tracking and audit capabilities. The solution extends to Customer Relationship Management (CRM) initiatives by enabling customers to review, dispute, approve and pay invoices online, while maintaining their existing workflow processes, authorization levels and organizational hierarchies.

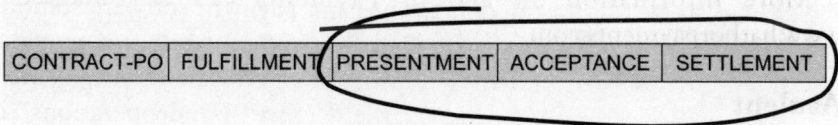

CONTRACT-PO	FULFILLMENT	PRESENTMENT	ACCEPTANCE	SETTLEMENT

Fig. 4.15 *Services of CheckFree focus on presentment, acceptance and settlement*

CheckFree has been vastly successful with many corporates in its bill presentment and payment model. CheckFree is also a part of IFX, one of the standards development organizations previously discussed, and is working towards the development of standards for exchange of invoice and payment information for EBPP applications between financial institutions and other intermediaries like themselves.

More information on CheckFree can be obtained from CheckFree.com.

Harbor Payments

Founded in 2000 and headquartered in USA, Harbor Payments provides technology solutions to the corporate sector in the following areas:
- Corporate disbursement solutions

- Electronic invoice presentment and payment solution
- Electronic bill presentment and payment solution

The corporate disbursement solution of Harbor Payments is linked closely with the accounts payable and EIPP solution of the company. The solution can process both electronic and paper payment and collection transactions. It also supports the function of converting a check to electronic collection through ACH.

The EIPP solution allows the accounts payable processes to capture and convert physical invoices into electronic data. Incoming invoices in soft copy upload format are also supported. These can then be processed for acceptance and payment approvals. For accounts receivables, the system supports electronic submission of invoices, automated workflow matching, dispute resolution and approval and automated processing of incoming approvals.

The EBPP solution is a B2C solution that is available to corporates and also to aggregators, and allows viewing and payment of bills online. It also provides support for online chat and collaboration capabilities.

The organization also provides solutions for claims workflow, reporting and payment solutions for insurance companies, third-party administrators, self-insured and managed care organizations.

The company has been successful because it has focused on pain areas with immediate solution benefits and has sold the above services to many large corporate organizations.

More information on Harbor Payments can be obtained at www.harborpayments.com.

Avolent

Founded in 1995, Avolent offers EIPP solutions to corporates on the sales and account receivable side. The EIPP solution comprises of the following key features.

- Invoice Design—Creates and manages the look and feel of invoices with an easy-to-use WYSIWYG design tool and allows definition of line details of the invoices.
- Invoice presentment:
  - ❏ Presents invoices electronically to customers, and sets up notifications to alert them to the arrival of new online invoices. Paper Bills and bill images can also be integrated with the systems, which can then be downloaded by customers or sorted and filtered for better reporting capabilities.
  - ❏ Consolidation—Invoices can be combined from multiple back-end systems into a single, consolidated invoice for a unified customer experience.

- ❏ Invoice printing.
- ❏ Multiple delivery channels—The system supports presentation and distribution of invoices via many methods including the Web, e-mail, etc.
- Dispute handling.
- Invoice payments.
- Accounts receivables tracking, penalty and trade terms management.

Avolent has specific offerings, customized and targeted towards the following sectors:

- Healthcare/insurance—Allows healthcare insurers to streamline employer group processes such as invoicing, member maintenance and reconciliation by replacing the manual tasks with an interactive online application.
- Retail/distribution—Helps retail organizations streamline invoice management and financial transactions with large corporate customers, e.g. for corporate purchases from Walmart, this solution helps Walmart to streamline its invoice management and payment processes with the corporate.
- Leasing/financial services—The solution for the leasing industry provides support to consolidate bills and provides access to underlying financial data for both the lessor and the customer.
- Manufacturing—This is the EIPP offering of Avolent, which supports the needs of manufacturers.

Avolent has been successful in implementing its EIPP services.

For more information refer to www.avolent.com.

BCE Emergis

BCE Emergis, a US-based company incorporated in 1988, focuses on settlement solutions for the health and financial services sector. The company has expertise in the following areas of operations:

- Health claim management
- Pharmacy benefit management
- Drug claim and dental claim processing
- Tax filing and payment services
- Financing and leasing services

It is thus evident that, BCE Emergis manages solutions that automate transactions and exchange of information to increase process efficiencies. The solution allows capture of the relevant information specific to particular industries and validates such information for accuracy before allowing it to be exchanged between the customer and its trading party, which in turn triggers the payment and settlement or a further action.

The health claim management solution helps both the insurance payers and health care providers to maximize efficiency through the entire claims management process. Emergis provides a Web-enabled health bill submission service to health and medical service providers by sending the health bills to the insurance companies or the government agencies, as the case may be. The solution fully automates the back-end processes of enrolment, bill submission, and adjudication and provider bill payment.

The Emergis solution for financing and leasing, streamlines the lien registration process to secure the financing and leasing transactions by offering a single entry point to each provincial registrar for proper lien registration. Each of these is tracked with a complete audit trail and the solution manages communication with the debtor when required by law.

The companies' services are used by many large corporates such as insurance companies, financial institutions, government agencies, pharmacies, etc.

BCE Emergis provides a very good model of linking together the trade and settlement processes in the specific verticals in which it operates.

For more information visit www.emergis.com.

SAP

Until recently, automation of the financial supply chain had been the domain of companies outside the realm of ERP firms. However, this has changed rapidly with companies like SAP now offering supply chain solutions within their product offerings. Founded in 1972, SAP is the world's largest business software company and third largest independent software provider overall.

The key offering of SAP related to supply chain management is mySAP Supply Chain Management (mySAP SCM). This application helps organizations to create supply chain networks, in which the dealer and vendor communities share information to adapt to changing market conditions and proactively respond to shorter, less predictable life cycles. This helps organizations to:

- Synchronize supply to demand—Balance the push and pull network planning processes and, replenish inventory and execute production based on actual demand.
- Sense and respond with an adaptive supply chain network—Drive distribution, transportation and logistics processes that are integrated with real-time planning processes.
- Provide network-wide visibility, collaboration and analytics—Monitor and analyze the extended supply chain.

SAP claims that the mySAP Supply Chain Management application can help organizations transform a linear supply chain into an adaptive supply chain network, in which communities of customer-centric, demand-driven companies share knowledge, intelligently adapt to changing market conditions, and proactively respond to shorter, less predictable life cycles.

This new offering from SAP draws its inputs from two other offerings namely, mySAP Supplier Relationship management and mySAP Customer Relationship management, and from product life cycle management solutions.

The mySAP customer relationship management solution supports the following functionality amongst others:

- Catalog and order management for B2B in e-commerce
- Complaints and returns management in e-commerce
- Contract management
- Service request management
- Channel management
- Sales management
- Information help desk

The mySAP supplier relationship management solution supports the following activities:

- Purchase planning
- Supplier qualification
- Supplier negotiation
  - ❏ Request for quotation
  - ❏ Reverse auction
  - ❏ Bid evaluation and awarding
- Contract management
- Requisitioning
- Order management
- Receiving
- Financial settlement
- Supplier enabling
  - ❏ Supplier network
  - ❏ Electronic document exchange
  - ❏ Supplier portal

The various modules of SAP are integrated with each other providing a powerful value proposition of linking the entire procurement to the distribution chain of the company. The offerings from SAP are focused on providing collaboration services between the corporate and its supply chain to facilitate and make the physical supply chain more efficient.

More information on SAP is available at www.sap.com.

Oracle

Founded in 1977, Oracle is the world's leading supplier of software for information management and the second largest independent software company. Like SAP, it has through acquisitions and development, developed a suite of products offering supply chain integration for corporates.

Oracle offers supply chain management (SCM) product lines that address requirements across procurement, order management, manufacturing, product life cycle management, maintenance, logistics, and supply chain planning and execution. Specific areas addressed by Oracle through its product offerings are shown in Fig. 4.16.

1	Collaborative demand forecasting
2	Procurement
3	Logistics
4	Manufacturing
5	Customer order management
6	Transportation management

Fig. 4.16 *Supply chain solutions offered by Oracle*

Although this supply chain appears linear, Oracle provides relevant connections to the various parties involved in the supply chain namely, the vendors, dealers, transporters etc. through the Internet, to allow the various participants to collaborate through the network.

Oracle Supply Chain Planning is part of the Oracle E-business Suite, integrating with other e-business suite applications, including Oracle Manufacturing, Oracle CRM, etc. The depth and breadth of penetration of such ERP systems, provides the providers with a tremendous advantage to further the supply chain integration. The services of Oracle are, like those of SAP, focused on improving efficiencies in the supply chain operations of the corporate.

The customer relationship management module of Oracle, which it acquired through acquisition of Siebel, has the following features:

- Sales
- Self-service and e-billing:
  - ❏ Online bill delivery
  - ❏ Interactive statements in HTML and PDF formats
  - ❏ Online payments
- Partner relationship management
- Contact center and service
- Business analytics

For procurement automation, as a part of its advanced procurement module, Oracle has recently launched, Oracle Supplier Network, an Internet based service that simplifies electronic document exchange with suppliers.

This supports the following key activities:
- Purchase order management
- Invoice management
- Shipment notices
- Payments management

The Oracle procurement modules support both purchasing and sourcing. Under purchasing it supports maintaining a central repository for suppliers chosen as per the policy of the company. The purchasing practices of the company can be configured and centrally maintained. For sourcing, Oracle supports online collaboration and negotiation to achieve more efficient sourcing.

For more information visit www.oracle.com.

SUMMARY—SERVICE POSITIONING OF VENDORS

The service offerings of the various technology solution vendors can be classified for easier understanding as shown in Fig. 4.17.

Almost all companies offer integration capabilities to other systems. Also, most of these systems profess capabilities to integrate using standard messages as proposed by various standard organizations, although they may not have these interfaces readily available at present.

A very interesting observation to be made relates to the various perspectives that these organizations incorporate in their offerings to support the automation of the supply chain. Each of these scenarios is relevant as they are real life conditions that have been met through these solutions. These situations offer both, a challenge and an insight into the organizations developing the standards, as these test cases need to be fulfilled in the process of development of standards. It is also no wonder therefore, that some of the standards forming organizations such as IFX have included organizations like CheckFree into their working group in order to benefit from such a perspective.

PLAYERS IN e-FINANCIAL SUPPLY CHAIN—BANKS

JPMorgan Chase

JPMorgan Chase & Co. is a leading global financial services firm with assets of $1.3 trillion and operations in more than 50 countries. The firm is a leader in investment banking, financial services for consumers, small business and commercial banking, financial transaction processing, asset and wealth management, and the private equity business. JP Morgan has also taken a

No	Vendor	Bank	Corporate	Cash	EIPP	EBPP	Receivable	Payable	Finance	Other
1	TradeCard	X	✓	X	✓	X	✓	✓	P	✓
2	Xign	X	✓	X	✓	X	X	✓	X	✓
3	Bottomline	✓	✓	✓	✓	X	X	✓	X	✓
4	Metavante	✓	✓	✓	✓	✓	✓	✓	✓	X
5	CashTech	✓	X	✓	✓	X	✓	✓	✓	✓
6	CheckFree	✓	✓	✓	✓	✓	✓	X	X	X
7	Harbor	X	✓	✓	✓	✓	✓	X	X	X
8	Avolent	X	✓	X	✓	X	✓	X	X	X
9	BCE Emergi	X	✓	X	✓	X	✓	X	X	X
10	SAP	X	✓	X	✓	X	✓	✓	X	✓
11	Oracle	X	✓	X	✓	✓	✓	✓	X	✓

Legend

1. Bank: Solution being offered to banks
2. Corporate: Solution being offered to corporate
3. Cash: Cash Management solution being offered for collections and payments
4. EIPP: EIPP B2B solution offered
5. EBPP: EBPP B2B solution offered
6. Receivable: Solution on the side of account receivables
7. Payable: Solution on the side of account payables
8. Finance: Solution offers trade finance capabilities
9. Other services: e.g. reconciliation, dispute handling, payment models, etc.

Fig. 4.17 Comparison of service offerings of the various technology solution vendors

leadership role in providing services for automation of the financial supply chain.

The acquisition of Vastera by JPMorgan Chase in 2005, and subsequent formation of JPMorgan Chase Vastera, caused substantial excitement in the supply chain and banking community. However, we will consider the other supply chain services offered by JPMorgan before we discuss this aspect of their business and the possible synergies.

JP Morgan offers the following solutions under its e-commerce solutions:
- Electronic bill resentment and payment
- Electronic invoice presentment and payment
- Online AP, procurement and supplier management network
- Online e-commerce transactions
- Receivables edge

As seen from this, JPMorgan offers a wide repertoire of services in the financial supply chain space. Some details of the offerings being provided by them are detailed in Figure 4.18.

1	EBPP—Accounts Receivable	Provides white-labeled service to automate business-to-consumer (B2C) billing and collection processes. Customers can initiate ACH direct debit or credit card transactions from a branded Website for one-time and recurring payments
2	EIPP—Accounts Receivable	Provides automation for business-to-business (B2B) invoice and collection processes. With EIPP, clients can view, accept or dispute and pay invoices online
3	Accounts Payable, Procurement and Supplier Management Network	The solution offers electronic invoice and payment service for business-to-business commerce, helping manage supplier terms, reduce accounts payable processing costs, avail early payment discounts and streamline operations
4	Online e-Commerce Transactions	The solution integrates with a client's front and back-end e-commerce enterprise applications. The solution enables clients' customers, vendors and other supply chain partners to conduct business, allowing customers Web access to their accounts to order goods and services, make deposits to e-fund accounts, track transactions, etc.
5	Receivables Edge	The solution consolidates all collection and transaction information from electronic and cheque collections into a single consolidated view for the corporate. The cheque images are also available for the corporate to view

Fig. 4.18   *Services offered by JPMorgan Chase*

For some of the above services, JPMorgan has tied-up with providers such as Xign for providing services to their customers.

Vastera

The acquisition of Vastera by JPMorgan surprised many.

"We have seen real interest and need to combine physical supply chain management with financial supply chain management to optimize the management of working capital", said Tod Burwell, vice president and global head of logistics for JPMorgan Chase, on the acquisition.

Vastera with large experience on handling trade processes for over 400 corporate offers the following outsourced services to the corporate:

- Import pre-entry management
  - ❑ Classification.
  - ❑ Special trade management.
  - ❑ Product specifications by country.
- Export management
- Import management
- Duty management

Global trade can be very complex and Vastera provides trade expertise in dealing with the complexity of global trade in various countries. Their outsource services propose to minimize duties, and reduce inventory, day sales outstanding, operations costs and third party fees. Their services also offer visibility into compliance and operations performance, as well as the ability to document procedures to withstand any government audit.

Coupled with these advantages, Vastera also provides the following services:

- Technology tool to monitor compliance for exports and imports, restricted party screening and also monitoring trade finance transactions.
- Consulting services in global supply chain management and other areas related to export and import compliance.

While the above areas are not directly linked to banking, the acquisition of Vastera provides the following key advantage to the bank and is possibly a very smart move in this respect:

- So far the CFOs of corporates and those who were not bolstered by the procurement and distribution chain of their organization, complained that the banks do not understand enough of their supply chain processes to provide them solutions on the supply chain. The backing of Vastera provides the following:
  - ❑ The corporates open their doors to the JPMorgan Vastera combine, who can demonstrate strong skills in the supply chain domain.
  - ❑ The bank can use this opportunity to further their supply chain offerings to the corporates.

- It provides JPMorgan with the opportunity to integrate their systems with real life systems of Vastera and further their skills in the domain.

More information on JPMorgan can be obtained from www.chase.com.

ABN AMRO Bank

Headquartered in the Netherlands, ABN AMRO is a leading multinational bank with presence in over 50 countries.

Among the key financial supply chain accomplishments of ABN AMRO are the electronic bridges that it has been building between its systems and the treasury management and ERP systems of its customers, thereby successfully increasing STP rates. AccessDirect, its e-payment gateway, can be accessed from treasury workstations such as SunGuard eTreasury Exchange, XRT, Trema, as well as ERP systems such as SAP and Oracle.

ABN also offers financial supply chain services through its MaxTrad offering, which is an Internet offering for facilitating financial supply chain services. The key offerings from MaxTrad are:

- Open account processing
- Supply chain financing

For open account processing through MaxTrad, buyers can upload purchase orders into the system. The subsequent invoice upload in the system can be compared with the purchase order against a pre-defined set of conditions agreed between the buyer and the seller. The discrepancies are tracked electronically and e-mail notifications are available to the buyer and the seller to facilitate the transaction. The reconciled transaction information can be downloaded for import into the ERP systems.

The supply chain finance module allows the buyer who is the client of the bank, to pre-pay the invoices and thereby enjoy early payment discounts. The system also supports upload of approved invoices to suppliers who can then issue online purchase requests for selected invoices. MaxTrad provides detailed status updates for each purchase invoice, whether paid or overdue.

Another solution from ABN AMRO Bank extends the traditional trade services offerings of the bank and provides the benefits of the existing LC offerings. Yet, it addresses some of the challenges faced by the importer and exporter in operating the traditional LC products namely, higher costs, potential delays in procurement because of the number of banks and parties involved in document handling, and a high administrative burden because of onerous documentary requirements.

The solution is useful for companies in the business of retailing textiles and apparels, electronics, footwear, etc., in the developed countries who, driven by fierce competition and reducing margins, are sourcing from Asian countries. ABN AMRO Bank has a good international network in both such geographies and deploys off-shoring and Internet technology to enhance efficiency for the benefit of clients with global supply chains. A case study of the solution model is presented as follows.

A Europe based retailer (buyer) with a significant supplier base in Asia (mainly, China and Hong Kong) was issuing a few thousands LCs every year. The retailer sells hundreds of different product lines, each of which is managed by a buying department that makes the commercial decision on purchasing. The finance department would then create the LC application for the bank using the standard LC process as outlined in Chapter 1. This paper process was resulting in high costs, a long procurement cycle and a high administrative burden, as is generally the problem when using LCs. Also, the suppliers would continuously make enquires about the status of the LCs with the procurement team who in turn, would make the same enquiries from the finance team.

Fig. 4.19 is a pictorial depiction of the solution implemented by ABN AMRO for its customer:

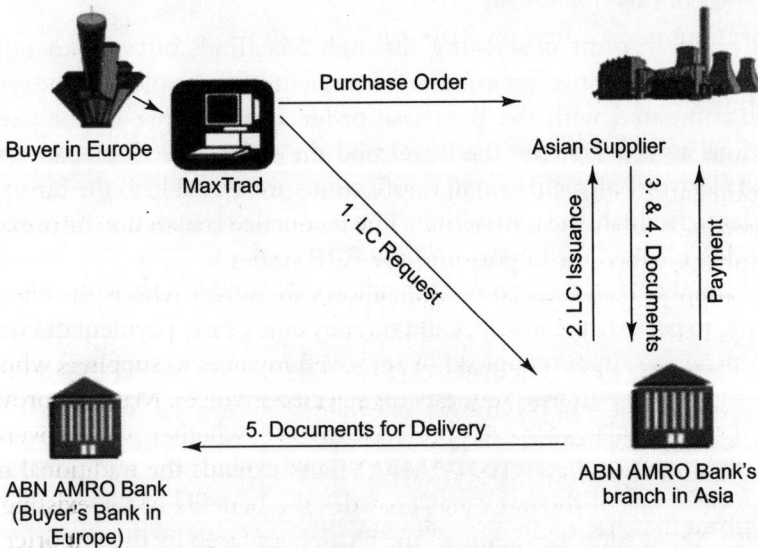

Fig. 4.19 *A structured LC solution implemented by ABN AMRO Bank*

The new solution proposed by ABN AMRO Bank had the following workflow steps and advantages:

1. Using the Internet offering of ABN AMRO Bank the procurement department of the retailer could directly make a request for an LC.

2. This LC request was routed to the relevant ABN AMRO branch in Asia, say Hong Kong, who would then directly issue the LC to the supplier.
3. When the supplier or his bank presented the documents at the ABN AMRO Hong Kong branch, these documents were scanned and made available to the centralized back-office in ABN AMRO India for verification.
4. If the documents were found discrepant they were rectified at source in the supplier's country in Hong Kong.
5. If the documents were found to be in order, they were directly couriered to ABN AMRO Bank in Europe where the retailer is the customer and where the documents were directly delivered without any further verification.

Simultaneously, the scanned images of the documents were also made available for the retailer to view over the Internet, which helped both the buyer and the seller to agree on any discrepancy and course of action. In the given situation, the above process substantially improved the operating efficiencies in the typical LC process.

For more information on ABN AMRO visit www.abnamro.com.

Citibank

Citibank, founded in 1812, is now one of the largest banks and provides consumer and corporate banking services around the world. Citibank is also credited with ushering in the cash management revolution around the world.

Citibank offers the following services under its umbrella of Global Transaction Services, which includes services around the financial supply chain as listed:

- Payments
- Collections and receivables reconciliation
- Commercial cards
- Vendor finance

Citibank has been a pioneer and extremely innovative in extending cash management and reconciliation services to corporates. To achieve this it focused on the overall services and also on niche services like dividend warrants, pension payments, etc. Citibank also pioneered the establishment of ERP linkages with the large corporates to facilitate straight through processing.

Around 1998, Citibank structured its organization to support emerging local corporates, which were provided support based on the relationships that these small and medium enterprises had with the large corporates, much like the financial supply chain discussed in this book.

In addition to conventional trade, Citibank is pushing its 'Enhanced Open Account Services' to leverage its relationship with large company buyers in the global supply chain to speed up payments to vendors. This capability positions buyers to negotiate better pricing and effectively reduces dependence on trade credit lines.

More information on Citibank can be obtained from www.citicorp.com.

Deutsche Bank

Founded in Berlin in 1870, to support the internationalization of business and to promote and facilitate trade relations between Germany, other European countries and overseas markets, Deutsche Bank is now a leading global provider of financial services.

Deutsche Bank has been a forerunner in providing sophisticated cash management services to its corporate customers in the areas of receivable and payable management. Deutsche Bank focused on specific industries such as telecom, to provide high value added services in the focused sector. It also provided good integration services with the corporate ERP systems.

Deutsche Bank has also been at the forefront of standards development and works with leading vendors of ERP and treasury workstations to integrate messaging standards.

Deutsche Bank introduced DB e-bills, and electronic invoice presentment and payments solution for the business-to-business market. The solution is available over the Internet, where the buyer and the supplier can be networked so that the buyer can verify and authorize the bills for payment to streamline the operations workflow.

More information on Deutsche Bank can be taken from www.db.com.

HSBC

Established in Hong Kong in 1865 and now headquartered in London, HSBC is one of the largest banking and financial services organizations in the world. HSBC's international network covers 76 countries and territories in Europe, the Asia-Pacific region, the Americas, the Middle East and Africa.

From the outset, trade finance and services has been a strong feature of HSBC's local and international business; an expertise that has been recognized throughout its history and by industry sources as well. With strong expertise in traditional trade services, HSBC's approach to supply chain has been to extend its trade services to more automation, and integration with corporates rather than extension of cash management services into the trade domain, which has been the approach of some of the other banks as well.

Paperless Trade

HSBC is currently piloting a paperless, open account platform based on an open communications infrastructure (BOLERO), to promote connectivity between the buyer, suppliers, HSBC and other supply chain parties such as freight forwarders, customs bodies, etc.

Document Imaging

This solution involves image scanning of the paper document presented by suppliers to HSBC, which are available for viewing and acceptance by the buyer. Suppliers will have online access to purchase order (PO) details, transaction status and finance products. Back office integration and PO reporting for the buyer is also possible.

Automated DC Issuance

This solution allows receipt of purchase orders from buyers and automatically creates documentary credit (DC) based on templates, for automated issuance.

Finance

HSBC provides trade finance services through its traditional trade finance offerings, which it has extended to provide finance for open account based trade.

Document In-sourcing

For large suppliers, HSBC can prepare and dispatch export documents on their behalf using a mix of technology and expertise, thereby allowing the corporate to outsource their trade operations back office to HSBC. This provides the benefit of cost savings, increased resource flexibility and superior expertise on trade processing capabilities.

Recently, HSBC has piloted a solution in the market, which uses the invoice processing infrastructure of Bottomline Technologies for providing services along the financial supply chain. The solution proposes to improve operations efficiencies along the vendor payments of large corporates. The proposed solution offers corporates the convenience to upload their purchase orders to the bank. Subsequently, the invoices are received from the solution of Bottomline Technologies and the system runs an automatic reconciliation between the terms and details of the purchase orders versus the information available in the invoices. If the two match, the payment is automatically scheduled as per payment terms. The solution also offers financing to vendors whose invoices are matched and where payment has been scheduled.

HSBC is also a forerunner in providing cash management services to its customers. More information on HSBC can be taken from www.hsbcnet.com.

US Bank—PowerTrack

U.S. Bancorp is among the 10 largest financial services holding companies in the United States. US Bank was one of the first movers in the space of management of account payables. In 1999, it launched PowerTrack an electronic business-to-business platform for electronic invoice presentment and payments. PowerTrack has been deployed as an ASP solution and is run as a separate business so that it can sell to non-US Bank customers as well.

PowerTrack offers the following key features:

- Allows access to the corporate and its buyers and suppliers.
- Stores contracts, catalogs and pricing information.
- Allows electronic submission of purchase orders, invoices and receipt information.
- A set of user-defined pre-payment audits ensures that transactions stay within established boundaries, such as price and spending limits. When an exception is detected, PowerTrack provides online collaboration tools to speed the review and resolution process.
- Allows dispute resolution on invoices.
- Supports electronic payments.
- Supports integration to ERP and accounting systems.
- Provides real-time visibility to operations, logistics and financial information.

Originally developed for the logistics and transportation industries (the U.S. Department of Defense is still its largest customer), PowerTrack has been expanded to meet the purchasing needs of companies as large as Cargill and John Deere and smaller ones as well.

US Bank also provides purchase cards, which enable the subscribing companies to set dollar limits and restrict the types of purchases that can be made with the card, thus ensuring that proper program purchases are made. The Internet offering from US Bank allows subscribers to manage the program and track purchasing trends.

US Bank has been a very successful first mover in the field of financial supply chain. For more information visit http://www.usbank.com/cgi_w/cfm/commercial_business/products_and_services/corp_payment/powertrack.cfm.

PLAYERS IN e-FINANCIAL SUPPLY CHAIN—OTHERS

Visa Commerce

Visa is a private, membership association jointly owned by more than 20,000 member financial institutions around the world. The organization is dedicated to serving these members, their cardholders and their merchant clients by facilitating payment anywhere, anytime and in any way.

Visa history dates back to 1958, when Bank of America launched its pioneering BankAmericard program in California. A decade later, Dee Hock, one of the leaders of a group of BankAmericard licensee banks proposed that the banks form an association—a joint venture that would allow members to enjoy the benefits of a centralized payments system, while competing fairly for their own interests. Hock became the new group's first president. In 1970, Bank of America transferred control and ownership of BankAmericard to the newly incorporated NBI (National BankAmericard, Inc.). In 1976, NBI changed the BankAmericard name to Visa.

To further its efforts on e-commerce, Visa is striving to leverage VisaNet, its global clearing, authorization and settlement system. With this back-bone, Visa is offering two products:
- Visa Purchase Card
- Visa Commerce

Visa Purchase Card

The Visa purchase card offers to reduce the time and costs associated with paying for goods and services by eliminating paper-based purchase orders and invoice processing. The solution offers to substantially reduce reconciliation requirements by:
- Allowing customized information capture and reporting solutions.
- Establish spending limits and controls by employee, department, or division.

The additional benefits of this approach are (a) it rides on the existing technology and clearing network, which is tested (b) the existing merchants and banks provide a convenient distribution network, and (c) the buyer enjoys temporary short-term finance as with a regular credit card.

Although the purchasing card is quite in use, one of the deterrents to its growth is the interchange fees that are applicable on the transactions. For business-to-business transactions, which are of high value and finely priced, this is a bugbear.

Visa Commerce

In 2002, Visa introduced a non-card based electronic payment and information management service designed to substantially increase the efficiencies on payment processing and reconciliation.

For suppliers, Visa Commerce allows submission of online payment requests on specified buyers accounts, much like the credit card account numbers at present. The buyers receive electronic payment requests from suppliers for which they can pay as per their agreement with the supplier or defer it as per their trade arrangement and practice. The payment instructions for this request can then be originated subsequently. The transaction limit is set at USD 10 million for a single transaction.

As for regular credit card transactions, there is a bank for the supplier (acquiring or merchant bank) and there is a bank for the buyer (card issuing bank).

The differences with respect to the existing card transactions are:

- The buyer and the seller need to integrate their systems with Visa to enable them to originate payment requests and make payment instructions.
- There is no interchange fee; the supplier can negotiate a fee with his bank depending upon the payment and credit arrangement that he agrees with his bank.

The key advantages of this model are as follows.

- Very high level of transaction information, which can be customised to the needs of the buyer and the seller. This can substantially help in increasing reconciliation efficiencies for both, the buyer and the seller.
- The payments can be made from anywhere to anywhere like with existing credit cards at present and these are not limited to the clearing systems available in a particular location. VisaNet supports a global infrastructure.
- The offering rides on the existing VisaNet infrastructure of technology, clearing and distribution, all of which is in place and tested.

However, in the implementation of Visa Commerce, Visa faces the following challenges:

- The existing clearing networks of ACH and Wire are very cheap and in many cases free for the banks when subsidized by the central banks. In a large number of cases, the domestic cash management payments get routed over this network. Banks and corporates have established systems for routing payments over these networks and are happy with the implementation and cost structure.
- The buyer and the seller have to undertake integration with Visa Commerce, which is an expense. They need to be ready to take on these costs.
- Finally the banks should be willing to sell services of Visa Commerce. This will happen if they can see clear profits for themselves, in the deal. On the one hand, there are the existing clearing systems with low costs and established linkages, but with lower information carrying capacity for support of reconciliation and customers who are demanding more at a lower price. On the other hand, there is Visa Commerce with better support for reconciliation requirements but

with a cost that the banks should be able to pass down and also make some money on it!

Therein lies the dilemma of Visa Commerce. For more information visit www.visa.com.

MasterCard

MasterCard was founded in 1966 in the USA as Inter-bank Card Association (ICA). As a critical link among financial institutions and millions of businesses, cardholders and merchants worldwide, MasterCard provides services in more than 210 countries and territories.

To further its offerings to support business-to-business payments, MasterCard has introduced the following solutions:
- Purchasing cards
- MasterCard eP3

Purchasing Cards

MasterCard introduced purchasing cards focused on various end requirements such as:
- Travel card
- Fleet card
- Travel and entertainment solution
- Employee fund solutions
- Multinational organizations

The purchase cards provide the following benefits:
- Provide detailed level of transaction information and reports on the spending, which helps in reconciliation.
- Assign cards to individuals or departments with variable controls, such as dollars per month and per transaction, number of transactions per day and per month, type of supplier(s), or specific supplier(s).
- Change purchasing authorization and spending criteria.

MasterCard provides a global, Web-based reporting application that helps companies to view and download financial data from MasterCard programs. The company can see details like hotel chain spending, flight legs, and other information on how money is being spent.

The MasterCard solution also supports data integration with the major ERP and accounting solution vendors.

MasterCard e-P3

This solution from MasterCard is available to subscribers of the purchasing card program. The solution integrates the EIPP offerings from vendors like

Xign and Burns, into the purchase card program of MasterCard. This is useful for typical business payments where purchase orders are issued and invoices and payments have to be verified against the purchase order before issuance of the payment instructions. The following is the process for payments through e-P3:

- Supplier submits invoices to the buyer.
- Buyer approves invoices on the EIPP solution and decides to pay using MasterCard e-P3.
- Buyer generates a payment file from his accounts payable system for settlement by MasterCard.
- Supplier receives e-mail notification and remittance information.
- Supplier receives funding via the acquiring bank account.
- Buyer receives monthly statement from the card issuing bank, which they settle.

The system also supports a payment channel for the supplier in case he does not utilize the services of an acquiring bank.

The challenges are similar to those being experienced by Visa Commerce. For one, the buyer needs to integrate the Xign or Burns offering with their ERP systems. Additionally, the acquiring and the issuing banks need to be provided with incentives to sell these services.

For more information visit www.mastercard.com.

DHL

Founded in 1969, DHL is the global market leader in international express, overland transport and air freight. It is also the world's number one in ocean freight and contract logistics. DHL has a comprehensive network combining air and ground transport for optimal delivery performance. On the one hand, this gives it worldwide reach and on the other, a strong local presence and unique understanding of local markets and customers. DHL operates in over 220 countries worldwide.

DHL offers a full range of customized solutions from express document shipping to supply chain management. In the logistics area, globalization is creating ever more complex supply chains and DHL's combination of global reach and local knowledge is a key competitive edge. DHL offers a wide range of standardized services as well as tailor-made industry solutions.

For managing the international supply chain, DHL offers the following services:

- Origin management, including vendor management; supplier collections; customs brokerage; consolidation services and value-added services.

- Global forwarding, including: air/ocean/road/rail freight forwarding and management; European managed transport.
- Destination management, including: port and demurrage management; customs brokerage; de-consolidation and pre-retail services; port to distribution center transportation; direct store delivery (US only).
- Supply chain visibility and management, including: purchase order management; RFID product tracking; exception management; planning and forecasting; inventory management.

Outsourcing involves DHL taking over and managing previous in-house logistics operations, including:
- Distribution centers
- Transport operations
- Back office functions
- Supply chain management functions
- After sales services

DHL not only provides physical logistics services but also manages other enhanced supply chain services, improving efficiencies and reducing costs.
- Order management—Receipt, management, execution, sequencing and dispatch of orders in a timely manner.
- Call center management—A call center manages orders, monitors sales activities, provides customer services and functions as a help desk.
- Global inventory management—DHL gives customers a global view of inventory, thus enabling informed decisions.
- Consolidated billing services—Offers creation of a consolidated and categorized invoice, based on all services performed in a specific time period by more than one service provider, in an agreed format.
- Freight and customs solutions
- Implementation and project management for a supply chain system.

Along with the above, DHL logistics e-services provide access to systems that ensure customers have control and visibility of their supply chains at all times. Products can be tracked, queried and ordered online.

And now DHL intends to offer trade finance services to further augment its transport offering, where it believes the margins are thin. The project is still in the concept stage and the key consideration is that, 'it is about managing risk and return and how DHL can take on more risks on behalf of its customers and then lay that off is some way to drive new innovative solutions'. DHL intends to involve some banks in its initiative in order to jointly offer integrated supply chain and financing services.

For more information on DHL visit www.dhl.com.

UPS

Founded in 1907 as a messenger company in the United States, UPS now manages the flow of goods, funds and information in more than 200 countries and territories worldwide. UPS is the world's largest package delivery company and a leading global provider of specialized transportation and logistics services.

UPS provides supply chain solutions through the following services:
- Manages suppliers and vendors, logistics, orders and shipment details from purchase order through to delivery.
- Manages a worldwide network of distribution centers.
- Manages inventory across the chain.
- Simplifies trade compliance internationally.
- Manages post sales and returns.

UPS also provides consulting services for making the cash management for the corporate more efficient through:
- Better working capital management strategies to accelerate cash flow.
- Reductions in aggregate cash requirements due to shortened order-to-cash cycles.
- Greater understanding of the costs to serve different customers.
- Superior utilization of assets through life cycle management.

With a view to integrating with the financial supply chain, UPS acquired Capital Business Credit Co. to form UPS Capital Corp., with the key business strategy of UPS to enable the flow of goods, information and funds. Combined with other UPS subsidiaries, UPS Capital's financial services can leverage technology, transportation, e-commerce and logistics solutions for total, efficient supply chain management, allowing companies to focus on their core businesses. UPS Capital has the following business groups: equipment leasing, distribution finance, payment solutions, card transaction solutions, global trade finance and insurance agency.

For more information on UPS visit www.ups.com.

TradeBeam

Founded in 2000, TradeBeam is a global trade management software and services company providing technology and outsourcing solutions that streamline global trading processes for corporates and their partners. TradeBeam's integrated solutions provide import and export compliance, inventory management, shipment tracking, supply chain event management, and global trade finance solutions such as open account and letter of credit management.

The solutions of TradeBeam cover the following aspects for a corporate:

- Export management
  - ❏ Order management, restricted party screening, compliance management, documentation, LC documentation, logistics tracking.
- Import management
  - ❏ Compliance facilitation, import document management, LC documentation, logistics tracking.
- Vendor managed inventory
  - ❏ Inventory replenishment models, notifications
- Purchase order management
  - ❏ Vendor collaboration, electronic PO distribution and management, PO to LCs, invoice, payment, packing list and PO reconciliation.
- Letter of credit management
  - ❏ PO and LC management, LC documentation, LC amendments, LC payments and reconciliation.
- Document management and legalization
  - ❏ Auto creation of trade documents, electronic document presentation, synchronizing and reconciling with letters of credits.
- Insurance and claims management
  - ❏ Cargo insurance management, synchronizing and reconciling cargo insurance management.
- Open account trade and finance management
  - ❏ Order management, document management, reconciliation of documents, involvement of banks in the supply chain, third party collaboration.
- Global trade content management
  - ❏ Product catalog, duty and fee calculation, currency exchange, restricted party list, trade documents, compliance documents, etc.

TradeBeam Holdings Inc. has ambitious sights on the supply chain. It acquired Open Harbor, an international trade logistics specialist, whose systems are used to gain pricing for international orders based on an aggregate of product costs, taxes and duties charged by the exporting and importing countries. TradeBeam also acquired SupplySolution, developer of a vendor-managed inventory application for the automotive industry, and Qiva, another trade logistics company that focused on retail and high-tech.

TradeBeam has over 3,000 customers with users in over 100 countries worldwide.

More information on TradeBeam can be obtained from www.TradeBeam.com.

CONCLUSION

Evidently, there is much energy and enthusiasm in the early explorers to seize the opportunity presented by significant changes in trade practices and technology. Various parties involved in the trade business are each looking at the change from their perspective and how they can extend their own services and domain to provide leadership in this field. The ultimate solution will have to encompass all these perspectives and will possibly have elements from each one of them.

Of all the forces that will drive the e-financial supply chain, the most fervent force will come from development of messaging standards. However, the standards themselves will be stoked by the emerging competitive offerings in the market. Presently, the offerings are just leaving the calm zone to generate a breeze that promises to turn into a full storm in the next decade.

Standards will rule because they offer simpler and efficient data exchange. Although there is a win-win situation in adoption of standards, present stakeholders with proprietary systems face considerable change and cost. Implementation is arduous and sometimes contentious when getting all parties on the same plane. Some agile and large corporates are beginning to demand these services from their banks, which the banks are finding difficult to ignore. Therein lies the future of the e-financial supply chain!

5

Case Studies on e-Financial Supply Chain

INTRODUCTION

The case studies on the financial supply chain have been drawn from real life situations witnessed across different banks and customers although the names of the companies have generally been altered. In many of these situations banks have either offered these solutions through an ingenuous use of Xls and their general ledger systems, or have offered solutions, which could partly meet the requirements of the case owing to lack of systems, processes and organization structures that facilitate such transactions.

In the ensuing case studies, a parallel has been drawn between the existing trade services and the new financial supply chain services in order to gain insight into how the trade services requirements are morphing to meet the needs of the modern physical supply chain.

Before we launch into the case studies,—we will digress briefly in order to understand what the benefits of the new financial supply chain services are and whom they benefit. We can then elaborate on these benefits and delve into our case studies.

BENEFITS OF THE NEW FINANCIAL SUPPLY CHAIN SERVICES

The corporate procurement and distribution chain consists of the vendors,

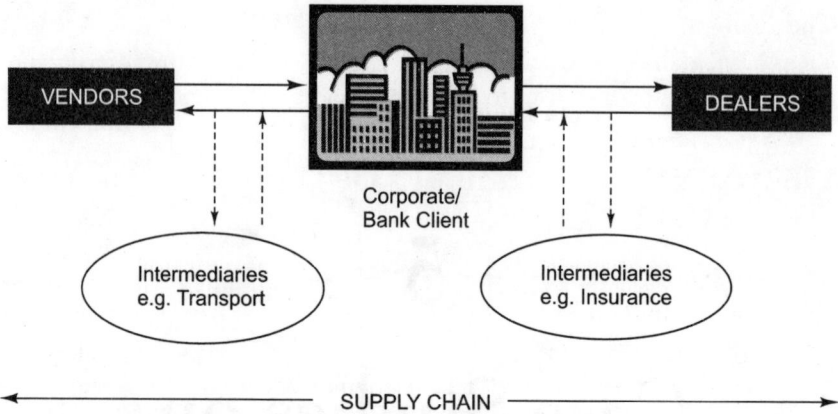

Fig. 5.1 *The various participants in the supply chain*

dealers and other intermediaries such as insurance companies, transport operators, warehouse operators, quality inspectors, etc.

The overall objectives of the financial supply chain products is to:
- Improve operations efficiency
- Improve financial efficiency

between the corporate and its physical supply chain. As each industry and each corporate, which is highly efficient, will have a supply chain which is largely customized to meet its business objectives, the case studies will highlight the various models that could lead to further improvement in efficiency. Broadly, the financial supply chain services are divided into two categories:
- Services
- Financing

SERVICES—INTRODUCTION

The services will generally result in increased operations efficiency in any of the following areas of operation:
- Reconciliation between the invoices raised and payments received.
- Faster delivery cycle on receipt of payment confirmation.
- Credit limit release of the dealers and subsequent efficient order processing.
- Payment reconciliation to vendors.

These are some of the large illustrative benefits in operations that can be realized. However, as will be seen from the case studies, the situations are varied and there are many small and large benefits to be realized by carefully scrutinizing the supply chain process for potential efficiencies.

The financing services on the other hand, lead to increased financial efficiency, i.e. reduced usage of working capital, reduced interest rates on borrowings, etc., and also lead to improved operations efficiency.

CASE 1: ADVANCE PAYMENTS OF OYSTER PETROLEUM DEALERS

Oyster Petroleum uses a large network of dealer franchisees who operate petrol pump stations to distribute petrol, diesel and other petroleum products. Oyster Petroleum is a large multinational company and the dealers are generally small individual operators who owned the appropriate real estate for a petrol pump station and were therefore drawn towards the business of operating such stations.

Oyster Petroleum supplies its dealers only on the basis of advance payments. The dealers either pay for their purchases by cheque or make electronic payments into Oyster Petroleum's account.

When dealers make electronic payment into the account held by Oyster Petroleum, they provide the payment reference along with the purchase order details to the regional sales support team of Oyster Petroleum. The finance team of Oyster Petroleum processes the release of the required goods to the dealer in its ERP system, after reconciliation of the receipt of money in the account with the payment reference and purchase order submitted by the dealer.

When payment is made by cheque, the dealer gives the cheque along with the purchase order. The finance department keys in the details of the cheque and the purchase order in their ERP systems and then presents the cheque to their bankers for clearing. Subsequently, on receipt of paid/unpaid information from the bank, the finance department reconciles the payment with the purchase order and then processes the release of the required goods to the dealer in its ERP system.

Both the above processes require reconciliation at the corporate and generally require 3–5 days from payment to processing the release of the goods to the dealer.

A banker friend of the CFO, from Creative Bank, offered to work with the company to make the process more efficient. The bank proposed to provide

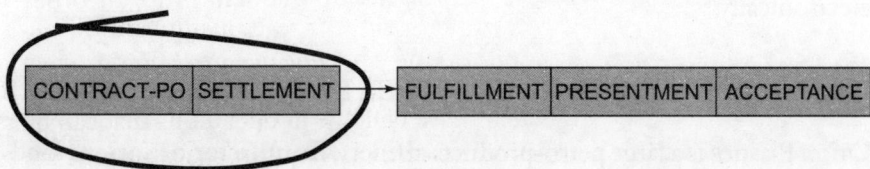

Fig. 5.2 *Parts of the supply chain of Oyster Petroleum being serviced by Creative Bank*

special payment facilities to the dealers of the company, through its Internet offering. The dealers could log on to the Internet facility of Creative Bank and give payment instructions in favor of Oyster Petroleum along with all the details of the merchandise they intended to buy. As soon as the dealer's account was debited, the bank passed on the payment information along with all the purchase details to the ERP system of Oyster Petroleum automatically, in an electronic format. The ERP system would then process the delivery of the goods immediately.

Thus, the operations process, which earlier took 3–5 days, was reduced to less than one hour.

The only constraint was that the dealers were required to maintain an account with Creative Bank. Considering the advantages, many dealers agreed to do this though not all dealers could join the program because of location and other constraints that they experienced. Overall, Oyster Petroleum benefited through:

- Much improved operations efficiency.
- Reduced cost on reconciliation and follow-ups.
- Better service to the customers.

The CFO and the bank agreed to mitigate this constraint of having the dealers to open their account with the bank in the second phase of the project. The modus operandi that they agreed to follow for such dealers was as follows:

- The dealers would provide the payment information and the goods required information through the Internet offering of Creative Bank.
- Creative Bank would then initiate direct debit instructions, which would be routed through the clearing network to the dealer's bank.
- On receipt of money from clearing, the Oyster Petroleum account would be credited and the relevant information would be routed to the ERP system of the company.

This is an example of achieving significant operations efficiency while making advance payments.

This example is highly oriented towards cash management, since the trade services of the bank are generally not utilized while making advance payments. However, it does provide useful supply chain solutions for high operations efficiencies, by linking together the buyer, sellers and the bank, electronically.

CASE 2: PAYMENTS GUARANTEE FOR ORION PLASTICS

Orion Plastics is a large petro-products refinery, manufacturing various kinds of base plastic chemicals that are sold to domestic dealers and manufacturers who buy these products in order to manufacture and sell various types of plastic products such as plastic buckets, containers, clips, etc.

As there were many such dealers and manufacturers, and they were generally small or medium-sized, Orion Plastics did not want to take a payment risk on these counter-parties, although in the past, it had set up small credit limits on some of these dealers and manufacturers. As there were other competitors in the market, Orion Plastics could not demand advance payment terms from these counter-parties.

It therefore contemplated the use of LCs from some of these counter-parties, but soon realized the futility of this after implementing it for a few dealers. After the dealers and manufacturers raised the purchase order, Orion Plastics normally required 1–15 days to ship the goods to them. The processing of the LC and the documents under the LC took far longer than this!

Orion Plastics then convinced some of the dealers and manufacturers to establish standby letters of credit (SBLC) and did manage to get this from some of these counter-parties. However, this too was not very successful, as many of them could not get their banks to set up the SBLC for them. In most cases the banks asked for 110% of the value of the SBLC as a fixed deposit, which they were not able to provide lest they block their working capital. The SBLC was intermittently used and it did not make sense to block capital for a full year for the SBLC; besides, the charges on the SBLC for the full period were also a waste!

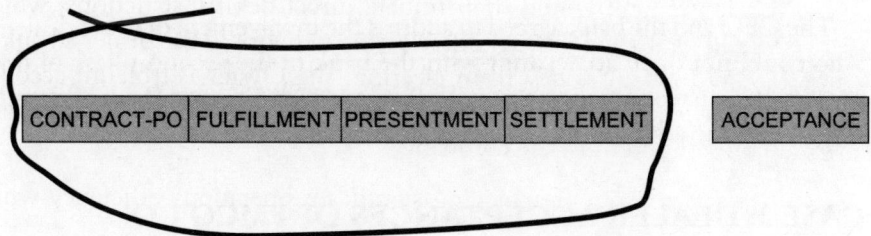

Fig. 5.3 *Parts of the supply chain of Orion Plastics serviced by Creative Bank*

The CFO of Orion Plastics also turned to Creative Bank for assistance. The bank worked along with the CFO and organized the following solution for them. When Orion Plastics received a purchase order from a dealer or a manufacturer, the user logged on to the new Internet offering of Creative Bank and posted the purchase order on the site. If the dealer were also a customer of Creative Bank, the system would check the balance in his account and block the account for the value of the purchase order.

When Orion Plastics had completed the shipment of goods they would log on to the Internet offering and confirm the shipment of goods for the specific purchase order, along with the invoice details. The system would then debit the account of the dealer based on the block that was created on the account earlier, and credit Orion Plastics.

This tripartite agreement between Orion Plastics, the dealer/manufacturer and Creative Bank is very similar to the constructs of an LC except that it is implemented differently in order to take into account the:

- Large number of transactions owing to there being a large number of dealers and manufacturers.
- Small purchase order to shipment cycle.

Orion Plastic is a large and successful company and comparatively much larger than their dealers. The shipment quality from them is generally good and the dealers are therefore not worried about the quality or quantity of goods being delivered to them. Disputes on either quality or quantity of goods are rare and are generally settled separate from the payment terms by the regional sales team.

The only constraint was that the dealers were required to maintain an account with Creative Bank. Considering the advantages many dealers agreed to this. The key benefits that Orion Plastics realized from this arrangement were:

- Reduction in dependency on paperwork required for establishing LCs
- Reduced cost of establishing LCs.
- Covered the payment risk.
- Improved reconciliation support.

The CFO and the bank agreed to address the involvement of other dealers who could not open an account with the bank in the second phase of the project. It is no wonder then that with this approach Creative Bank is getting richer with the addition of more customers to its fold.

CASE 3: DEALER ACCEPTANCES OF FMCG CO.

FMCG Co. is a large multinational company manufacturing many of consumer items such as packaged foods, detergents, toiletries etc. It has a large distribution network of hundreds of dealers who serve large geographical areas in countries like the USA, India, China, etc. FMCG Co is an AAA rated company whose products are very fast moving and the dealership of FMCG Co. is always very much sought after. The dealers are generally much smaller companies and agree to payment terms and conditions stipulated by FMCG Co.

Since there are many brands in many different sizes and packaging, the order traffic from each individual dealer is very high. To smoothen its operations and eliminate any payment risk on the part of the dealers, FMCG

Co. started the practice of taking signed cheques from its dealers in the 70s. Based on the requested order, FMCG Co. would fill in the cheque and put it in for clearing. It would then ship the goods to the buyer on receipt of the clearing information and payment confirmation.

By the late 90s, there was pressure to improve these operations as:

- Volumes grew significantly with a growth in the number of dealers and increase in the number of brands thus, putting large pressure on operations and costs.
- Handling blank cheques was a key security issue.
- The paper process was time-consuming and costly.
- Some of the dealers, especially in the metros, had grown in size and were asserting that they would not like their account to be debited in such a manner as they had problems in managing their cash flows.

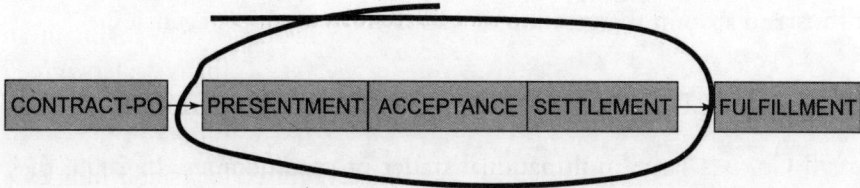

Fig. 5.4 *Parts of the supply chain of FMCG Co. serviced by Creative Bank*

The CFO of the company called on Creative Bank to devise a solution to improve their operations. The Bank, as earlier, worked with the CFO and introduced another offering on their Internet site, which the CFO was happy to subscribe to.

Instead of taking blank cheques from the dealers, FMCG Co. would take a one-time mandate from the dealers to debit their accounts held with Creative Bank. FMCG Co. would provide a file from its ERP system containing all the transactions for which the various dealers had to be debited. The bank would debit the accounts of the dealers based on the mandates provided by them and credit the account of FMCG Co. While processing the debits the bank would also consider some of the conditions laid down by the dealer for debiting the account such as:

- Maximum amount that can be debited to the account.
- Maximum number of times in a month that the account can be debited.
- If the transaction is more than a reference amount specified by the dealer, the transaction is made available to the dealer for approval, who then logs on to the Internet site and approves the transaction for further debit into his account.

The bank provides the status of the direct debit instructions to FMCG Co. indicating the instructions that have been successfully debited to the account of the dealer and those that have been rejected. The company then directly uploads this in soft-copy format, into their ERP system for further processing of dispatches.

The above structure substantially improved the operations efficiency of FMCG Co. as it could convince a large number of its dealers to establish their account with Creative Bank. It also addressed the key security issues raised by the treasury of FMCG Co and provided the dealers with control over their accounts so that they could monitor and plan their cash flows.

The transaction is a hybrid of the advance payment and document/delivery against payment (DP) structure of trade services provided by banks. As in previous cases, this structure works best when both the company and the dealer have accounts with the same bank. However, these structures can be made extensible by proper and adequate standards, and highlights the enthusiasm around the creation of standards by multiple agencies!

CASE 4: DELIVERY ORDERS FOR WAREHOUSE DELIVERY

Argyll Co. is a large multinational trader of commodities. In 2000, they identified an opportunity to import edible palm oil from Malaysia into India. The oil was off-loaded on the eastern coast of India at Chennai port, and distributed to the southern region of India. Argyll Co. being a trader, did not own the tanks in which the edible oil was stored. They rented the storage tanks at a location close to the port and also appointed a surveyor to guard the oil and release it to the buyers based on delivery orders issued by Argyll.

Small shop owners, restaurants and distributors would come from the hinterland of southern states with company cheques, banker's cheques and sometimes LCs, for purchase of the edible oil. The surveyor in Chennai would take these along with the purchase order, and based on the stock available in the tanks, he would send these to their centralized processing center in Delhi. Argyll's finance department in Delhi would present these cheques through a bank and await the realization status whence the information was forwarded to the surveyor. He, in turn, would then issue delivery orders to the buyers for presentation and obtaining release of the oil.

The CFO of Argyll wished to make this process more efficient and identified the following issues with the present structure:

- There was a delay of at least 3–4 days due to the transit time of the cheque from Chennai in South India, to Delhi in the North, and back again to Chennai or other southern states. As the sales took place in South India, most of the cheques were drawn on some city in the south, and the company would ideally therefore, prefer to deposit them there rather than have them travel to Delhi.

- However, the surveyor in Chennai was not conversant with the cheque handling processes and did not have access to the system for information related to this. Argyll did not want to pass over this reconciliation activity to the surveyor without adequate processes and system in place.
- To reduce inventory and float of 3–4 days, it was very tempting to place an Argyll resource from the finance team with access to system, in Chennai. However, this would be expensive as such a resource would be required in each of the cities where they operate. The trading business of Argyll was fickle and the trading opportunity could be here today and gone tomorrow and hence, building a permanent infrastructure in such a scenario was difficult.
- The other problem experienced by their buyers was the uncertainty on the fund realization and therefore delivery dates.

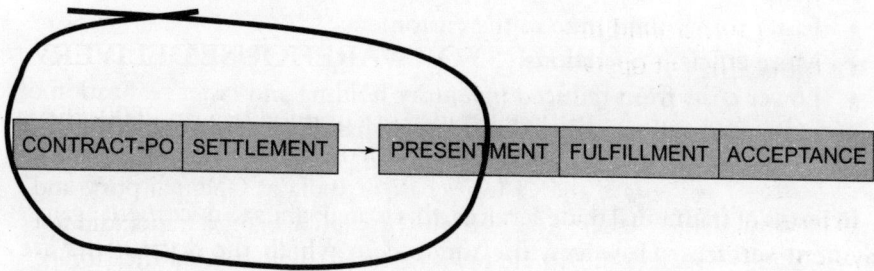

Fig. 5.5   *Parts of the supply chain of Argyll Co. serviced by Creative Bank*

The CFO had been informed about the ingenuity of Creative Bank and made an appointment with them to discuss these problems. The bank proposed the following solutions.

- The branch network of Creative Bank would be made available to the buyers of Argyll Co. where they could come and deposit the cheque along with the purchase order in a pre-specified format. The bank staff would accept the deposits based on the availability of stocks in the tankers.

In turn, the bank provided Argyll with a statement of cheques accepted daily and the delivery of goods promised on behalf of the company.

The stock position would be updated by Argyll every day on the new Internet service of Creative Bank based on arrivals, bookings and delivery, and the system did not allow the bank tellers to accept deposits if the stock position did not permit it. Argyll also updated the price of goods on a regular basis since commodity prices fluctuated, and the bank could use this information to calculate the quantity of goods being requested by the buyers in their purchase order, which in turn aided the bank teller in deciding whether or not to accept the deposit being placed by the buyer.

The bank took an identity proof of the people making the deposit so that the delivery orders could be issued to the same individuals.

- The cheque would be sent to clearing and the bank would also advise the buyer of the expected date of realization.
- On realization, the bank would issue a delivery order for the buyer who would come to the branch and on providing proof of identity, pick up the delivery order and take delivery of the goods from the tankers.

Implementation of the new workflow provided Argyll with the following advantages:

- Larger distribution points through the branch network of Creative Bank.
- Faster turnaround time to the customers.
- More efficient operations.
- Lower costs from reduced inventory holding and faster realization of money as well as, reduced operations handling of cheques and their reconciliation at its office in Delhi.

In terms of traditional trade services, this is analogous to document against payment services. However, the method in which the documents are presented and processed is entirely different.

CASE 5: INVOICE PRESENTMENT, PAYMENT AND RECONCILIATION

One of the key models, which are expected to substantially improve processing efficiencies, is electronic invoice presentment and payment. However, the problem presented by Rose Mall Management incorporated a few new twists.

Rose Mall was in the business of constructing malls and letting these to companies, shops, banks, etc. as showrooms. On the 28th of each month, it raised invoices on the lessees for rent, electricity and utilities, which they were expected to pay by the 15th of the next month. Rose Mall also raised invoices for 'pay per use' kind of services such as common parking bays for unloading, common pantry and cleaning services, etc.

The invoices for the 'pay per use' services were often contested—although they were later resolved—and were generally within 10–15% in variance of the invoice. The payment for these was very often delayed and any subsequent overdue interest charges for delayed payments only added to more disputes and reconciliation problems.

The payment for these came in through multiple sources such as cheques, electronic collections and account transfers.

The CFO faced the following problems with the existing system:

- The reconciliation of payments and invoices was time-consuming and not smooth.
- Often the customers complained of not receiving invoices or of having forgotten to pay on time.
- The 'pay per use' services were a great hit with the showrooms but the implementation of the operational aspects of it were very cumbersome.

The CFO in partnership with Creative Bank decided on the following objectives.

- The invoices would be presented over the Internet offering to the shop owners. They could accept the invoices in full or part and then make payment for the accepted amount. The disputed amount could be accepted and settled subsequently.
- The bank would provide a single source reconciliation of all deposits for the various clearing methods whether they were cheques, electronic payments or electronic transfers.
- The shop owners would receive e-mail and SMS alerts to remind them to pay on time.

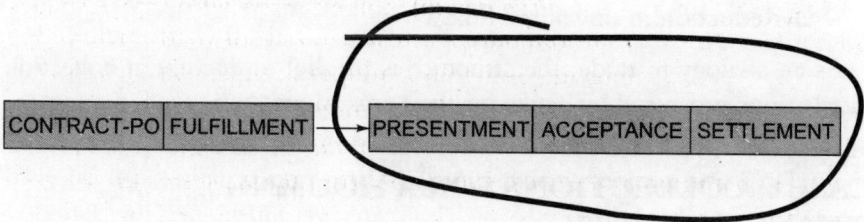

Fig. 5.6 *Parts of the supply chain of Rose Mall Management serviced by Creative Bank*

Creative Bank, through their Internet offering, proposed the following solution.

- Rose Mall would upload all their invoices periodically through the Internet channel. The shop owners could accept the invoices fully or partially.
- Shop owners having an account with Creative Bank could log on to the Internet offering and place payment instructions for settlement of the invoices directly on the Web.

- All cheque collections from shop owners who did not have an account with Creative Bank were also routed through Creative Bank. On realization of the cheque, the outstanding invoices were reconciled against the realization based on shop owner codes.
- For all other electronic collections received into the account of Rose Mall, the following was implemented:
  - ❑ Shop owners were advised to provide reference details as 'MallRent *ShopOwnerCode*' of the transaction in the electronic payment message.
  - ❑ Creative Bank uploaded all such payments received into the new system offering, which reconciled the outstanding invoices.
- Any remaining outstanding invoices could be manually marked as paid, by Rose Mall if they were subsequently, found to be paid.
- A Report of all reconciled and unreconciled invoices for a period could. be generated by the CFO as required, through the Internet offering.
- The system also generated e-mail and SMS alerts on outstanding invoices to the various shop owners.

Implementation of this system helped the CFO in several ways as follows:
- Single view and better visibility on paid and unpaid invoices.
- Efficient reconciliation and follow-up, leading to reduced operations cost.
- Improved customer service through:
  - ❑ Easier medium to deliver payment instructions.
  - ❑ Generate timely follow-up.
  - ❑ Reduction in unwanted follow-ups.

As an analogy to trade, the structure is parallel to document collection instructions processed by banks for their customers.

CASE 6: COLLECTIONS FOR A HOUSING FINANCE SOCIETY

This case, similar to the previous one, is based on a Housing Finance Company, Rio Development Agency, which sells plots of land and also flats and shops on long term leases that are generally repaid over a period of 100 months, through monthly payments. The CFO of Rio Development Agency faced many challenges, of which the key ones were:
- Payment was forced through cheque and cash only. However, the company faced a large reconciliation problem between its bank books and the actual outstanding.
  In some cases, the customer deposited the cheque on time, but by the time it was deposited and collected the books of Rio Development Agency would reflect it as overdue.

In quite a few cases, there were complaints of payments having been made by the customers that were not reflected in the books of Rio Development Agency.
- The company had one collection center for payment where it accepted cheques and cash. Customers complained about long queues and inaccessibility of the collection center.
- Customers complained about the lack of alternate means for easier electronic payment.

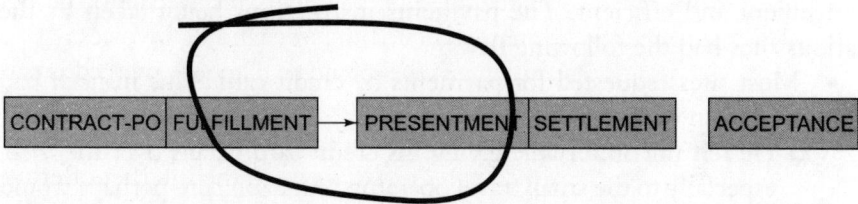

| CONTRACT-PO | FULFILLMENT | → | PRESENTMENT | SETTLEMENT | | ACCEPTANCE |

Fig. 5.7   *Parts of the supply chain of Rio Development Agency serviced by Creative Bank*

Sure enough, Creative Bank had a solution and offered to implement the following:
- Make available its branches where the tellers could receive the payments and simultaneously apply it against specific invoices.
- Reconcile the cheque realizations and the invoices.
- The bank system calculated the overdue interest based on the outstanding invoices and payments, and this was used for reconciliation of outstanding dues.
- Make available payments of the invoices through its Internet offering.
- Make available reconciliation information to the system at Rio Development Agency.

The solution provided Rio Development Agency with the following benefits:
- Large network of collection points for the customers to pay their dues.
- Reconciliation at source, resulting in more efficient and better control on reconciled and un-reconciled items.
- Facilitated payments through larger option on payment channels.

As earlier above, from an analogy to trade, the structure is parallel to document collection instructions processed by banks for their customers.

CASE 7: e-PAYMENTS EXCHANGE

During his visit to USA in early 2002, the Technical Director (TD) of the Central Bank of Malaysia was very impressed with the growth of e-commerce in America. He liked the way in which corporates like Amazon.com, the airline companies, gift companies, stock-broking companies, etc. were expanding their business by providing facilities to transact on their websites and the way such websites were growing by the day.

Eager to learn more about the customer conveniences offered by these sites, he transacted on a few of these sites. While he found the overall experience quite amazing, being a banker and familiar with the risks in payment processing, he noticed that making payments was not very convenient and efficient. The payments instructions being taken by the various sites had the following flaws.

- Most sites requested for payments by credit card. This in itself had two main draw-backs.
  - ❏ He felt uncomfortable giving his credit card details over the Web, especially to the small travel operators. Amazon.com perhaps would have safe systems and processes for protecting the credit card details of customers on their websites, but could one trust the small companies soliciting credit card information!

    Extending his thoughts of promoting such a practice in his country, he felt that while this may be possible for payments to the larger and well established corporate it might not work for small and medium enterprises. However, the Internet promised small and medium enterprises a powerful distribution mechanism in the future.
  - ❏ A charge of 2% was being levied for use of credit cards for purchase of some of the commodities. He felt that this was very high for a payments transaction.
- Some of the sites offered to accept payments through a few selected banks. On choosing a bank, he was re-directed to the website of the bank where he was required to provide his user id and password to make the payment. He liked the fact that some of the key transaction details such as, the invoice number and the seller were transferred to the payments instructions page. This would help him in reconciling the payments in his account statement and also help the seller in reconciling the payments in his books. The medium also had very low costs.

While making payment through the bank had its advantages, he found that the system was not widely used. On investigation he found that the real problem was the connectivity that had to be established between the banks and the merchants, i.e. if Amazon.com wanted to accept payments through Citibank and Manhattan Bank they would have to each of the merchants to connect their Web servers to the servers of the banks.

This same exercise had to be done by National Airlines and with all the sellers with both these, as well as other banks. Thus, assuming that there were 50 banks and 100,000 merchants, this integration exercise would have to run 5,000,000 times!

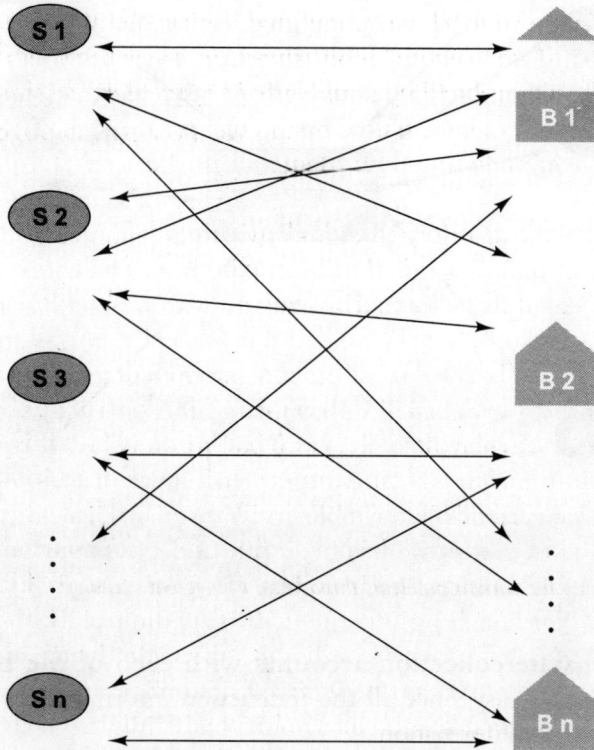

S – Seller
B – Bank

Fig. 5.8 *The problem of connecting many merchants to many banks*

Naturally, the spread of this convenience was being hampered by such costly and time-consuming integration. On his return to Malaysia he therefore, proposed an e-payment exchange with the following structure:

- Set up a national Web server for e-payments exchange.
- Each of the banks and each of the merchants will tie-up with this exchange. In relation to the earlier example of 50 banks and 100,000 merchants, this would require 100,050 integrations to be established.
- The bank distributed standards and tool kits for connectivity to its national Web server to the merchants and banks.

The key benefit to the merchants was that, by tying up with the national Web server they were immediately linked to all the banks that were connected to the national e-payments exchange. Additionally, they did not have to

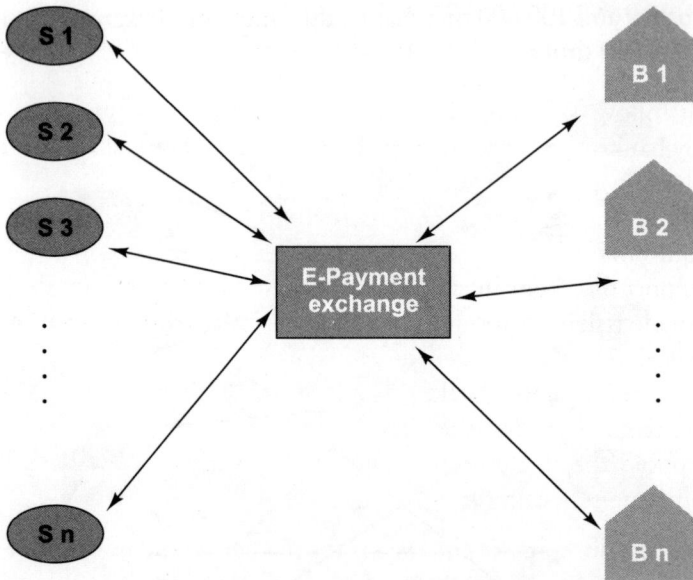

S – Seller
B – Bank

Fig. 5.9   *Solving the various problems through an e-payment exchange*

maintain separate collection accounts with each of the banks. The reconciliation was easy since all the transaction information was available with the payments information.

The key benefit offered in the above solution is that the transaction information flows along with the payments information and thus makes the reconciliation very simple.

From an analogy to trade, the structure is parallel to document collection instructions processed by banks for their customers. As in the case of trade, it involves a buyer bank that makes the payments and a seller bank that receives the payments.

FINANCE—AN INTRODUCTION

In financial supply chain services we saw that, Creative Bank could provide services by getting involved in various different parts of the physical supply chain and linking the settlement process with some of the other trade processes within the chain. Some of the transactions appear to be more closely coupled with the trade processes, while others appear to be linked closer to the cash management processes within the bank. The cases discussed, merely illustrate the exciting possibilities and the wide range of services that can be provided by banks through financial supply chain services.

The same ingenuity can be extended to the financing services. Financing is generally done against invoices or the purchase order and these processes are included and can be observed in the types of services discussed in the cases that follow. By using the e-financial supply chain financing services offered by banks, the corporate can achieve financial efficiencies in some of the following ways:

- Support the vendors in helping them to manage their working capital requirement.
- Support the client in smoothening their cash flows from dealers.
- Provide risk mitigation to the clients by insuring them against defaults by dealers.
- Allow the dealers to take advantage of the rebate program for early payments offered by the client.
- Support the dealers in financing the inventory while paying the corporate seller on time.

These illustrate some of the means for furthering the financial efficiency between the corporates and their value chain. Besides these, the corporates and their supply chain too, would generally experience improvement in operations efficiencies as well.

CASE 8: DEALER FINANCE TO SUPPORT SALES

Lube Oil is a large multinational company manufacturing and distributing industrial and automobile lubricants. It has over 800 dealers in the Indian network, to distribute lubricants to the remotest locations. The products of Lube Oil have a good market reputation and its dealership is highly coveted. Most of the dealers have stuck with the company and have grown with them over decades.

Lube Oil gives its dealers, 21-days suppliers' credit, for payment of invoices, i.e. when Lube Oil dispatches the lubricants to the dealers it draws an invoice on them allowing payment 21 days after the date of the invoice. The company normally takes from them a blank, signed cheque or a direct debit mandate into their account and initiates the collection process on the 15th day after the invoice date. The payment terms are on an open account basis.

The 21 days credit given by Lube Oil is accounted for as follows:

- 4–8 days transport time for dispatch and receipt of goods by the dealers.
- Approximately 15 days for the dealers to sell some of the lubricants and collect some money with which they can pay Lube Oil.

However, the dealers have to put in their own money as well, since all the lubricants cannot be sold within 21 days. The dealers carry the stock, which they will sell over a period of time and collect their dues. Also, the dealers need to give their buyers a credit of 10–30 days. In any event, they have to pay Lube Oil on the 21st day.

The sales department of Lube Oil wants its dealers to stock more, especially during the festival periods, as they believe that the off-take and sales could be higher if inventory is readily available with the dealers. However, many of the dealers requested them to provide a longer credit period to enable them to stock more. Lube Oil is guided by its global credit policy and cannot therefore, provide any more credit support to its dealers.

Most of the dealers were small enterprises and they expressed their inability to garner loan limits from banks and borrowing money from the informal market was usurious! The CFO of Lube oil had a very convenient relationship with their bankers and he approached his banks for assistance. He made the following value proposition to the banks:

- The bank would have access to business with over 800 dealers of Lube Oil, most of whom had a long relationship and credit history with Lube Oil.
- The bank was required to extend loans of 20 days to dealers against the invoices raised by Lube Oil for payment on the invoice due date.
- In case any of the dealers defaulted and did not pay the loan within 60 days after the due date, either (a) Lube Oil would pay the bank or (b) discontinue the dealership of the dealer. The latter was presumably a more serious penalty for long-standing dealers, as their livelihood and prosperity depended on their dealerships.

Creative Bank was excited with this business opportunity and it proposed the following offering to Lube Oil.

- Creative Bank would set up limits on those dealers who had more than 3 years relationship with Lube Oil. The limit would be based on their average turnover with Lube Oil.
- All collections of Lube Oil would be routed through Creative Bank.
- On supply, Lube Oil would upload invoices through the Internet offering, to Creative Bank.
- The dealers could request for finance against such invoices up to the 15th day from the invoice date. If a dealer requested for a loan against a particular invoice, the collection for such an invoice was deferred to the 35th day. However, Lube Oil was paid on the 21st day and a loan was created for the dealer on the 21st day, with repayment due on the 40th day.
- If the dealer did not make a finance request against a particular invoice, the collection process was initiated on the 15th day as per the regular process, and Lube Oil generally received money on the 21st day.

On implementation of the process, the CFO of Lube Oil proudly announced the following benefits in the AGM:

- The company was able to achieve higher turnover and 5% of it was attributed to this innovative arrangement. This had also led to higher customer satisfaction.
- The reconciliation process at the company had improved with all payments and reconciliation information coming from the bank.

From a trade perspective this is equivalent to an import loan or buyer's credit transaction.

CASE 9: VENDOR FINANCE FOR PROCUREMENT SUPPORT

Duke-mart is a large departmental store with presence in many malls across the country. It stores and sells almost everything—branded apparels, packaged foods, toiletries, furnishings, kitchen utensils and consumables, furniture, electronic items, medical and hygiene items, sports goods, books and stationery, etc. In all, it stocked more than 8,000 different items and many of them were in different types and sizes of packing. Its vendor base for procuring such a wide array of products was over 1,500.

One of the key challenges faced by Duke-mart was the size of its inventory and the fact that much of its working capital was locked up in inventory. One way in which Duke-mart addressed this was by negotiating large credit terms from its buyers. Generally, Duke-mart asked for credit terms of at least 60–90 days on the fast moving items and this was higher for some other slow moving items. Payment terms were on an open account basis. Thus, Duke-mart would pay the vendors 60–90 days after the invoice date or receipt date.

Many of the vendors selling to them are small enterprises and requested Duke-mart to pay them sooner in order to help them manage their working capital. The CFO of Duke-mart realized the problems being faced by the vendors but was aware that their own working capital management depended very much on the credit provided by these small suppliers. However, being a humble and obliging person he heard them and assured them that he would try to find some solution to the problem.

He had heard of Creative Bank through a cocktail circle round and he decided to approach them. Creative Bank heard him out enthusiastically, and after a week offered the following proposal:

- The vendors of Duke-mart could upload their invoices on the Internet offering after they had made supplies to Duke-mart.

- After verification of the delivered goods, Duke-mart would provide acceptance of the relevant invoices to Creative Bank and these would then be uploaded on the Internet offering.
- The vendors could request for finance against these accepted invoices through the Internet offering and the bank would then provide the finance to them based on their request and the accepted invoices.
- When Duke-mart made the payments to the vendors on the 10th and 25th of each month as per their payment cycle, the money to be paid to the vendors would be adjusted against the loan, if any.
- All vendor payments of Duke-mart would be routed through Creative Bank.

The CFO of Duke-mart found the proposal very interesting and with the consensus of the vendors implemented it in record time and soon realized the following benefits.

- The vendors were naturally very pleased and were willing to sell and provide more stocks to Duke-mart since they now had a solution to their working capital problem. This in turn helped Duke-mart to stock more liberally.
- There was not much change in process or additional work at Duke-mart in the entire offering.

From a trade analogy, this is akin to invoice financing. With some technical nuances it is also known as bill discounting, factoring, post-shipment loan, etc. The key difference lies in the large volume and small values of the transactions and the way in which these transactions are processed to keep the costs low.

CASE 10: DEALER PRE-PAYMENTS

Technolux is a large sized corporation manufacturing kitchen appliances. These are distributed through a large network of dealers and distributors. The company normally gives them 60 days credit and payment terms are on open account basis.

As an incentive for early payment, the company gives the dealers and distributors a rebate for pre-payment. The terms for pre-payment are: e.g. if the invoice value is 500 and the dealer pays within the first 10 days of drawing the invoice, he gets a rebate of 3%, i.e. 15. He can then just pay 485 and the bill would be considered as settled. The rebate structure offered by Technolux was as follows:

On delayed payments the dealers were supposed to pay interest at the rate of 25% per annum. However, there was no sufficient system within the

Days	Rebate
0–10	3.0%
11–20	2.5%
21–30	2.0%
31–40	1.5%
41–50	0.75%

Fig. 5.10 *Rebate structure of Technolux for early payment incentive to its dealers*

company to track and receive overdue interest payments, when they became overdue.

Despite the rebate and penalty structure, the dealer payments were still not regular and there was pressure on Technolux from shareholders, to reduce its days receivable in its books.

The CFO of Technolux decided to meet with Creative Bank, whom he knew previously. After discussions and many rounds of negotiations, Technolux found the following proposal acceptable:

- Creative Bank set up credit limits on the dealers and distributors of Technolux based on their past history with the company.
- Technolux would upload all invoices into the Internet offering of Creative Bank.
- The dealers could request for a loan against these invoices during the credit period of 60 days to pre-pay Technolux. This would be beneficial to the dealers as the rate of interest charged by banks was much lower than the rebate offered by the company.
- Irrespective of whether the dealer had taken a loan or not, Creative Bank would pay Technolux on the 60th day, within the limit of the dealer. The bank would do all the follow-up for overdue payments and charges on these in order to recover money from the dealer.
- All collections would be routed through Creative Bank and these will be used to repay the loans.
- The loans were proposed on a non-recourse basis, i.e. if the dealers did not pay then the bank would take the loss. However, the bank had a right of recourse to the company for the first 10% of the losses suffered by the bank.

On implementation, Technolux and its dealers found immense benefit as follows:

- Technolux was able to reduce its days receivable substantially.

- It received payments on time and did not require operations for follow-up on over-dues.
- The dealers benefited from taking a loan from the bank and enjoying early payment rebates.

In trade analogy, this transaction is similar to invoice financing.

CASE 11: DEALER FINANCE—INSURED

Organic Chemicals is a large multinational, manufacturing industrial chemicals and pesticides, which are distributed through a large network of dealers.

Payments are on open account and the company gives 30 days credit to its dealers. To improve its cash flows and to enhance its balance sheet, the company wanted to sell its receivables to a factoring company. After discussion with various organizations including banks and insurance companies, it decided to do this through Creative Bank as the collections could then be routed through the bank and also because the reconciliation of invoices and payments received, would then happen in one place. In addition, since Creative Bank was also providing cash management services, it offered the following benefits:

- There was much closer control on the limits and outstanding for a dealer with collections and realizations quickly repaying the outstanding loan, consequently freeing up the limit for additional discounting.
- Creative Bank offered much better pricing as a result of packaged cash management collection and financing service.
- Through the Internet offering, Creative Bank offered superior MIS and control over the receivables to Organic Chemicals who had a very good visibility on the outstanding and risks on a dealer, with good understanding of expected collection flows. This helped them in planning their sales and dispatches to the dealers.

Creative Bank offered to buy the receivables of Organic Chemicals on a non-recourse basis, meaning that, in case the dealers did not pay, it would be a loss for the bank who would not be able to recover the money from Organic Chemicals. To protect itself in such an eventuality, Organic Chemicals decided to insure itself with an insurance company.

All Situation Insurance agreed to insure the receivables of Organic Chemicals. They placed the following operations requirements for executing the insurance:

- A list of all invoices financed and outstanding should be provided to them on a weekly basis.

- For a single invoice of over USD 25,000 the bank should seek prior permission of All Situation Insurance before financing this.
- All dues that were more than 7 days overdue, should be reported to them on a daily basis.
- Dealers blacklisted by All Situation Insurance should not be financed again.

Since there were many dealers, it was operationally a challenge to execute these conditions. In the past, Creative Bank had faced situations where the insurance companies had denied payment because they had not met some of the reporting requirements, and this, despite having paid all premiums as required by the insurance policy. Creative Bank decided to enhance its Internet offering to include All Situation Insurance in its net! This was the flow of the transaction:

- Organic Chemicals uploaded the invoices on the Internet offering of Creative Bank.
- Based on limit availability, invoices less than USD 25,000 were financed by Creative Bank.
- Invoices over USD 25,000 were made available to All Situation Insurance for their approval and on their confirmation, the transaction was financed by Creative Bank.
- All the collections of Organic Chemicals were routed through Creative Bank.
- The MIS required by All Situation Insurance was made available to them through the Internet offering. Thus, All Situation Insurance was responsible for downloading the information required by them for providing the insurance cover.

On implementation of the proposed offering, the following benefits were realized:

- Organic Chemicals showed reduced working capital assets on its balance sheet.
- It also smoothened its receivables, reconciliation and overdue follow-up processes.
- Creative Bank was able to better manage its risk through involvement of the insurance company in the transaction.
- The insurance company was able to service its insurance business through better availability of information.

In traditional trade services, these services are typically offered through the factoring route. However, the benefits of e-financial supply chain services results from keen focus on efficient operations for such low value, high volume transactions and controlling the operations risks involved.

CASE 12-: PRE-SHIPMENT VENDOR FINANCE TO SUPPORT PROCUREMENT

Kea Furniture is a large manufacturer and distributor of ready-made household furniture items. To support its growth and to maintain its profit margins, Kea Furniture had taken to outsourcing the manufacture of furniture items to small carpentry shops across the country. To ensure quality and delivery reliability, it has strict selection criteria for vendors and check their track record for delivery and quality apart from financial strength and viability.

However, the vendors require a large amount of working capital to process the orders from Kea Furniture. This is needed to buy raw materials such as ply-board, veneer, glue, etc. and, also need to pay the wages of their workers. To make matters worse Kea Furniture pays them 60 days after delivery of the goods. To cope with these growing business requirements they met with the CFO of Kea and sought his help to mobilize money from banks.

The CFO of Kea Furniture was acquainted with Creative Bank and approached them for a solution to this problem.

After a few days of deliberation, Creative Bank makes the following proposal:

- Kea furniture would upload the confirmed purchase orders issued by them to the various vendors over the Internet offering of Creative Bank.
- The vendors could make a request for financing against these purchase orders to finance their need for raw material and wage payments.
- When the vendors ship the goods they would upload the invoice information on the Internet offering. On acceptance of the goods and invoices by Kea Furniture, the pre-shipment loan would be converted into a post-shipment loan.
- When Kea Furniture made payment to the vendor, their loan outstanding would be settled before the residual is paid to them.
- All payments of Kea Furniture would be routed through Creative Bank.

The CFO of Kea Furniture liked the proposal and implemented it quickly, to realize the following benefits:

- The vendors and in turn, Kea Furniture could grow their business without blocking additional capital into the business.
- Kea Furniture did not have to get involved with financing the vendors to support its growth. The CFO firmly believed that financing was not their core competency.

The above structure is similar to the packing loans or pre-shipment loans given by banks through their trade services at present.

CASES OF BUSINESS PROCESS OUTSOURCING TO BANKS

The cases discussed above demonstrate to a great extent how the physical and the financial supply chain are linked together at various points. There are, however, many other examples where the evidence of linkage is not so evident and which have been generally processed under the extension of cash management or trade services within the bank.

FMCG Collections

This is one of the earliest cases of introduction of cash management services in India.

In 1987, the CFO of FMCG Co. was directed by the board to reduce the number of people working in his department from about 135 to 100. FMCG Co. has large operations in India and sells its product in over 5,000 locations through a large distribution network of over 1,500 stockists and distributors.

The CFO was scratching for ideas to implement this without affecting his operations. He realized that most of his staff was occupied with collections and reconciliation of the many accounts that they had with the banks. FMCG Co. was maintaining accounts with multiple banks in various locations to facilitate speedy collections of the cheques that they received from their dealers. However, reconciling these accounts for return credits, return cheques and charges was a huge operations overhead. The company also maintained many office boys to collect cheques from dealers or to return them in the case of bounced cheques. The CFO anticipated that he could outsource some of these functions:

- He would maintain a relationship with just one bank for all his collections. The company would thus have to deal with reconciliation with just one bank and this function too could be centralized. In turn, the bank would tie-up with multiple partner banks for ensuring that it could provide collection services for all locations serviced by FMCG Co.
- The cheque pick-up and delivery functions could be outsourced to a courier company or alternatively, even this function could be performed by the bank, so that adherence to the clearing time lines while depositing the cheques would be under the control of a single entity namely, the bank.

This earliest outsourcing of some of its business processes by FMCG Co. set the tune of cash management services in India.

Vendor Payment Factory for a Truck Manufacturing Company

In the late 1990s, a large truck manufacturing company, which was buying components from many vendors, wanted to streamline its payment processes to vendors. The CFO figured that a lot of time and resources was being wasted first in follow-up by vendors and then, in internal investigation processes while replying to such follow-ups.

The typical payment process was as follows:

- Acceptance for the material would come from the purchase department. This acceptance was checked versus the already approved purchase order so the payment was already approved.
- The treasury department would prepare cheques and covering letters for these payments. These cheques were to be signed by the authorized signatories as per the board resolution.
- Subsequently, the cheques were (a) couriered to the beneficiary, or (b) picked up by the beneficiaries at a central outlet of the company.

Typical problems faced in the above payment operations were:

- The signatories were not always available in time for signing the cheques.
- There were operational challenges in moving cheques from one desk to another or couriering the cheques and there were always some cases of cheques being lost in transit.

The truck manufacturing company decided to outsource all these operations to a bank as follows:

- The company gave the bank an ERP file containing all payments to be made to the vendors, from its system.
- The bank printed all the cheques along with the relevant signatures on the cheques as per the authorized signatory matrix and also the payment advise detailing the reason for the payment.
- The bank then couriered the cheques to the vendor, held them at its counters in various branch locations for the vendor to collect, or sent it directly to the vendor's bank, based on the instructions given by the vendor to the company.
- The bank also provided an additional service by sending an alert to the vendor on receipt of payment instruction from the truck manufacturing company and also when the cheques were dispatched to the vendors.

This vendor payment process, which was outsourced to the bank, substantially smoothened and streamlined the vendor payment process at the truck manufacturing company.

Salary Payments

While offering banking services to its customers, Creative Bank realized that almost all their customers in the organized sector who were paying salaries were doing so in multiple sections such as:

- Salary
- Provident funds
- Social security funds
- Loan repayments, etc.

Creative Bank further identified that while some of the larger corporates had put in place systems to track and monitor such payments, many other large and mid-size corporates were grappling with manual systems to process these transactions. Creative Bank decided to provide outsourced services for salary payment processing to address the following pain points in salary processing:

- Paying salary through multiple bank arrangements.
- Providing salary slips and other salary related information to the employees.
- Paying provident funds, loan repayments and other social security payments on behalf of the employers.
- Linking up with various service providers as provident fund, loan bodies, etc., to provide them with information on payments being made to them and providing reconciliation information back to the company.

Such outsourced salary processing, substantially improved the payment processing of salaries at the corporate.

Telephone Bill Collections

Telephone companies service the deepest areas in a country and collecting monies from such largely spread and deep areas is a major logistical challenge. The payment challenge is for both:

- Regular subscription payments, as well as for
- Over the counter new sales, pre-paid cards, etc.

Telephone companies would like to support multiple payment methods such as cheques, cash, credit card, electronic payments, etc. At the same time, the activation and availability of services is often, directly linked to realization of money to be collected from the buyer of the services.

In the eighties and early nineties, many of these collection centers were managed and run by the telephone companies themselves. However, with substantial growth in business this model became increasingly unviable. Companies then started to look at ways of outsourcing this activity to third

party providers. Although this has been implemented differently in different countries, some of the third party providers for such services presently are:
- Banks who collect on behalf of telephone companies.
- Retail chains and hyper-mart stores.
- Third party collection agencies.

Some banks have focused on this segment to provide:
- Specialized services
- Specialized software

Such services and software are further customized to suit the needs of the retail chain and third party collection agents, in order to provide effective collection and reconciliation information to the telephone companies. Banks also offer specialized software to telephone companies to help reconcile and manage their collections from such various sources.

This process outsourcing has substantially improved services to the consumers by providing them with a larger collection network. Simultaneously, it has also substantially cut down its operations cost and reduced errors like terminating connections or delayed connections in its operations.

Dividend Payments

Dividend payments is a regular activity for all corporates and the challenges faced by them are as follows:
- Dividends are paid to large number of shareholders and often in areas across the globe. The shareholders are mostly unknown to the corporate and delivering the dividend amount to them in the most efficient and cost effective manner is often a challenge for the corporate.
- There are regulatory requirements surrounding payments of dividend.
  - ❑ Companies need to report to regulatory authorities on unclaimed dividends periodically.
  - ❑ Some countries require that the physical warrants be preserved for a minimum period of say, 7 years.
- There are operations issues surrounding dividend payments:
  - ❑ The value is small and same for similar number of shares held. There is high possibility and incidence of fraud through forged instruments.
  - ❑ There is book closure date on which basis the dividend is paid to the registered shareholders. When the share registrar books of records are not accurately reflected there are transaction reversals.
  - ❑ In the case of some shares the dividend may need to be transferred in a different name if, for example, the shareholder is deceased, etc.
- Handling of return instruments, etc.

Many of these activities are done by the corporate in conjunction with the share registrars. Over time, banks have started offering services surrounding payment of dividends and banks handle many of the activities mentioned, on behalf of the corporate. Many corporates are outsourcing such dividend and interest payment activities to the banks as this does not form part of their core competence and it enhances the efficiencies of their operations.

Industrial Lubricants Collections

The market for industrial lubricants is a highly competitive and Good Lubes generally gives a credit period of 21 days to its dealers and distributors. Good Lubes has about 800 dealers. However, these are not exclusive dealerships and the dealers often stock and sell competitor products as well.

While Good Lubes gives 21 days credit to its dealers, it also maintains a strict credit management and monitoring system to ensure that there is no over-exposure on any of the dealers. So, based on the past and projected business turnover with Good Lubes and assessment of the dealer strength, it sets a credit limit of, say USD 100,000 for a particular dealer. Thus, Good Lubes supplies goods up to a value of USD 100,000 to the dealer and will supply additional goods only when the payment of the earlier consignment has been cleared.

From an operations point of view, Good Lubes collects cheques from its dealers and sends it for collection through the banks. When the bank credits their account, the accounts department verifies the credits and releases limits for the dealers in the ERP system. This last manual process presently takes 5–10 days. During this period, there is considerable follow-up from the sales team and the dealer to release the goods as they have made payments and their account has been debited.

Considering the competitive industry that Good Lubes is in, they wished to make this process more efficient. They worked with Creative Bank and developed a system to ensure that the information on paid cheques was made available to Good Lubes 3 times in a day, in a format, which could be uploaded directly into their ERP system. This automation substantially reduced the delays of reconciliation and release of limits for the dealers into the client ERP system.

LC Process Outsourcing

The verification of documents against the letter of credit is a very knowledge intensive process. The verification of documents against the LC is done at two ends:
- By the seller bank
- By the buyer bank

Any mistake in verification of documents has a direct risk and financial loss implication to the banks.

At the same time the trade business of banks has been besotted with the following challenges:

- Trade is conducted from all remote locations and buyers and sellers in remote locations need to be able to access trade finance services in these locations.
- Having trained people is difficult in large numbers and in remote locations for such a knowledge intensive industry and especially where financial implications for the bank are large; and the problem is further compounded by a demand for similar talent by other banks as well.
- Managing such resources and teams in remote locations is expensive and there is also a lack of control and consistency in the service delivered.

As a result, and with increasing availability of bandwidth and IT solutions, some banks have worked towards first centralizing their trade processes from various locations and countries into a central location. From a customer perspective, they still have a local branch to deal with, to whom they give LC applications or from where they receive documents presented by the seller. However, all these documents are scanned and transmitted to a centralized processing unit for verification and processing. The centralized team has a group of experts who ensure that the verification and other processes are handled professionally and with uniformity.

Recently, some large banks have started offering these services on an outsourced basis to other banks so that the back office processing of the documents are outsourced. Although at present this is not very popular, such an outsourcing arrangement promises tremendous value benefits considering the complex processes involved in letters of credit.

WHAT DIFFERENTIATES e-FINANCIAL SUPPLY CHAIN SERVICES

Many of the services mentioned, appear very similar to the trade or cash management services provided by banks in the usual course of action. So the reader may wonder as to what it is about e-financial supply chain services that is so different from the trade or cash management services.

A key business diversity, which the financial supply chain attempts to address, is the much larger group of counter-parties. In all of the previous examples, one common premise that a discerning reader will have observed is the large number of dealers or vendors who are participating in the process. In summary, these are low value, high volume transactions. Each corporate may have hundreds of dealers and vendors and each transaction size can be as small as USD 500 with more than 1,000 transactions each day! This is a big departure from traditional trade services, which are generally structured to handle high value, low volume transactions.

The other key difference is the operations and delivery models of supply chain that is supported by the traditional trade services versus what is being attempted in the new financial supply chain services. The traditional services are still relevant for large structured transactions, which require customized handling for example, purchase of a machinery or software worth USD 10 mln. Such a large transaction requires the documents to be legally perfect and many of the transaction stages to be handled manually, through various parties, in order to ensure proper verification and judgment at various stages in the life cycle of the transaction. On the other hand, the financial supply chain products are targeted towards a more mass market type of situation where the operations rules are packaged and templated so that, each time they can be executed with minimum human intervention. In a sense, these make assumptions on the relative strength and standing of a trade counterparty to simplify the traditional trade service transaction.

Because of the volume of transactions and the nature of the service being offered, the delivery of the service to the end consumers, the corporate and its supply chain, is very different from traditional trade services. Much of it is being offered as self-service over the Internet. Moving ahead 10 years, it is expected that much of this will change from Internet offerings to host-to-host connectivity type of connections between the systems of various counterparties involved in the trade, so that in many cases even the Internet interaction could be made redundant. This helps is servicing the large number of counterparties and transactions while also keeping the operations cost down.

As will be obvious by now, this type of service will have a large requirement for reconciliation between various stages of the transaction life cycle—the purchase orders, invoices, the loans and the payment or settlement. This can be a very huge problem. Imagine that there are 10 invoices, and 10 payments are received. To reconcile the 10 payments with the 10 invoices, one will have to take each payment and see which of the 10 invoices it can be matched against. Roughly, this will require 100 matches, or n^2 operations in technical language.

If there are four stages possible in a transaction as mentioned earlier—the purchase orders, invoices, the loans and the payment or settlement—then we are looking at a potential n^4 reconciliation problem! This can be very complex when the number of transactions is large say, 5,000 transactions a day. The new e-financial supply chain services attempt to bundle in EIPP, trade, cash management and other services, to provide a single source of reconciliation across all these services.

CONCLUSION

That solutions through automation in the e-financial supply chain can significantly improve the operations and financial efficiencies of the corporate supply chain is evident from the given examples. At the same time, clearly the e-financial supply chain is not just about providing an Internet channel for facilitating traditional trade finance and other related products. Helping to dematerialize trade related data into electronic format is seen as an important support function, along with the key objective of supporting trade and making the operations process of trade more efficient.

While the adventures of Creative Bank may appear exciting and motivating, it is not all smooth sailing for banks and corporates. In some situations, corporates have shunned the overtures and reacted with lukewarm or cautious response of banks, like Creative Bank, expressing the following concerns.

- The processes are working presently. Automation should not disrupt the existing processes with their trade partners. Like any commercial enterprise, corporates are sensitive to the reactions of their customers and vendors.
- Corporates want the offerings from the bank to fit in to their existing processes rather than them having to modify their processes to fit the product offerings from the bank.
- Changes proposed should be incremental so that these can be implemented gradually, but with certainty, and can be rolled back selectively, if required.
- Sales pitch around information technology—with its string of delayed and sometimes failed projects, and at others, not returning sufficient value to the corporate—may not excite the corporate CFO any more.

Banks need to work closely with the corporate, to understand their objectives and processes in order to propose what can be realistically achieved. Such realistic projections still have a significant ground for optimism and benefits in the emerging area of automation of the financial supply chain.

6

Legal Aspects of e-Financial Supply Chain

BACKGROUND

Finance of trade business and providing trade services is in itself not a new business for banks. However, when one considers the type of services proposed to be delivered under the umbrella of e-financial supply chain the following key differences are evident:

- The operations and delivery method of these services is very different from the traditional trade finance and services. Most of this is proposed on the electronic medium over the Internet.
- The products and services offered are parallel to the traditional trade products but they are however, different in form, if not in spirit.

As a result there is considerable discussion and consternation amongst banks over the legal protection and structure for such new products and services that are being proposed by the product manager. This chapter outlines some of the key legal aspects surrounding the e-financial supply chain services by banks.

It is inevitable that the law will lag behind the technological developments and business innovations and will evolve as practices become more and more well-defined. However, financing and settling contracts of such magnitudes clearly requires some basic framework to be put in place in order to facilitate processing of such transactions. To understand the basis of legal aspects surrounding the e-financial supply chain, we will delve into the following aspects in this section:

- Contract Act
- Electronic evidence
- Security Issues related to e-commerce
- Electronic Commerce Law
- Negotiable Instruments Act
- Other related laws
- Law of Jurisdiction
- Challenges on adoption of laws relating to electronic commerce
- Legal cases on cyber crimes

Although most laws require that some form of written contracts should exist, they do not unduly hinder the facilitation of e-commerce. However these are un-chartered territories and not many such transactions have presently been tested in the courts, so there are not many precedents to follow.

The succeeding discussion is not aimed at furnishing accurate legal advice, but coming from a non-lawyer it aims to provide a high level perspective in which such transactions are to be viewed.

CONTRACT ACT

The most important document binding any two or more parties involved in a trade transaction is the contract. Every agreement, which has consideration or benefits to both the parties and is mutually agreed upon by both the parties, forms a contract.

If a contract has been established, each of the parties is required to fulfill the contract as per the conditions laid out. Each of the parties has the freedom to initiate legal action and approach the courts in case they believe that there is a breach of contract conditions and the counter-party has not fulfilled the conditions specified in the contract.

It must be noted that the contract need not be in writing, unless there is specific provision in law that it should be so. For example, in India, the Contract Act states that (a) contract for sale of immovable property must be in writing, stamped and registered, (b) contracts which need registration should be in writing, (c) bill of exchange or promissory note must be in writing, (d) trusts should be created in writing, (e) promise to pay a time barred loan should be in writing, as per the Limitation Act. Such provisions are important and cause difficulties for providing e-financial Services, as we will discuss in a later section. In other cases, a verbal contract is equally enforceable, if it can be proved.

With regard to e-financial supply chain transactions, it is pertinent to note that banks have been allowing electronic banking for a long time through the following methods:

- Internet banking
- Phone banking
- Fax banking
- Mobile banking
- Credit cards
- ATM cards
- Host-to-host banking, etc.

In each of these cases, the bank and the customer agree on a written document—a contract with the customer—that outlines the terms and conditions under which the services are made available to the customer. So, just as a customer is expected to handle his cheque book with care and not leave it around, in the case of an ATM Card too, the customer is expected to handle the card and the ATM PIN with care. On its part, the bank agrees to make available to the customer, specific services in a certain manner, if he processes the ATM card in an ATM machine.

Both the parties then adhere to this contract. Each one of the parties enjoys legal protection under the Contract Act.

ELECTRONIC EVIDENCE

While this kind of contract is fine, the challenge is in handling situations where for example, the client contests that a telephone instruction for debit to his account was not really given by him!

The bank would then possibly have the following evidence to prove its point:

- Record of the phone pin used by the subscriber.
- Record of the instructions given by the subscriber through his digital phone key board.

However, two big problems with this type of electronic evidence are:

- The bank provides such evidence from its own systems and the bank is one of the interested parties in the dispute.
- The electronic evidence can be tampered with and the subscriber can genuinely claim that the electronic evidence being provided by the bank is spurious; so there is no way for the court to have an un-biased opinion on this matter.

Although, cases on electronic evidence are not new to courts and the legal system, where in the past, recorded voices or photographs have been used to prove evidence of complicity or infidelity, electronic evidence has generally been viewed with circumspection in court and many jurisdictions do not allow such evidence or consider this only as circumstantial evidence.

This poses a challenge to the basis of e-commerce. Admission of electronic evidence is generally stringent, as can be seen in the sample text of, 'Admissibility of electronic records in courts', as defined in India and included in Exhibit 4.

Another related law on evidence—Banker's Books Evidence Act—stipulates that, 'a certified copy of any entry in a banker's books shall in all legal proceedings be received as prima facie evidence of the existence of such entry, and shall be admitted as evidence of the matters, transactions and accounts therein recorded in every case where, and to the same extent as, the original entry itself is now by law admissible, but not further or otherwise.' This position facilitates offering of e-commerce offerings from banks. However, these laws vary by country and state and there has therefore, been a great deal of interest and work in perfecting the electronic evidence.

In USA the laws regarding, 'Searching and Seizing Computers and Obtaining Electronic Evidence in Criminal Investigations, Criminal Division, United States Department of Justice', provides a good overview of the legal provisions and indicates that law makers are progressing on the subject. The document in itself is very large. To give the readers an idea of what the document contains the table of content of the Law is included in Exhibit 11. Details of the same can be taken from www.usdoj.gov/criminal/cybercrime.

SECURITY ISSUES RELATED TO e-COMMERCE

Despite the challenge, e-commerce has been growing rapidly and considering its adoption, it just goes to show the need for better security framework to support such a convenience. To address the concerns of courts on electronic evidence, technologists have proposed the following four pillars of security framework, which can conclusively provide the required evidence for a transaction.

Authenticity	During transaction processing, this process verifies the initiator to ensure the identity and authenticity of the initiator. This is done through the use of User Id, Password, ATM PINs etc.
Integrity	Ensuring that the data is the same as that submitted by the user, and has not morphed or spoofed during transmission over the channel. This is achieved through hashing and hash checks.
Non-Repudiation	Being able to conclusively prove in a court of law, subsequently after the transaction has been completed, that the data being presented as evidence was indeed the data that was presented by the user for the transaction.
Confidentiality	That the data is kept confidential, during and after the transaction has been completed and only the intended users can view the data.

Fig. 6.1 *The four pillars of security for electronic commerce*

The security infrastructure proposed by technologists is based on public key cryptography. Each user of the system is issued with a key pair or (two PINs), a private key (which is kept secret by the user) and a public key (known to all other users in the system). All messages are digitally singed with the private key of the sender and these are verified by the receiving system at the bank with the user's corresponding public key. Only the public key, mathematically related to the users private key is technically able to verify his signed message. The recipient thereby knows that the message originated from the sender.

The question then arises as to how the recipient knows that the public key was issued to the sender of the message. Also, how does a bank system know the private key of the user with which the message is signed. This is achieved through the use of a Certification Authority or trusted third party. The Certification Authority issues a digital certificate to each of the users that provides the recipient with the confirmation that the public key used to sign the message was in fact, the one issued to the sender. When the digital signature is applied to the message, it creates a unique mathematical signature of the message known as 'hash'. Any tampering with the message or the use of a different key will produce a different hash result.

On verification by the recipient, if the hash result remains unchanged, the recipient knows that the message has not been changed in the transmission. The recipient can also store the transaction data along with the hash result and the Certification Authority has a store of the digital signatures issues to a user so that if at a later date, the transaction is contested in court, they can provide the certificates and the recipient will provide the transaction data and the original hash result The transaction data and hash will be computed with the signatures provided by the certification authority and matched with the hash result stored along with the transaction, to prove non-repudiation. The same signatures can also be used for encrypting the transaction, on the transaction medium, to ensure confidentiality of the transaction.

It is of course, essential that the user ensures that his private key remains secure and the operational contract makes it clear that the user is responsible for any misuse in this regard.

ELECTRONIC COMMERCE LAW

In view of the growing number of transactions in international trade being carried out by means of electronic data interchange and other means of communication, commonly referred to as e-commerce, which involve the use of alternatives to paper based methods of communication—UNCITRAL, a section of The United Nations Commission on International Trade Law—formulated the Model Law for e-commerce in 1996, and this has subsequently been accepted by many countries.

The e-commerce Law at the outset recognizes electronic information. It states that, 'information shall not be denied legal effect, validity or enforcement solely on the grounds that it is in the form of data message'.

On signatures it states that, 'where the law requires a signature of a person, and the requirement is met if a method is used to identify the person as described in the above section on security then the signature requirement would have been met.'

The Law covers the following sections:
- Recognition of data messages
  - ❏ Writing
  - ❏ Signature
  - ❏ Requirement of original document
  - ❏ Admissibility of data messages as evidence
  - ❏ Retention of data messages
- Communication of data messages
  - ❏ Formation and validity of contracts
  - ❏ Recognition by parties of data messages
  - ❏ Attribution of data messages
  - ❏ Acknowledgement of receipt
  - ❏ Time and place of dispatch and receipt of message

The Model Law is a framework for the adopting countries and allows them to make modifications to the law as per their existing legal framework and their development in electronic commerce.

Governments of certain countries e.g. India, while implementing the Act have included the following considerations:
- Amendments in Contract Act, Negotiable Instruments Act, Evidence Act, Banking Regulation Act, etc.
- Appointment of certifying authorities and controller of certifying authorities including recognition of foreign certifying authorities to control and monitor the issuance of digital certificates.
- Establishment of Cyber Appellate Tribunal.
- Act to apply for offences or contraventions committed outside country.
- Network service providers not to be liable in certain cases.

The Model Law for (a) electronic commerce (b) electronic signatures as outlined by UNCITRAL is included in Exhibit 7. A list of countries that have legislation implementing provisions of the Model Law for electronic commerce is included in Exhibit 8.

The United Nations Commission on International Trade Law (UNCITRAL) was established by the General Assembly in 1966. In establishing the Commission, the General Assembly recognized that disparities in national laws governing international trade created obstacles to the flow of trade, and it regarded the Commission as the vehicle by which the United Nations could play a more active role in reducing or removing these obstacles. The Commission is composed of sixty member states elected by the General Assembly. Membership is structured so as to be representative of the world's various geographic regions and its principal economic and legal systems.

More information on UNCITRAL can be obtained from www.uncitral.org.

NEGOTIABLE INSTRUMENTS ACT

The Jews are the first to be accredited with the use of bills of exchange in the middle of the thirteenth century. In the year 1697, inland bills of exchange were, for the first time, declared legal instruments: this had been necessary in order to enable the Bank of England to advance money upon them.

Negotiable Instruments generally provide a better security over the Contract Act. There are two key reasons for this:

1. In case of Negotiable Instruments, the transferee can get a better title than the transferor. The normal principle is that a person cannot transfer better title to property that he himself has. For example, if a person steals a car and sells the same, the buyer does not get any legal title to the car, as the transferor himself had no title to the car. The real owner of car can at anytime obtain possession from the buyer, even if the buyer had purchased the car in good faith and had no idea that the seller had no title to the car. This provision is no doubt sound, but would make free negotiability of an instrument difficult, as it would be difficult to verify the title of the transferor in many cases. Hence, it is provided that if a person acquires a 'negotiable instrument' in good faith and without knowledge of a defect in the title of the transferor, the transferee can get better title to the negotiable instrument, even if the title of the transferor was defective. This is really to ensure free negotiability of instruments so that persons can deal in instrument without any fear.

   The most salient feature of the instrument is that it is negotiable. Negotiation does not mean a mere transfer. After negotiation, the holder in due course can get a better title even if the title of the transferor was defective. If the instrument is 'to order', it can be negotiated by making an endorsement and if it is 'to bearer', it can be negotiated by delivery. As per definition of 'delivery', such delivery is valid only if made by the party making, accepting or indorsing the instrument or by a person authorized by him.

2. In many countries, there are separate courts to quickly settle the disputes regarding negotiable instruments. It is generally presumed that the negotiable instrument has to be honored.

While negotiable instruments are very convenient and secure, for bankers however, in many places:

- A negotiable instrument is required to be stamped, or drawn on government stamp paper or stamp duty needs to be paid on it.
- They are required to be in writing and are specifically excluded from the provisions of laws of electronic commerce.

This poses a dilemma for banks wanting to extend lending services through the use of the electronic medium. In such cases it would mean that the banks would need to draw their security and comfort from the provisions of the Contract Act through assignment of receivables in their favor and may not get cover under the provisions of the Negotiable Instruments Act. One way around this, followed by certain banks, is to get the promissory notes, bills of exchange or cheques subsequently from the borrower, though it still remains a pain.

OTHER RELATED LAWS

Many other Commercial Acts could impact transactions. Some of these are:
- Contract of Carriage Act
- Banking Regulation Act
- Sale of Goods Act
- Assignment of Receivables
- Islamic Laws
- Insurance Act
- Customs and Excise Acts
- Revenue, Stamp Duty Act, etc.

The position with regard to contracts of carriage is more complicated as a shipper's bill of lading is also construed as a negotiable instrument. However, electronic contracts of carriage are likely to be accepted as electronic contracts in most states. Contracts of carriage i.e. lorry receipts, rail receipts, shipping way bills, and air way bills generally act as receipt of goods shipped, as per applicable contractual terms and establish the carriers obligation to deliver.

The Banking Regulation Act varies by country and state and could impose some very specific conditions in respect of banking practice with respect to borrowing, e.g. in some countries there are regulations such that all loans over 200,000 should be supported by a written promissory note.

Depending on the transaction and the countries involved in the transaction, each of these need to be examined to ensure due security on the transaction. However, it can generally be said with comfort that it would be most important for the bank to cover themselves under the Contract Act, apart from compliance specific acts, from a legal perspective.

LAW OF JURISDICTION

This can be another important consideration while transacting electronically. The positions of countries in respect of adoption of electronic commerce is different as:

- Some have adopted the model law for electronic commerce, as per UNCITRAL, into their constitution.
- Many countries have yet not adopted laws on electronic commerce.
- Some countries have adopted these laws with modifications.

However, many of these considerations are similar to the challenges faced while drawing contracts on paper. The transacting parties need to agree on a jurisdiction based on their mutually acceptable level of comfort.

CHALLENGES ON ADOPTION OF LAWS RELATING TO ELECTRONIC COMMERCE

The laws and practices relating to electronic commerce are still in their nascent stage as courts and other authorities face the following challenges:

- There are no precedents against which they can judge any disputes that are presented to them for resolution.
- Most of the people and processes in the courts are knowledgeable and support the paper processes. There is very little knowledge of the framework of the information technology systems and the tools that support the audit and extraction of data from such systems.

As such, if cases of cyber crimes do come up, which has started happening sporadically now, there is very little knowledge on how to react to these.

In some cases, where the laws on electronic commerce have been adopted with modifications, these have not been integrated with other acts such as the Negotiable Instruments Act. This makes transaction processing on an electronic platform difficult, as the existing practices and safeguards of commerce are there for a reason and altering them is not always easy.

In some cases the framework and certifying agencies for digital signatures are yet to be established. Additionally, after the initial euphoria, the growth in use of digital signatures has been slow. The fact that this is related to growth of electronic commerce, makes it a chicken and egg story.

LEGAL CASES ON CYBER CRIMES

www.usdoj.gov/criminal/cybercrime/cccases.html is a very good site to visit for a collection of cases executed on cyber crimes. Broadly, the cases covered under this site can be categorized as follows:

- Propagating spam through e-mails.
- Distributing computer worms and viruses.
- Juvenile pornography.
- Defacing other companies websites.
- Pulling down the network/websites.
- Stealing sensitive information like marks from schools and companies.
- Hacking into computers.
- Financial misappropriation.

In general, one does not find cases relating to the problems of business-to-business electronic commerce. However, this is also not to be expected, as most of the electronic commerce today is generally well covered and supported through paper trail. However, some cases involving bank frauds are detailed, to provide a sense of the crime committed and the punishment meted out for the same.

CASE 1: CLEVELAND, OHIO MAN SENTENCED TO PRISON FOR BANK FRAUD AND CONSPIRACY

On October 18, 2005, a federal grand jury in Cleveland, Ohio, indicted Flury for defrauding CitiBank between 15 April 2004, and 4 May 2004. Flury obtained stolen CitiBank debit card account numbers, PINs and personal identifier information of the true account holders, which he then fraudulently encoded onto blank ATM cards. After encoding blank cards with the stolen account information, Flury used the counterfeit ATM card to withdraw cash and obtain cash advances totaling over $384,000 from ATM machines located in the Greater Cleveland area over a 3-week period. After fraudulently obtaining the funds, he transferred approximately $167,000 of the fraud proceeds via Western Union money transfers to the individuals supplying the stolen CitiBank account information located in Europe and Asia.

The investigation was conducted through a long-term online undercover investigation conducted by the U.S. Secret Service targeting domestic and international subjects engaged in identity theft, credit card fraud and production of false identification documents. Flury was sentenced to 32 months in prison, to be followed by 3 years of supervised release.

CASE 2: SHADOWCREW ORGANIZATION—'ONE-STOP ONLINE MARKETPLACE FOR IDENTITY THEFT'

Six men who administered and operated the "Shadowcrew.com" website, one of the largest online centers for trafficking in stolen credit and bank card numbers and identity information, pleaded guilty in federal court, the Department of Justice and U.S. Attorney's office for the District of New Jersey. The one-stop online marketplace operated by the defendants was taken down in October 2004 by the U.S. Secret Service, closing an illicit business that trafficked in at least 1.5 million stolen credit and bank card numbers that resulted in losses in excess of $4 million.

A year-long investigation by the Secret Service led to the arrests of 21 individuals in the United States, in October 2004.

Both the conspiracy and unlawful transfer counts carry maximum prison sentences of five years and a maximum fine of $250,000.

CONCLUSION

Legal processes are in their infancy and will take time to stabilize when driven by maturity of business practices. After all if one looks at history of Bill of Exchange, it took almost over 400 years after their introduction and substantial growth in use for about 100 years prior to legalization, before bills of exchange were accepted in the legal system. The regulators, apart from creating the basic framework, must themselves:

- Gather the typical problems from test cases being presented to them and determine how these can be solved in the fairest possible way.
- Accumulate knowledge on the subject in order to set up an organization structure that can address the legal issues. It would be unfair to expect a court judge who for 30 years of his life has deliberated on other acts, to suddenly become proficient in digital signature and data extraction methodologies.

Simultaneously, the basic structure for monitoring, control and enforcing electronic law could itself require a very different approach.

At the same time if one examines the legal cases on cyber crimes, one will come to the conclusion that even with the best security measures it would not have been possible to prevent the crimes that were committed. The wily criminal will exploit the laws or the lacuna therein in order to further his goals. However, as has been proved by the intelligence agencies, their endeavors to unearth such crimes have not been found wanting and they have succeeded in nabbing the perpetrators of crime. The law agencies also acted with flexibility to book these criminals.

Such progress will continue. The early explorers will just need to take these in their stride for the sake of advancement of mankind and to gain ownership of un-chartered territories.

EXHIBIT 1

RECOLLECTIONS OF PINE GULCH, 1840–1890, TAKEN FROM THE MEMOIRS OF GUS MAHLER

With the discovery of gold at Sutter's Mill in 1848, the new American dream of sudden wealth taken from the ground resulted in a population boom in Northern California. Where before there had been barren wilderness and small homesteads, this discovery gave rise to "boom towns" and "mining camps" filled with men (and some women) who believed that they were going to be the ones to strike it rich. As some of these opportunists came to realize that they were not going to find the big strike, they saw the need to provide services for those who continued to try to find the Mother Lode. Among those who felt that they could do better in some form of the service industry was Gus Mahler, who saw that he could make a living by providing to the miners, a service that there would always be a demand for—he opened a saloon. The following is Gus' story.

"I had one of the first permanent buildings in Pine Gulch. When every other business was set up in tents, I built a two-storied saloon that had rooms for paying customers to sleep it off and a poker room in the back of the first floor. Business was good; too good. I constantly worried about the amount of gold dust I had on hand. We didn't use money in Pine Gulch; that was too inconvenient. If a person found some gold, he would have to ride 85 miles to the nearest assay office in San Francisco, or go to one of the banks there, to get money for the gold. Since the only reason for being in Pine Gulch had to do with gold, everyone had gold. We just used gold for money. Well, there were others in Pine Gulch who were even worse off than me in prospecting for gold, and they weren't so particular as to how they were going to make a living."

"Every businessman in town, me included, was worried about getting robbed, especially those who didn't live in a room located where their business was. We had many of our businessmen get hit over the head on their way home at night, especially after a good day of selling their wares. Something had to be done."

"Sometime in early 1851, six or seven of us got together and discussed the problem. I didn't have to worry about going home with the receipts at night like my fellow businessmen, but I was worried about a raid on my saloon. The saloon in Red Mountain had been knocked over late one night and the owner, a Swede named Ole Svenson, had lost a large supply of dust because he hadn't been to San Francisco in 5 months. I was afraid that the crooks that had done that job would hit my place one night, even though I made the trip to Frisco once a month and never kept as much on hand as Svenson had that

EXHIBIT 1   **161**

night. Moon Jenkins, the dry goods supplier, came up with possibly the best idea that Bible-thumping moron ever had.

He suggested that we find the biggest, toughest, best-shooting, most honest piece of man-flesh that we could find and offer him a job. He takes care of our gold dust for us, and we give him some of it in exchange for his protection. The only problem, according to Moon, was that he didn't know anyone who was man enough and mean enough to handle the crooks in the area and at the same time honest enough for us to trust."

"Smithy Perkins, the blacksmith, said that he knew a man who fit the bill—Slim Johnson. We all agreed with no reservations. Slim Johnson was a giant of a man, 6 foot, 7 inches tall and weighing 300 pounds, if he weighed an ounce. Slim would have stood out in Pine Gulch just by his size, but what folks around here think about when they think of Slim is the time he dropped a deer at the crest of Skillet Mountain with a single shot from 400 yards below. Those who saw the shot said that no man could ever match it. Slim was liked by everyone. There weren't many in Pine Gulch who hadn't been befriended by Slim at some point. We all felt a little sorry that a nice guy like that had had such rotten luck in searching for gold. Slim never seemed to find more than enough to keep him in vittles and the occasional beer. After discussing how we felt about Slim, we adjourned our meeting and went to make him a proposal."

"We found Slim working his claim over on the Elbow Creek and asked him if he was willing to listen to a job offer. He said that since his luck had been running about normal that day, he might as well take some time out to talk with us. We described our problem, and explained that we wanted someone we could trust and have confidence in to take care of our gold dust. Slim asked us what he would earn from this and we told him that we would each give him 1/2 of 1% of our gold that he held each month in exchange for him safeguarding it for us. Slim asked us how much we would be asking him to guard each month and after doing a little calculating, he figured that he would see a lot more gold tending after ours than he ever would working his claim. He agreed to our deal and asked us give him the weekend to make preparations."

"Slim spent that weekend making arrangements in Pine Gulch. He rented a small house in town, and all weekend people heard the sound of hammering and sawing coming from the house. When we went to see Slim on Monday, he showed us his work. He had put iron bars on the three windows in the house and cut a hole in the floor and placed sheets of steel all around the hole. He told us that he intended to keep our gold in this hole. When Moon Jenkins asked him what was to keep someone from crawling under the house and trying to get into the hole from the outside, Slim told him to go outside and crawl under the house and try. Moon came running back in within seconds, and I think I actually heard him cuss for the first time. It was such a shock that I wasn't sure what I heard. I did hear him say something about a monster and realized that Slim wasn't living in the house alone; he had brought Daisy to town with him. Daisy was a creature of indeterminate breed. Some thought she was a dog, while others considered her a wolf. The only thing I was sure of was that Slim was the only one who Daisy got along with. I knew that if anyone was going to try to break into Slim's strongbox from the outside, Daisy was a big obstacle that they were going to have to overcome. Satisfied, we all went back to our businesses and brought most of the gold dust we had on hand and deposited it with Slim. He gave us receipts for the amount we placed with him and told us to return whenever we needed to put more in or get some out."

"Thus began Slim's banking career. As more and more of Pine Gulch's businessmen saw the advantage of having Slim take care of the gold dust that they made, they made the same deal with him. In exchange for Slim taking care of the gold dust (and the occasional nuggets that they took in), Slim would receive 1/2 of 1% of the dust that he held with them. Slim, being a sharp businessman, began offering his services to the prospectors in the area also, and slowly they too began using his services. As his customers expanded, Slim slowly started on his way to becoming the wealthiest man in Pine Gulch. But as the years went on and his list of customers grew, he began to realize that the demands on his time were becoming so much that he wasn't able to enjoy his new found wealth."

"The final straw came the night that Orville Kanter got involved in a poker game in the back of my saloon. I closed the saloon at around two in the morning, but allowed the game in the back to continue. Somewhere around four in the morning, Orville, who had been losing steadily for quite some time, got involved in a show down with Two-Fingers Bradley. Bradley had been the game's big winner that night, and I think that he thought he could buy the pot from Orville. When Orville wouldn't back down and couldn't match Two-Fingers' bet, he turned to me and asked me to hold his cards while he went to get the money required to match the bet. I agreed and we waited about 20 minutes until Orville returned with the dust necessary to match the bet. It was a good thing that Orville's straight was better than Two-Fingers' three kings because I sure didn't want Orville to suffer the black eye he had gotten for nothing. It seems that when Orville went to get the dust he needed to match the bet, he barged into Slim's house to wake him up and get what he needed. Normally, I don't think would have been a problem, but Slim wasn't alone when Orville burst in, and I think he was a little embarrassed to be found embracing Bessie Nordstrom with both of them in various stages of undress. Anyway, Slim's first reaction when Orville burst in the door was to leap up and land a haymaker on Orville that gave

EXHIBIT 1   **163**

him a beaut of a shiner. After helping Orville up off the floor, Slim withdrew the gold dust that Orville needed but I understand that he wasn't very happy about being disturbed at that particular time."

"The next day Slim stopped by the saloon and told me that he was going to be gone for a couple of days and that I would need to hold on to my dust until he returned. He rode off that night without telling us where he was going."

"When he returned, he summoned me to his house and told me where he had been. It seems that he had ridden to San Francisco looking for something that could help him keep from being interrupted at all hours of the night and also from having to be on call for all the people who had left their dust with him. He told me that he had searched all over San Francisco and finally found something that would fit his needs. He had found a stationery shop just off Nob Hill, and he had asked the owner if there was any paper and ink that the owner had in stock that was unique. The owner of the stationery shop said that he had had an eccentric old widow who had special ordered a unique combination from him and then died before she had picked up the order. The order was green paper and purple ink. Slim looked the material over and, after determining that there was no paper and ink like it on the West Coast, he bought the entire supply."

"Why?" I asked him. Slim answered that from that point on, whenever we left gold dust with him, he would write out a receipt for the amount of dust we had left. He said that he would even fill out receipts for different amounts. If I left $100 worth of dust with him, for example, he could give me one receipt for $100, or 2 receipts for $50, or whatever combination I wished. Then whenever I needed to purchase anything, instead of coming to Slim to withdraw some of the dust I had left with him, I could just give a receipt to whomever I was doing business with and that person would know that if they wanted the dust, they could go to Slim and withdraw it. If they didn't want the inconvenience of carrying the dust around, they could just hold on to the receipt and use it to purchase something that they wanted. Slim guaranteed me that he had the only supply of green paper and purple ink on the West Coast and that everyone would know that the receipt was good because of his signature on the receipt. When I asked Slim if this writing of receipts would be worth all the trouble that he would have to go through, he replied that they were going to make his job much easier because now people wouldn't be bothering him at all times of the night to get their dust. In fact, he said that he was only going to be open on Monday through Friday from 9:00 am to 4:00 pm for people to leave their dust with him or withdraw dust. In this way he could still protect the deposits and have a life of his own.

"I was skeptical at first but gradually everyone in Pine Gulch accepted Slim's receipts as 'money' and Slim's life began to approach what would be considered by some to be normal. If it had been anyone else but Slim, I don't think the plan would have worked, but since everyone knew Slim to be an honest and virtuous man (Bessie Nordstrom notwithstanding), Slim's currency became the medium of exchange in Pine Gulch. Some even joked that Slim should add a slogan to the receipts, one that said 'In Slim, we trust'."

"About a year after Slim introduced his currency into Pine Gulch, he stopped into my saloon to have a glass of sarsaparilla. I had been doing some thinking about how to improve my business, since Pine Gulch was growing and I no longer had the only saloon in town. I had a few ideas about what would bring more business into my place, but I sure didn't have the money I needed. I brought Slim his glass of sarsaparilla and took him over to the corner booth to discuss my particular problem. I wanted to add on to the saloon and build a big stage where I could bring in some of them fancy dancers from San Francisco for a hoochy-koochy show. The type of fancy place I envisioned would have a mirror running the length of the bar and fancy curtains and all the baubles I saw in those fancy places in San Francisco. The only trouble was that everything I wanted was going to cost around $5,000 and I didn't have anywhere near that amount of money, especially since the other saloons were taking a large part of my business away. I asked Slim if there was some idea that he had that could help me with my problem."

"Slim thought for a while, and then he said that he didn't have enough to lend me either. He had spent a large part of his earnings on the new building he bought for his bank. But, he said, if I would stop by the bank the next day, he might have a way for me to get what I needed to expand. I went to the bank the next day, and Slim welcomed me and took me into his back office. After we sat down, Slim told me that he had a solution to my problem. He reached into his desk and pulled out a stack of receipts totaling $5,000. He pushed the stack across his desk and told me that the receipts were mine to use for the expansion of my place.

"I was shocked! 'Where,' I asked Slim, 'did the money come from? I thought you said you didn't have any you could lend me. What is this?' I was not prepared for Slim's answer. He told me that he had written up the receipts that morning."

"I couldn't believe my ears. We had come to Slim to care for our gold because we trusted him. Now he was offering to hand me receipts for gold that I didn't have. It had to be stealing."

"Slim told me not to worry. He explained that he had around $20,000 worth of gold dust in his safe, and he had written $20,000 worth of receipts that we were circulating in Pine Gulch as currency. But few people ever came into the bank and cashed the receipts in for gold dust anymore. In fact, he said that the biggest demand for gold dust in the previous year had been

EXHIBIT 1   **165**

a $1,000 redemption of receipts. Since he had more dust on hand than anyone ever wanted to redeem, he felt that he could write out enough receipts to give me a loan for my expansion and never worry because the people wouldn't demand their gold."

"I was thinking that somehow what we were talking about was illegal. Slim was writing receipts for gold that I hadn't put into his bank and allowing me to spend the receipts. Something was wrong here. Slim explained to me that I wasn't going to get the receipts for nothing. He reached into his desk and pulled out a piece of paper and handed it to me. The paper said that I, Gus Mahler, was borrowing $5,000 in receipts from Slim's bank and that in six months I would repay the $5,000 plus $1,000 in something called interest. He explained that the $1,000 was going to be my cost of borrowing from his bank. I was nervous about this, but as long as Slim assured me that he would stick the paper away where no one would see it and wouldn't tell anyone about it, I felt that I could improve my business and make enough to repay the loan without anyone learning about it."

"I accepted the receipts and began ordering what I needed from the businesses in town. The materials to expand my saloon got to Pine Gulch within a month, and the expansion took about another 2 weeks. By the end of the 6-month period of the loan, my business had improved to such a point that I could repay the loan in full plus the interest that I owed Slim. I walked into Slim's office one Monday morning and, after we had gone back into his office, I took the $6,000 in receipts out of my pocket, set it on his desk, and demanded that he give me the note that I had signed. Slim reached into his desk and withdrew the note. When he handed it over to me, I immediately ripped the note up into little pieces so that it could never be recognizable again. I breathed a sigh of relief (that note had worried me so much for the past 6 months that I had not had a decent night's sleep) and started laughing, as much from relief as anything else. Slim looked at me, started laughing too, and then, to my dismay, he took the receipts that I had put on his desk, set aside $1,000 worth and ripped up the rest! I was shocked! I started choking as my laughter got caught in my throat.

"'What are you doing?' I screamed. Slim just kept laughing at me, laughing in such a way that I worried about his sanity. I ran out of his office and back to the saloon. Over a couple of shots of whiskey, I calmed down and thought about what had happened. Slim had, by loaning me $5,000 of receipts increased the money supply in Pine Gulch. Then, when I no longer had the need for the money and repaid the loan, he decreased the money supply back to what it had been before. The only difference, as I saw things, was that now Slim had $1,000 that he didn't have before he made me the loan. Somehow, I wasn't sure exactly, Slim's control of the money supply made him more wealthy. Everyone in town still trusted Slim, and had faith in his receipts as our currency, but I was a little leery. Somehow, something wasn't right."

"As the years went along, Slim made loans to many others in Pine Gulch. I never felt good about borrowing from him again, but I knew many others who went to Slim whenever they needed something and couldn't afford it. I was sure that if he was making money off their loans the way he did off mine, he had to be the richest man in Pine Gulch. But the gold strikes were starting to peter out and I wondered if Slim had anywhere near the gold dust in his safe as the amount of receipts that were in circulation."

"In the late 1860's a stranger rode into town. With my first glance at him, all thoughts of Slim being a big man left my head. This monster was bigger than most bears I had ever seen. He sat in my saloon, tossing back beers with the regulars, and telling jokes and laughing louder that anyone I had ever heard. His name was Bart McQueen, but everyone referred to him as Big Bart. After partying all over town for a couple of days, Big Bart announced his intentions to settle down in Pine Gulch. He said he was going to need a job, and he wanted the best job in town. 'What is that job?' he asked, and everyone in town knew what the answer was."

"Slim Johnson has the best job in town," they said. "He's the banker." After listening to the townspeople talk about Slim and his job, Big Bart decided that this was the job for him.

"You can't do that," Smithy Perkins said. "Slim is the banker and he's the one we go to for finances. We can't have two bankers and two different kinds of money. That would make things confusing."

"No problem," said Bart, "just tell Slim that I'll be waiting for him in the street at 3:00 this afternoon. After we're done, there will only be one person who wants to be banker in Pine Gulch."

"Like wild fire, the news spread through Pine Gulch. When I heard it, I knew that Slim was in trouble. No one had challenged him for years, and I had begun to wonder if he was living off his reputation. Big Bart was impressive looking, and if he could handle a six-gun, I had a feeling that Slim might have seen better days."

"That afternoon, there was no one on the only street that ran through Pine Gulch, but if you looked behind the curtains that looked out on the street, you would have found everyone who lived within 5 miles of town. A lot of people were wondering if Slim would show up, but at 3:00 he walked out of his office and took up a position in the middle of the street. About a minute later Big Bart walked out of the office of the Pine Gulch Gazette (I found out later he was helping the copy boy write Slim's obituary), and took up a position opposite Slim."

"I heard him tell Slim that this fuss could be avoided if Slim chose to leave town. Slim's reply was that the person who should leave was the person

EXHIBIT 1

167

who was new to town. I'm not really clear about what happened next. I think Bart told Slim that he should draw first, but I did see the one shot that was fired. Slim went for his gun, but he didn't even get it out of his belt before Bart had drawn and fired. Slim fell immediately, but we knew he wasn't dead. The scream that he let out informed all of us that he was still alive. Bart had shot him in the knee cap and the bullet had shattered his knee."

"Immediately the street was filled with people. About 5 guys picked up Slim and carted him off to his office, all the while yelling for Doc Adams to come and patch up his knee. The others milled around Big Bart and went with him to my saloon to join in some celebratory drinks. The liquor sure flowed that afternoon. Big Bart announced that he would be opening his bank on Monday morning and that he would be issuing his own receipts for deposits that he expected to be used as currency in Pine Gulch. Everyone in town thought that Big Bart's new bank was the way to go, and they went running down to Slim's bank to cash in their receipts and get their gold dust to put in Big Bart's bank the following Monday."

"In just a few minutes a huge crowd had developed outside Slim's bank. No one was being allowed inside and after about 15 minutes, Doc Adams came out and said that Slim was closing the bank for the day because of his wound, but that the bank would be open at 8:00 Monday morning for anyone who wanted to redeem his receipts for gold dust. The crowd dispersed (many of them coming back to my saloon to drink with Big Bart and congratulate him on his impressive handling of Slim) and things settled down for the weekend."

"The next Monday a long line developed in front of Slim's bank by 8:00. Everyone in town was waiting to cash in the funny green receipts with the purple ink and get their gold dust to put in Big Bart's bank. When the doors didn't open at 8:00, there was some grumbling. When the doors didn't open by 8:30, the grumbling turned into action. The doors were kicked in, and we were greeted with a terrible sight. Slim's vault was open, and the only thing in it was a pile of promissory notes that almost everyone in town had signed. Oh, there was one other thing found in the vault; a sealed letter addressed to me. Sensing the mood of the crowd around me, I didn't think it would be a good idea to take the letter and read it privately. I got up on the counter, yelled at everyone to be quiet, tore open the letter, and began reading aloud."

"'My old friend Gus', the letter began, 'I'm writing this to you because you are probably the person in this town who will best understand what has happened. My unfortunate run-in with the impressive Mr. McQueen this afternoon (the letter must have been written Friday evening after the gunfight) has left me unable to handle the financial needs of this community. As you may suspect, Pine Gulch has been in existence financially because everyone used my receipts as their currency. Whenever anyone in town needed money, I was willing to write out new receipts in exchange for their promissory notes, which I held in my vault. Over the years more and more people came to me for loans for longer and longer periods of time. I realized that there were far more receipts in circulation in Pine Gulch than I could ever cover with the gold dust that I had available, but as long as people retained their faith in me and didn't all come in to redeem their receipts at the same time, we would have no problems. The people of Pine Gulch no longer have the faith in me that is required, as is evidenced by the fact that they all wish to withdraw their gold dust and place it in Mr. McQueen's new establishment. Well, I am unable to redeem all of the receipts in the community. As you can see by the notes here in this vault, there are almost $200,000 worth of receipts outstanding in Pine Gulch. Unfortunately, I have never had more than $40,000 worth of gold dust in my vault. Thus, I am faced with a dilemma. Do I stay in Pine Gulch, pay off the fortunate few who arrive first on Monday morning, and then, after the gold dust is gone, say that I'm sorry to the others who did not get the chance to redeem their receipts? Or do I leave town, realizing that a man of my skills can get away with a 2-day head start? If I do the first, I have no doubt that I will be swinging from a tree before lunchtime. If I do the second, I will undoubtedly have a guilty conscience for the rest of my days. After a great deal of reflection (and a generous dose of Doc Adams' pain reliever), I have decided to take the second course. I feel that my conscience can be greatly eased by the gold dust that I feel I am honor bound to take with me. If I leave the gold, only a small section of the population in Pine Gulch will receive what they feel they are owed, and those who receive none of the gold will feel antagonistic to those who have received some of the gold. If the people of Pine Gulch are to be antagonistic to anyone, let it be to me. I wish the people of Pine Gulch well. They are all in the same boat now. I hope that Mr. McQueen will be able to do for them what I have tried to do for the past 20 years. Goodbye, old friend. Please don't think ill of me. Signed, Hector, 'Slim', Johnson."

"As I finished the letter, there was an angry uproar from the crowd around me. There were cries of anguish and shouts of revenge and a push to gather up a posse to chase after Slim and string him up. However, most people in the crowd realized that the chances of catching someone like Slim after he had 2 days head start were slim indeed and thoughts of chasing after him gradually died out."

"The next few months after Slim vanished, things were tough in Pine Gulch. Most people heard about silver strikes over in Nevada and decided that maybe they should try their luck elsewhere. By the time a year had passed, only about 20 of us still lived in Pine Gulch. I stayed on. The occasional traveler through the valley always wanted to wet his whistle before he moved on. I never was very wealthy again, but I never let anyone else take care of my money (or my gold) either. I always wondered what would have happened if Big Bart had never come to Pine Gulch. I guess I'll never know."

EXHIBIT 2

HISTORY AND IMPORTANCE OF BANKING

Since this book is about involvement of banks in the financial supply chain, it would not be out of turn to briefly understand the role of banks and their antecedents. Banks have played a key role in building and supporting the financial supply chain since their inception, although the financial supply chain is in a considerable stage of evolution at present.

'Among the instruments of Civilization which the ingenuity and industry of man have given to his species, not one has been so completely characterized by the elements of potency of effects and universality of application as Money. No people is so barbarous as not to recognize its use: none so daring as to contemplate its discontinuance'
—Lawson John, *History of Banking*

And banks have held this responsibility as guardians of money and to further perpetuate and create money. It is indeed both tempting and astonishing that banks can create money! There have been many historical incidents of ferocious consequences challenging such money creation. However, over a period of time, it has been well accepted that the money creation does add to the well being of the economy and society at large—both emotionally and physically—and this function has been largely taken over by the central banks in the country.

To the readers who may not be very familiar with banking and would be grappling with questions such as, 'what is money', 'how can it be created or shrunk' and 'what do the bankers in striped suits really do', there can be no better resource than the story titled, 'Recollections of Pine Gulch', set in the background of gold discovery in the middle of 1800, in a small town in the Americas. The story is included as Exhibit 1 so that readers familiar with banking can progress without obstruction.

Banking, as we know it today came into existence only in the seventeenth century. The banking, and in particular the money lending, business was primarily controlled by the goldsmiths, the pawnbrokers and the Jews. The first joint stock bank with activities similar to present day banks was possibly the Bank of England, which was formed in 1694. It is interesting to understand the motivations and the activities of the formation of such an institution. However, here is a brief digress to discuss some of the important events leading up to the formation of the Bank of England.

ORIGINS OF MONEY

Trade of goods, commodities and services happened long before the origin of money and the earliest form of value exchange was through barter.

Writing was invented in Mesopotamia in around 3,100 BC and during the period between 3,000 BC and 2,000 BC primitive banking originated in Babylonia out of the activities of temples and palaces, which provided safe places for the storage of valuables. Initially, deposits of grain were accepted and later other goods including cattle, agricultural implements, and precious metals were traded. In the period around 330 BC in Egypt, grain had been used as a form of money and state granaries functioned as banks. An elaborate system was put in place, where payments were made through the transfer of grain held by the warehouse, from one account to another!

Till about 1910 AD, the Kirghiz people in central Asia used horses as their main monetary unit and store of value; sheep was used as subsidiary units and small change was given in lambskins. Till date, cattle are used in some parts of Africa as a monetary value for exchange. Barter continued as a popular method of value exchange upto the early thirteenth century.

Coins

Amongst the first permanent forms of money in the form of porcelain tablets or coins, was possibly first used in China around 2,700 BC. About 600 BC, round base metal coins of iron and clay were introduced. However, as these were made of base metal and were of relatively low value, they were inconvenient for expensive purchases.

The earliest coins made in Lydia, present day Turkey in Asia Minor, around 640 BC, consisted of electrum, a naturally occurring amalgam of gold and silver. Very soon the usage of coins spread rapidly from Lydia to Greece and around 550 BC, pure metal coins of silver and gold were produced in Lydia.

However, in about 405 BC, Athens in Greece issued bronze coins with a silver coating. The Athenian public hoarded the silver coins, which quickly disappeared from circulation.

The Romans were a little late in adopting coins and used bronze bars until about 275 BC and around 270 BC there was regular issue of silver coins by the Romans and these were widely circulated. During the war between Rome and Carthage near about 210 BC, because of the enormous demand for coins to pay troops the Roman rulers debased their coinage in purity and weight, causing inflation. Then during his reign between 30 BC and 14 AD, Augustus Caesar reformed the Roman monetary and taxation systems issuing new, almost pure, gold and silver coins as well as brass and copper ones. However, succeeding rulers like Nero and others regularly

EXHIBIT 2   **171**

debased the coins and by 270 AD the silver content in the coin was only about 4%!

Pure coins were once again introduced in Rome by Aurelian and then later by Constantine. During the rule of Constantine, about 320 AD, Britain was a part of the Roman province. As a result of the Anglo Saxon invasions about 435 AD, Britain ceased to use coins as money for nearly 200 years. When coins were re-introduced from the continent they were used initially for ornaments. After the conquest of Kent by Offa in 765 AD, the Anglo Saxon King of Mercia, Central England, production of the silver *penny* increased enormously and it replaced the older, more crudely designed *sceat* as the main English coin. During his reign, in around 960 AD, King Edgar reformed the English coinage system by controlling the issue of dies and strictly regulating the mints to ensure that the coinage was of uniform type and standard.

Because of their convenience as a royally authenticated means of payment the value of coins was higher than the value of their silver content. During 973 AD, King Edgar started recalling, melting down and re-minting coins and thus he and his successors not only maintained the quality of the currency but also made handsome profits from the operation.

During the reign of Henry 1, the quality of England's silver currency fell drastically. On Christmas day in 1124 AD, all the mint masters were punished and their right hands cut off. Not surprisingly this produced a temporary improvement in the quality of the coinage.

Previous to and immediately after the Norman conquest of England in 1066, there was little money in use in England and most obligations were discharged by personal service and by payments, such as cattle, horses, dogs, hawks, etc. Rent of Land was reckoned in kind, as "the rent of Hicklinge is ten measures of malt, five of groute, five of white meale, eight gammons of bacon, sixteen cheeses and two fat cows".

Down to the period of Henry I in the early twelfth century, the rents, taxes and fines due to the king were paid in provisions that were necessary for his household. In succeeding reigns later, the revenues of the crown were chiefly paid in gold and silver, but sometimes made up with horses, dogs and birds for the game.

But even gold and silver were subject to adulteration by the admixture of baser metals. Sometimes when money was paid in to the Exchequer, if it was suspected to be alloyed beneath the legal standard, it was brought to the fire to be tested.

Around the middle of the thirteenth century, Henry III caused a grain of wheat gathered from the middle of the ear to be the standard weight; and 32 of these well dried, were to make one penny weight, twenty-two penny weights made one ounce and 12 ounces were equivalent to one pound. Since then, it has been thought advisable to divide the pennyweight into 24 equal parts called grains.

With such reforms, the prestige of English money was maintained at a high level for some time. In 1282 AD, the first public trial of Pyx was recorded, a public test of the purity of gold and silver coins, which continues in Britain to this day.

Around the same time in about 1250 AD, gold coins were issued by several Italian states. In 1489, Henry VII issued the first gold sovereigns. Up to 1489 the English pound had simply been a unit of account. Now, with the issue of the sovereign, it was also a coin.

Coin acceptance and circulation increased rapidly around this time although there continued to be debasement of coins from time to time. The generally accepted practice was that, the metal content in the coin constituted its equivalent values. Around 1526, Nicholas Copernicus the great astronomer argued that, it is the total number of coins in circulation, rather than the weight of metal they contain, that determines the level of prices and the buying power of the currency.

Amongst the drawings of Leonardo da Vinci, 1452 to 1519 AD are designs for a press to produce more uniform coins quickly using a water-driven mill. This innovation was widely adopted and the new money is termed *milled money*.

By 1645, with the replacement of the ancient technique of hammering coins, minting became fully mechanized. Improved productivity is not the only advantage. The milled edges prevent clipping and cutting and make counterfeiting more difficult.

Because tokens had become common the British government decided that the free market could probably supply copper currency better than the Royal Mint and in 1797, the initial contract for 50 tons of two-penny and one-penny pieces was awarded to Mathew Boulton. His partnership with James Watt eventually resulted in the use of steam-powered machinery for producing 4,200 tons of copper coins.

The advancement of the coin system in other parts of the world happened more slowly than in Europe. The USA passed the Coinage Act in 1792 and adopted the dollar as its unit of account, based on a bi-metallic standard. However in 1848, following the discovery of gold in California there was a massive increase in the production of gold coins by the mint with the result that in practice the US moved away from bi-metallism towards a gold standard. In 1871, the German states united and adopted the mark as their common currency and based it on the gold standard. Japan passed its currency act in 1871 and established a national mint at Osaka and introduced the decimal system of yen and sen. In 1878, France adopted a gold standard for its currency. By the end of 1870s, the gold standard had become an international standard with London as the world's main financial center.

EXHIBIT 2   173

In 1914, Britain issued new one pound and 10 shilling notes, and postal orders and Scottish and Irish banknotes were made legal tender. The success of the new notes allows banks to withdraw gold gradually from internal circulation, thus putting a quiet end to the gold standard.

Bank Notes

The first paper money or rather non-metallic money seems to have been issued in China in 118 BC. This consisted of a piece of white deer skin, about one square foot, with a value equivalent to 40,000 of the base metal coins (cash).

It is interesting that China continued with the issuance of paper money for a long period of time, much before it became popular in Western Europe. In about 960 AD, the issuance of paper money became regular in China. However by 1032 AD, there were about 16 note issuing houses in China and the excessive supply of notes caused inflation. Around 1160 AD, emperor Kao Tsung replaced the earlier notes with a new issue, as the earlier notes became useless with prolonged inflation. However, additional note issuance continued and by 1448 AD, the Ming note nominally worth 1,000 cash had a market value of only three! In 1455 AD, China abandoned the use of paper money and re-introduced it only in the early twentieth century. Thus, after well over 500 years of experience with paper currencies, during which there were repeated episodes of inflation and currency reform, China stopped the use of paper money.

In the meanwhile during the thirteenth and fourteenth century, there were attempts to issue notes in many countries such as Russia, the Middle East states, Iran, India, Japan, etc. under able leaders like Kublai Khan. However, these attempts failed mainly because of high inflation of the currency resulting from wars perpetrated by these successful rulers.

The present day currency notes, which were formalized under the British Empire have their origin in 'Goldsmith's notes', which were issued around 1633 AD by goldsmiths and were used not only as receipts for reclaiming the gold deposits but also as evidence of ability to pay. Because goldsmiths' notes were a convenient alternative to handling coins or bullion and the borrowers found them just as convenient and secure as depositories, these began to be used as banknotes in England in around 1660 AD.

In 1695 AD, the Bank of England was incorporated and issued bank notes, initially of twenty pounds and above in value. In 1697 AD, the Bank of England ran into difficulty when it issued notes against clipped and diminished silver coins before receiving new silver coins from the mint for their daily demands. This led to the notes falling to a seventeen to twenty percent discount, against the issuance price. This resulted in a loss to the bank, which was made up by subscription for additional capital.

However, for a long period of time advances of the Bank of England to the government were 4 to 5 times more than the commercial discounts, which helped the government to support their expenses and fund the war with France. In 1745, 1793 and then again in 1797, there was a run on the bank and there was a large demand for gold against deposits. In 1793, the bank then started issuance of 5 pound notes and in 1797, it issue 1 pound notes.

On each of these occasions, when there was run on the bank, the bank proclaimed that, "they would continue the usual discounts for the accommodation of the commercial interests, paying the amount in bank notes, and that dividend warrants would be paid in the same manner". This was strongly protested as the very basis of the bank notes was the convenience of converting it into gold or silver on demand. It was considered a farce that the bank's promise to pay on demand was paid by another promise to pay at some undefined period. However, as a large portion of the monies were owed by the government and who was not able to refurnish the monies that it had borrowed from the bank on demand, such measures had the tacit support of the government. Such restrictions on payment in gold and silver were placed from time to time to prevent a run on the bank. The provisions of the Bank Restriction Act passed in 1797, when notes were made non-convertible into gold, was initially expected to be for a very short duration but, it was 24 years before convertibility was restored.

In 1809, owing to excessive issues of bills by the British government, the value of the pound had fallen in exchange for other currencies versus the French franc. However, this resulted in the gold price going up in England, thus reflecting the depreciation in the value of the pound. The Governor of the Bank of England suggested in his opinion, "I cannot see how the amount of bank notes can operate upon the price of bullion or the exchange; and I am therefore, individually of the opinion that the price of bullion can never be a reason for lessening the amount of bank notes to be issued".

Accordingly in the year 1819, a resolution was passed to the above effect, de-linking the issuance of bank notes and the price of gold. The resolution of 1819 was cancelled in 1827, when the bank note issuance was governed by the state of the exchanges, i.e. they are increased when gold is received in the bank and reduced when gold is removed from the bank.

In 1826, the Bank of England opened more branches outside the city of London and thus, the notes issued by the Bank of England began to be circulated outside London. Several other county banks, which were until then issuing their own notes outside London, undertook the circulation of Bank of England notes instead of their own.

Meanwhile the Bank of Sweden issued notes in 1660 and became the first bank in Europe to do so. Similarly, a note-issuing bank was founded in the

EXHIBIT 2 **175**

USA in 1681. In 1716, John Law started the first public bank in France and issued notes. Again, in 1789 the French government introduced paper notes called 'assignats' which were backed by property confiscated during the revolution. However, owing to indiscreet issuance of notes, most economies were faced with hyperinflation and prices rose, but wages did not.

In 1797, the 'assignats' were withdrawn in France and replaced by a new system based upon gold. Until 1846, the minimum legal denomination in France was 250 francs, or more than a month's wages for the average worker. In the following years it gradually reduced as it was found to be too high for most purposes. Until 1848, the Bank of France enjoyed a monopoly of note issues since its foundation was only in Paris. The rest of the country was largely dependent on the note issues and bill discounting of local banks, many of which were weak. On failure of many local banks in 1848, the national bank was given a monopoly of note issuing. The Bank of France also began to develop a large network of branches in different parts of the country.

During 1809–1831, Ohio State Government issued paper warrants of 5, 10 and 20 dollars as currency, because of shortage of coins. In 1836, President Jackson issued a circular stating that future purchases of government land must be paid in gold or silver, or their strict equivalent, rather than in local notes or promises to pay. This had the effect of swelling the US government's coffers with specie.

During 1850s in the US, many thousands of different types of banknotes, both genuine and counterfeit, were in circulation causing considerable problems for bankers and traders. To finance the US Civil War during 1861–1865, the Confederacy financed its war effort mainly by printing money. In addition to the confederate notes, the states, railway, insurance and other companies also issued notes. The resulting hyperinflation rendered the confederate paper worthless. In 1862, The United States Treasury started issuing notes that were not convertible into silver or gold but were legal tender for all purposes except payment of customs duties and interest on government securities. Following the US Civil War the value of the dollar had depreciated a great deal and the government passed an act in 1875 to withdraw these from circulation. However, this caused an economic depression and a compromise was reached in 1879, where the circulation of dollars continued and the government also passed an act to restore conversion of dollars to gold.

In 1914, the Government Treasury of Britain issued new British notes and not the Bank of England, and gold was withdrawn from circulation. The success of the new notes allowed banks to withdraw gold gradually from internal circulation, thus putting a quiet end to the gold standard. In 1921, the note issuing by commercial banks in England ceased.

THE ORIGIN OF BANKS

As early as 1792 BC during the reign of Hammurabi in Babylon, the code of Hammurabi included laws for governing banking operations. During 350 BC, the normal rate of interest in Greece was set at 10% except for risky businesses such as shipping, for which it was placed higher at 20% to 30%.

During 320 BC, the empire of the Ptolemies in Egypt used the state granaries as banks, with a central bank in Alexandria. During 200 BC, Delos a barren Greek island, capitalized on its magnificent harbor and famous temple of Apollo to become a financial center. Its rise was aided by the defeat of Carthage, one of its main rivals, by the Romans.

When Rome fell to the Visigoths in the fifth century AD, banking was abandoned in Western Europe and did not develop again until the times of the Crusades. During the 11th and 12th century, the need to transfer large sums of money to finance the Crusades provides a stimulus to the re-emergence of banking in Western Europe. The rulers experimented with issuance of coins to facilitate collection of taxes and loans from the public at large. Around the same time the money lending business was primarily facilitated by the goldsmiths, the pawn-brokers and the Jews.

The first public institution remotely similar to our present-day bank was the exchequer founded by William I in about 1080 AD. A great portion of the yearly revenue received by the king consisted of taxes, which were paid for grants of lands and confirmations of liberties and franchises of various kinds. When the collectors of the taxes lodged the money in the exchequer, they received a receipt called 'tally'. The 'tally' was a pair of prism shaped pieces of wood on which notches were cut for the amount of the money deposited and the same amount was also written on the piece of wood. The 'tally' was used as a receipt and was also used for tracking the amount collected. On presentation, the holder of a 'tally' could demand gold or silver from the exchequer.

The first regular institution, resembling the present day bank was founded in Venice, Italy, in the early 14th century. In its origin, its objective being to raise funds for the war engaged in by the Republic, the merchants were forced to loan money to the ruler against annual interest of 4%. A corporation entitled 'Chamber of Loans' was formed at this time and undertook this activity. Soon the Chamber started to finance some commercial bills of exchange, with surplus money that it had from time to time. The Chamber being of undoubted standing, having been founded by the Republic, the merchants soon started to keep their money with the Chamber for safe keeping. Subsequently, money transfer from one account to another was initiated when it was found cumbersome to count and move so much money physically. This method of doing business was found to be so favorable that

EXHIBIT 2   **177**

it was subsequently, made a law and every merchant was obliged to open an account with the Chamber. All payments of bills of exchange for wholesale transactions were settled in the Chamber.

Similar institutions were founded in the beginning of the fifteenth century, notable among them being the Medici Bank, the Bank of Barcelona and the Bank of St George, Genoa. A few other banks were formed in Italy towards the end of the sixteenth century namely, the Bank of Genoa in 1585 and Banco di Rialto, Venice in 1587.

Despite the traditional Christian prohibition of usury, charging interest on loans was ruled legal in Florence, Italy in about 1403 AD. In 1545 AD, Henry VIII legalized interest charges on loans and set an upper limit of 10% per annum on the interest charges.

At the beginning of the seventeenth century, the Dutch were the leaders in European commerce and Amsterdam was the central point of trade. In 1602, the Dutch East India Company was founded, to provide the financial backing for Dutch companies competing against British companies for the pepper market in the Far East. In 1609, the Bank of Amsterdam was founded. Subsequently, other new private and public banks were founded in Netherlands between 1610 AD and 1635 AD namely, Bank of Middelburg, Hamburg Girobank, Bank of Delft, Bank of Nuremburg and Bank of Rotterdam.

In 1656, the Bank of Sweden was founded for accepting deposits and granting loans and mortgages and issuing bills of credit.

The period between 1630 and 1670 saw the rise of many goldsmith bankers in Britain. Some British goldsmiths gradually evolved into bankers by dealing in foreign and domestic coins and by letting their safes be used for deposits of valuables. Goldsmith's deposit notes came to be used not only as receipts for reclaiming deposits but also as evidence of ability to pay.

The Government of England experienced considerable financial difficulties in 1691, during its war with France. A scheme was laid before the government for formation of a Joint Stock Bank wherein forty merchants subscribed a total of 500 thousand pounds of the total capital of 1,200,000 pounds, to be lent to the government in consideration of 8% interest. The Bank of England was incorporated on 25 April 1694 and the public subscribed to its full capital by 17 June 1694.

Although a latecomer to the banking practice, the key contributions of Britain, which led to subsequent and significant progress of banking worldwide, were as follows.

(a) Issuance of bank notes—Although bills of exchange were convenient for commercial trade, they were useful only where the drawer had a good reputation and his signature still required verification. With the bank note, both these risks were addressed. Also, the transfer of a bank note did not leave any liability on the transferor, unlike the bill of exchange.

(b) Issuance of government debt—As a large part of the borrowings of the bank were from government debt, over a period of time this created a liquid market for government debt and consequently government stock.

During the eighteenth century, the banking industry gained further momentum with its spread in USA, Germany and France albeit with some hiccups. The nineteenth century saw rapid development of banking in many parts of the world along with variations such as savings banks, industrial finance banks, industrial credit co-operatives, etc.

Banking presently is a well-established and large industry and adds, according to some estimates, about 1–3% to the national GDP.

Origin of Cheques and Clearing

Clearing is one of the key services offered by the banks for moving money from one holder to another.

About 320 BC, in the empire of the Ptolemies in Egypt grain had been used as a form of money and state granaries functioned as banks. Payments were made by transfer of grain from one account to another without money passing.

The earliest British cheque is supposed to have been issued in 1659 AD through an order drawn on a goldsmith. The first printed cheques are traced to 1762 and British banker Lawrence Childs. The word "check" also may have originated in England in the 1700s when serial numbers were placed on these pieces of paper as a way to keep track, or "check" on them. The concept of writing and depositing checks as a method of arranging payments, spread in England around 1780. However, there was skepticism about use of these instruments as they were easily forged or replicated. The initial cheques were used for high value and commercial transactions only.

In the very early days of the cheque, the drawer had to present himself to the bank for honoring the cheque. As they became more widely accepted bankers wondered how to move these pieces of paper to collect the money due from so many other banks. At first, each bank sent messengers to the other banks to present cheques for collection, but that meant a lot of traveling and a lot of cash being hauled around in insecure conditions.

As folklore goes, the solution to this problem was found in the 1700s at a British pub. The story goes that a London bank messenger carrying cheques for clearing stopped for a pint (or two) and noticed another bank messenger. They got talking, realized that they each had checks drawn on the other's bank, and decided to exchange them and save each other the extra trip. The pub and subsequently the practice evolved into a system of cheque

EXHIBIT 2   **179**

"clearinghouses" or paper networks of banks that exchange cheques with each other. The first clearinghouse was set up in London, in 1770.

As usage of cheques developed, the clearinghouses had to physically handle very large amounts of cheques every day. The MICR standard, which provided tremendous boost to cheque processing, was developed in the US in the 1950s, by a consensus group of banks. The MICR contains information such as the routing number identifying the drawee bank, the payment amount and the customer account number of the payer, and this lends itself to easy and automated processing at the clearinghouse.

In 1906, Austria established the first postal giro system in the 1883. This was followed by Switzerland and Japan, in 1906. France introduced the giro system in the 1918, and this proved very successful for money transfers, as cheques were not very commonly used in France then. By the time England's giro system was established in the 1960s, the French giro system had become the largest in the world.

By late 1980s and early 1990s, many of the developed countries had well developed electronic clearing systems. By the 1990s many of the countries such as Netherlands, Sweden, Germany, Japan, etc. had over 90% of their transactions settled electronically without the use of paper based instruments like cheques. In 2004, in the USA for the first time the number of electronic transactions exceeded the number of cheque-based transactions.

EXHIBIT 3

ELEMENTS OF PHYSICAL SUPPLY CHAIN

The following classifications have been created in an attempt to understand the various types of services involved, which are in themselves independent transactions and yet form a part of supply chain services of other transactions. While structuring financial supply chain solutions for these parties, it is important to understand the perspective of the solution, i.e. is the party involved the key buyer/seller in the transaction or is it involved as a party in facilitating the services being exchanged between a pair of buyers and sellers.

It is also possible that in some cases these services are the beneficiaries of the financial supply chain services from banks, e.g. a transporter has drawn an invoice which the buyer of the transportation services pays after 30 days. In such a case, the transporter may seek post-shipment finance from the bank.

1. Transportation Services

There is a vast area of services offered under transportation:

A. Transport operators

These are companies, which generally have access to various means of transportation as:

❑ Lorries and roads
❑ Ships
❑ Planes
❑ Railways
❑ Multi-modal transport such as a combination of these

B. Couriers and freight consolidators

The couriers generally receive small shipments from various parties and then consolidate these. They then use the transport operators to ship the goods.

C. Freight forwarders

Freight forwarders act as agents of the transport operators and release and forward goods as per the instructions of the transport agents.

D. Packagers and forwarders

Packagers also take responsibility of packaging goods and then moving them to the target destinations using their own transport or through using the services of transport operators.

EXHIBIT 3   **181**

2. Insurance Services

Insurance companies provide cover against various types of risks e.g. life insurance, medical insurance, transit insurance, plant and machinery insurance, credit insurance, etc.

3. Tertiary Services

These are services to facilitate the physical flow of goods. Typically, these would be the quality inspectors, warehouse operators, security services, software services, etc.

4. Distribution Services

These services are required for distribution of goods and sometimes services as well. There are different types of arrangements:
  A. Dealer—Generally understood as a party who buys and then sells the goods.
  B. Stockists or distributors—They do not buy, but stock the goods on behalf of the sellers and then help in distribution.
  C. Original equipment manufacturers—They buy the goods and do substantial value add-on to these before selling the finished products.

5. Financial Services

Banks and other institutions provide various types of services to customers, e.g. deposits, loans, share trading, foreign exchange services, trade services, etc.

6. Regulatory Services

Regulators collect money for various types of services offered, e.g. customs, taxes, certifications and licenses, etc.

In all these cases, there is a buyer and a seller of the services. The buyer of the services normally pays the seller based on agreed conditions of payments. In effect, these are like the regular physical supply chain albeit the goods and services being exchanged are of a different nature.

EXHIBIT 4

ADMISSIBILITY OF ELECTRONIC RECORDS IN COURTS AS IN INDIAN LAW

1. Notwithstanding anything contained in this Act, any information contained in an electronic record which is printed on a paper, stored, recorded or copied in optical or magnetic media produced by a computer (hereinafter referred to as the computer output) shall be deemed to be also a document, if the conditions mentioned in this section are satisfied in relation to the information and computer in question and shall be admissible in any proceedings, without further proof or production of the original, as evidence of any contents of the original or of any fact stated therein or which direct evidence would be admissible.

2. The conditions referred to in sub-section (1) in respect of a computer output shall be the following, namely:

   (a) The computer output containing the information was produced by the computer during the period over which the computer was used regularly to store or process information for the purposes of any activities regularly carried on over that period by the person having lawful control over the use of the computer;

   (b) During the said period, information of the kind contained in the electronic record or of the kind from which the information so contained is derived was regularly fed into the computer in the ordinary course of the said activities;

   (c) Throughout the material part of the said period, the computer was operating properly or, if not, then in respect of any period in which it was not operating properly or was out of operation during that part of the period, was not such as to affect the electronic record or the accuracy of its contents; and

   (d) The information contained in the electronic record reproduces or is derived from such information fed into the computer in the ordinary course of the said activities.

3. Where over any period, the functions of storing or processing information for the purposes of any activities of any regularly carried on over that period as mentioned in clause (a) of sub-section (2) was regularly performed by computer, whether:

   (a) By a combination of computers operating over that period; or

   (b) By different computers operating in succession over that period; or

EXHIBIT 4   **183**

(c) By different combinations of computers operating in succession over that period; or

(d) In any other manner involving the successive operation over that period, in whatever order, of one or more computers and one or more combinations of computers.

All the computers used for that purpose during that period shall be treated for the purposes of this section as constituting a single computer; and references in this section to a computer shall be construed accordingly.

4. In any proceedings where it is desired to give a statement in evidence by virtue of this section, a certificate doing any of the following things, that is to say:

(a) Identifying the electronic record containing the statement and describing the manner in which it was produced;

(b) Giving such particulars of any device involved in the production of that electronic record as may be appropriate for the purpose of showing that the electronic record was produced by a computer,

(c) Dealing with any of the matters to which the conditions mentioned in sub-section (2) relate,

and purporting to be signed by a person occupying a responsible official position in relation to the operation of the relevant device or the management of the relevant activities (whichever is appropriate) shall be evidence of any matter stated in the certificate; and for the purpose of this sub-section it shall be sufficient for a matter to be stated to the best of the knowledge and belief of the person stating it.

5. For the purposes of this section:

(a) Information shall be taken to be supplied to a computer if it is supplied thereto in any appropriate form and whether it is so supplied directly or (with or without human intervention) by means of any appropriate equipment;

(b) Whether in the course of activities carried on by any official, information is supplied with a view to its being stored or processed for the purposes of those activities by a computer operated otherwise than in the course of those activities, that information, if duly supplied to that computer, shall be taken to be supplied to it in the course of those activities;

(c) A computer output shall be taken to have been produced by a computer whether it was produced by it directly or (with or without human intervention) by means of any appropriate equipment.

EXHIBIT 5

UNIFI—ISO 90022—SAMPLE MESSAGE FLOWS CUSTOMER CREDIT TRANSFER INITIATION

SCENARIO

The customer credit transfer initiation messages are sent from the initiating party to the debtor agent. Depending on the service level agreed between the debtor agent and initiating party, the debtor agent may send a payment status report message to inform the initiating party of the status of the initiation. Other than the scenario depicted here diagrammatically, there could be different types of scenarios as:

(i) One actor playing roles of initiating party, debtor and ultimate debtor and one actor playing roles of creditor and ultimate creditor

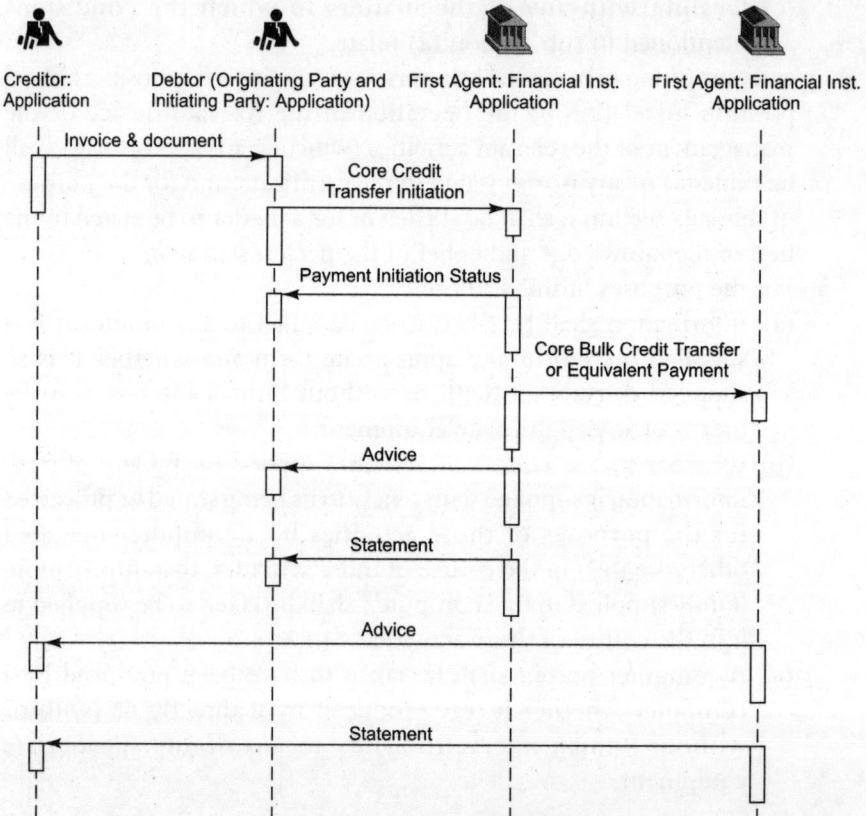

Creditor: Application	Debtor (Originating Party and Initiating Party: Application)	First Agent: Financial Inst. Application	First Agent: Financial Inst. Application

Invoice & document

Core Credit Transfer Initiation

Payment Initiation Status

Core Bulk Credit Transfer or Equivalent Payment

Advice

Statement

Advice

Statement

The message flow between various counter-parties under ISO 90022

EXHIBIT 5   185

(ii) One actor playing roles of initiating party and debtor, with a different actor for the role of ultimate debtor

(iii) Three different actors playing the roles of initiating party, debtor and ultimate debtor

Scenario A—ISO 90022 currently supports the following messages: credit transfer initiation, FI-to-FI customer credit transfer, payment initiation status.

The anticipated message flows for this scenario are expected to be:

Step 1: The seller sends the invoice message to the buyer.

Step 2: The buyer gives payment instructions through credit transfer to his bank.

Step 3: The buyer bank gives payment instructions to the seller's bank through bulk credit transfer or equivalent payment.

The transactions status can be obtained at various times through the following messages:

Step 4: Payment initiation status to buyer/payer.

Step 5: Payment advice to buyer.

Step 6: Statement of account to buyer.

Step 7: Payment receipt by seller bank to buyer/payer.

Presently message formats for Step 2, 3 and 4 have been developed by ISTH.

EXHIBIT 6

UNIFI-ISO 20022—SAMPLE MESSAGE DEFINITION SAMPLE MESSAGE: CUSTOMER CREDIT TRANSFER INITIATION

SCOPE

The customer credit transfer initiation message is sent by the initiating party to the forwarding agent or debtor agent. It is used to request movement of funds from the debtor's account to a creditor.

To enable the user to read the message, a high level structure of the type of payment instructions supported by the message is as follows:

```
+ Message Header                    – One in the message
|
 + Payment Batch 1                  – Multiple, e.g. Salary Payment
 | (Key Information at Batch Level – Dr Account, Dr Bank, Payment Method, etc.)
 + Payment Batch 2                  – e.g. Vendor Payment
 | |
 | + Instruction 1                  – Multiple e.g. Beneficiary – Joseph
 | | (Key Information at Instruction Level – Amount, Beneficiary Bank, Beneficiary etc ..)
 | + Instruction 2                  – e.g. Beneficiary – Martin
 | | |
 | | + Remittance Information       – Multiple, e.g. Salary Details
 | | | |
 | | | + Payment Amount Break-up    – Multiple, e.g. Salary Break-up
 | | |
 | | + Regulatory Reporting         – Multiple, e.g. Tax Reporting
 | | |
 | | + Information to Beneficiary bank  – Multiple
 | | |
 | | + Related Remittance Information – Multiple, Maximum 10
 | |
 | + Instruction n
 |
 + Payment Batch n
```

EXHIBIT 6   **187**

The values in the 'Mult' column in the Table are to be read as under:

[1..1]   – This field or group must appear once

[0..1]   – Optional, can appear once

[1..n]   – This field or group must appear at least once, and can be repeated multiple times

[0..n]   – Optional, can appear multiple times

[0..10] – Optional, can appear maximum 10 times in the group

Table 6.1

Index	Or	Message Item	<XML Tag>	Mult. Represent./Type
1		GroupHeader	<GrpHdr>	[1..1]
1.1		MessageIdentification	<MsgId>	[1..1] Text
1.2		CreationDateTime	<CreDtTm>	[1..1] DateTime
1.3		Authorisation	<Authstn>	[0..2] Text
1.4		BatchBooking	<BtchBookg>	[0..1] Indicator
1.5		NumberOfTransactions	<NbOfTxs>	[1..1] Text
1.6		ControlSum	<CtrlSum>	[0..1] Quantity
1.7		Grouping	<Grpg>	[1..1] Code
1.8		InitiatingParty	<InitgPty>	[1..1] +
1.9		ForwardingAgent	<FwdgAgt>	[0..1] +

Index	Or	Message Item	<XML Tag>	Mult. Represent./Type
2.0		PaymentInformation	<PmtInf>	[1..n]
2.1		PaymentInformationIdentification	<PmtInfId>	[0..1] Text
2.2		PaymentMethod	<PmtMtd>	[1..1] Code
2.3		PaymentTypeInformation	<PmtTpInf>	[0..1]
2.4		InstructionPriority	<InstrPrty>	[0..1] Code
2.5	{Or	ServiceLevel	<SvcLvl>	[0..1]
2.6	{{Or	Code	<Cd>	[1..1] Code
2.7	Or}}	Proprietary	<Prtry>	[1..1] Text
2.8	Or}	ClearingChannel	<ClrChanl>	[0..1] Code
2.9		LocalInstrument	<LclInstrm>	[0..1]
2.10	{Or	Code	<Cd>	[1..1] Text
2.11	Or}	Proprietary	<Prtry>	[1..1] Text
2.12		CategoryPurpose	<CtgyPurp>	[0..1] Code
2.13		RequestedExecutionDate	<ReqdExctnDt>	[1..1] DateTime
2.14		PoolingAdjustmentDate	<PoolgAdjstmntDt>	[0..1] DateTime
2.15		Debtor	<Dbtr>	[1..1] +
2.16		DebtorAccount	<DbtrAcct>	[1..1] +
2.17		DebtorAgent	<DbtrAgt>	[1..1] +
2.18		DebtorAgentAccount	<DbtrAgtAcct>	[0..1] +
2.19		UltimateDebtor	<UltmtDbtr>	[0..1] +
2.20		ChargeBearer	<ChrgBr>	[0..1] Code
2.21		ChargesAccount	<ChrgsAcct>	[0..1] +
2.22		ChargesAccountAgent	<ChrgsAcctAgt>	[0..1] +

Index	Or	Message Item	<XML Tag>	Mult. Represent./Type
2.23		CreditTransferTransactionInformation	<CdtTrfTxInf>	[1..n]
2.24		PaymentIdentification	<PmtId>	[1..1]
2.25		InstructionIdentification	<InstrId>	[0..1] Text
2.26		EndToEndIdentification	<EndToEndId>	[1..1] Text
2.27		PaymentTypeInformation	<PmtTpInf>	[0..1]
2.28		InstructionPriority	<InstrPrty>	[0..1] Code
2.29	{Or	ServiceLevel	<SvcLvl>	[0..1]
2.30	{{Or	Code	<Cd>	[1..1] Code
2.31	Or}}	Proprietary	<Prtry>	[1..1] Text
2.32	Or}	ClearingChannel	<ClrChanl>	[0..1] Code
2.33		LocalInstrument	<LclInstrm>	[0..1]
2.34	{Or	Code	<Cd>	[1..1] Text
2.35	Or}	Proprietary	<Prtry>	[1..1] Text
2.36		CategoryPurpose	<CtgyPurp>	[0..1] Code
2.37		Amount	<Amt>	[1..1]
2.38	{Or	InstructedAmount	<InstdAmt>	[1..1] Amount
2.39	Or}	EquivalentAmount	<EqvtAmt>	[1..1]
2.40		Amount	<Amt>	[1..1] Amount
2.41		CurrencyOfTransfer	<CcyOfTrf>	[1..1] Code
2.42		ExchangeRateInformation	<XchgRateInf>	[0..1]
2.43		ExchangeRate	<XchgRate>	[0..1] Rate
2.44		RateType	<RateTp>	[0..1] Code
2.45		ContractIdentification	<CtrctId>	[0..1] Text
2.46		ChargeBearer	<ChrgBr>	[0..1] Code
2.47		ChequeInstruction	<ChqInstr>	[0..1] +
2.48		UltimateDebtor	<UltmtDbtr>	[0..1] +
2.49		IntermediaryAgent1	<IntrmyAgt1>	[0..1] +
2.50		IntermediaryAgent1Account	<IntrmyAgt1Acct>	[0..1] +
2.51		IntermediaryAgent2	<IntrmyAgt2>	[0..1] +
2.52		IntermediaryAgent2Account	<IntrmyAgt2Acct>	[0..1] +
2.53		IntermediaryAgent3	<IntrmyAgt3>	[0..1] +
2.54		IntermediaryAgent3Account	<IntrmyAgt3Acct>	[0..1] +
2.55		CreditorAgent	<CdtrAgt>	[1..1] +
2.56		CreditorAgentAccount	<CdtrAgtAcct>	[0..1] +
2.57		Creditor	<Cdtr>	[0..1] +
2.58		CreditorAccount	<CdtrAcct>	[0..1] +
2.59		UltimateCreditor	<UltmtCdtr>	[0..1] +

EXHIBIT 6   189

Index	Or	Message Item	<XML Tag>	Mult. Represent./Type
2.60		InstructionForCreditorAgent	\<InstrForCdtrAgt\>	[0..n]
2.61		Code	\<Cd\>	[0..1] Code
2.62		InstructionInformation	\<InstrInf\>	[0..1] Text
2.63		InstructionForDebtorAgent	\<InstrForDbtrAgt\>	[0..1] Text
2.64		Purpose	\<Purp\>	[0..1]
2.65	{Or	Code	\<Cd\>	[1..1] Text
2.66	Or}	Proprietary	\<Prtry\>	[1..1] Text
2.67		RegulatoryReporting	\<RgltryRptg\>	[0..10]
2.68		DebitCreditReportingIndicator	\<DbtCdtRptgInd\>	[0..1] Code
2.69		Authority	\<Authrty\>	[0..1]
2.70		AuthorityName	\<AuthrtyNm\>	[0..1] Text
2.71		AuthorityCountry	\<AuthrtyCtry\>	[0..1] Code
2.72		RegulatoryDetails	\<RgltryDtls\>	[0..1]
2.73		Code	\<Cd\>	[0..1] Text
2.74		Amount	\<Amt\>	[0..1] Amount
2.75		Information	\<Inf\>	[0..1] Text
2.76		Tax	\<Tax\>	[0..1] +
2.77		RelatedRemittanceInformation	\<RltdRmtInf\>	[0..10]
2.78		RemittanceIdentification	\<RmtId\>	[0..1] Text
2.79		RemittanceLocationMethod	\<RmtLctnMtd\>	[0..1] Code
2.80		RemittanceLocationElectronicAddress	\<RmtLctn ElctrncAdr\>	[0..1] Text
2.81		RemittanceLocationPostalAddress	\<RmtLctnPstlAdr\>	[0..1]
2.82		Name	\<Nm\>	[1..1] Text
2.83		Address	\<Adr\>	[1..1] +
2.84		RemittanceInformation	\<RmtInf\>	[0..1]
2.85		Unstructured	\<Ustrd\>	[0..n] Text
2.86		Structured	\<Strd\>	[0..n]
2.87		ReferredDocumentInformation	\<RfrdDocInf\>	[0..1]
2.88		ReferredDocumentType	\<RfrdDocTp\>	[0..1]
2.89	Or	Code	\<Cd\>	[1..1] Code
2.90	Or}	Proprietary	\<Prtry\>	[1..1] Text
2.91		Issuer	\<Issr\>	[0..1] Text
2.92		ReferredDocumentNumber	\<RfrdDocNb\>	[0..1] Text
2.93		ReferredDocumentRelatedDate	\<RfrdDocRltdDt\>	[0..1] DateTime

Index	Or	Message Item	<XML Tag>	Mult. Represent./Type
2.94		ReferredDocumentAmount	<RfrdDocAmt>	[0..n]
2.95	{Or	DuePayableAmount	<DuePyblAmt>	[1..1] Amount
2.96	Or	DiscountAppliedAmount	<DscntApldAmt>	[1..1] Amount
2.97	Or	RemittedAmount	<RmtdAmt>	[1..1] Amount
2.98	Or	CreditNoteAmount	<CdtNoteAmt>	[1..1] Amount
2.99	Or}	TaxAmount	<TaxAmt>	[1..1] Amount

Index	Or	Message Item	<XML Tag>	Mult. Represent./Type
2.100		CreditorReferenceInformation	<CdtrRefInf>	[0..1]
2.101		CreditorReferenceType	<CdtrRefTp>	[0..1]
2.102	{Or	Code	<Cd>	[1..1] Code
2.103	Or}	Proprietary	<Prtry>	[1..1] Text
2.104		Issuer	<Issr>	[0..1] Text
2.105		CreditorReference	<CdtrRef>	[0..1] Text
2.106		Invoicer	<Invcr>	[0..1] +
2.107		Invoicee	<Invcee>	[0..1] +
2.108		AdditionalRemittanceInformation	<AddtlRmtInf>	[0..1] Text

The payment message format in the ISO 90022 format

EXHIBIT 7

UNCITRAL—MODEL LAW ON ELECTRONIC COMMERCE

Part One—Electronic Commerce in General

Chapter I—General Provisions

Chapter II—Application of Legal Requirements to Data Messages

Chapter III—Communication of Data Messages

Part Two—Electronic Commerce in Specific Areas

Chapter I—Carriage of Goods

PART ONE—ELECTRONIC COMMERCE IN GENERAL

Chapter I. General Provisions

Article 1. Sphere of application★

This Law★★ applies to any kind of information in the form of a data message used in the context★★★ of commercial★★★★ activities.

★The Commission suggests the following text for States that might wish to limit the applicability of this Law to international data messages:

"This Law applies to a data message as defined in paragraph (1) of article 2 where the data message relates to international commerce."

★★This Law does not override any rule of law intended for the protection of consumers.

★★★The Commission suggests the following text for States that might wish to extend the applicability of this Law:

"This Law applies to any kind of information in the form of a data message, except in the following situations: [...]."

★★★★The term "commercial" should be given a wide interpretation so as to cover matters arising from all relationships of a commercial nature, whether contractual or not.

Relationships of a commercial nature include, but are not limited to, the following transactions:

Any trade transaction for the supply or exchange of goods or services; distribution agreement; commercial representation or agency; factoring; leasing; construction of works; consulting; engineering; licensing; investment; financing; banking; insurance; exploitation agreement or concession; joint venture and other forms of industrial or business co-operation; carriage of goods or passengers by air, sea, rail or road.

Article 2. Definitions

For the purposes of this law:

(a) "Data message" means information generated, sent, received or stored by electronic, optical or similar means including, but not limited to, electronic data interchange (EDI), electronic mail, telegram, telex or telecopy;

(b) "Electronic data interchange" (EDI) means the electronic transfer from computer to computer of information using an agreed standard to structure the information;

(c) "Originator" of a data message means a person by whom, or on whose behalf, the data message purports to have been sent or generated prior to storage, if any, but it does not include a person acting as an intermediary with respect to that data message;

(d) "Addressee" of a data message means a person who is intended by the originator to receive the data message, but does not include a person acting as an intermediary with respect to that data message;

(e) "Intermediary", with respect to a particular data message, means a person who, on behalf of another person, sends, receives or stores that data message or provides other services with respect to that data message;

EXHIBIT 7   **193**

(f) "Information system" means a system for generating, sending, receiving, storing or otherwise processing data messages.

Article 3. Interpretation

1. In the interpretation of this law, regard is to be had to its international origin and to the need to promote uniformity in its application and the observance of good faith.
2. Questions concerning matters governed by this law which are not expressly settled in it are to be settled in conformity with the general principles on which this law is based.

Article 4. Variation by agreement

1. As between parties involved in generating, sending, receiving, storing or otherwise processing data messages, and except as otherwise provided, the provisions of chapter III may be varied by agreement.
2. Paragraph (1) does not affect any right that may exist to modify by agreement any rule of law referred to in chapter II.

Chapter II. Application of Legal Requirements to Data Messages

Article 5. Legal recognition of data messages

Information shall not be denied legal effect, validity or enforceability solely on the grounds that it is in the form of a data message.

Article 5 bis. Incorporation by reference

(As adopted by the Commission at its thirty-first session, in June 1998)

Information shall not be denied legal effect, validity or enforceability solely on the grounds that it is not contained in the data message purporting to give rise to such legal effect, but is merely referred to in that data message.

Article 6. Writing

1. Where the law requires information to be in writing, that requirement is met by a data message if the information contained therein is accessible so as to be usable for subsequent reference.
2. Paragraph (1) applies whether the requirement therein is in the form of an obligation or whether the law simply provides consequences for the information not being in writing.
3. The provisions of this article do not apply to the following: [...].

Article 7. Signature

1. Where the law requires a signature of a person, that requirement is met in relation to a data message if:

(a) A method is used to identify that person and to indicate that person's approval of the information contained in the data message; and

(b) That method is as reliable as was appropriate for the purpose for which the data message was generated or communicated, in the light of all the circumstances, including any relevant agreement.

2. Paragraph (1) applies whether the requirement therein is in the form of an obligation or whether the law simply provides consequences for the absence of a signature.

3. The provisions of this article do not apply to the following: [...].

Article 8. Original

1. Where the law requires information to be presented or retained in its original form, that requirement is met by a data message if:

(a) There exists a reliable assurance as to the integrity of the information from the time when it was first generated in its final form, as a data message or otherwise; and

(b) Where it is required that information be presented, that information is capable of being displayed to the person to whom it is to be presented.

2. Paragraph (1) applies whether the requirement therein is in the form of an obligation or whether the law simply provides consequences for the information not being presented or retained in its original form.

3. For the purposes of subparagraph (a) of paragraph (1):

(a) The criteria for assessing integrity shall be whether the information has remained complete and unaltered, apart from the addition of any endorsement and any change which arises in the normal course of communication, storage and display; and

(b) The standard of reliability required shall be assessed in the light of the purpose for which the information was generated and in the light of all the relevant circumstances.

4. The provisions of this article do not apply to the following: [...].

Article 9. Admissibility and evidential weight of data messages

1. In any legal proceedings, nothing in the application of the rules of evidence shall apply so as to deny the admissibility of a data message in evidence:

(a) On the sole ground that it is a data message; or,

(b) If it is the best evidence that the person adducing it could reasonably be expected to obtain, on the grounds that it is not in its original form.

EXHIBIT 7   **195**

2. Information in the form of a data message shall be given due evidential weight. In assessing the evidential weight of a data message, regard shall be had to the reliability of the manner in which the data message was generated, stored or communicated, to the reliability of the manner in which the integrity of the information was maintained, to the manner in which its originator was identified, and to any other relevant factor.

Article 10. Retention of data messages

1. Where the law requires that certain documents, records or information be retained, that requirement is met by retaining data messages, provided that the following conditions are satisfied:
   (a) The information contained therein is accessible so as to be usable for subsequent reference; and
   (b) The data message is retained in the format in which it was generated, sent or received, or in a format which can be demonstrated to represent accurately the information generated, sent or received; and
   (c) Such information, if any, is retained as enables the identification of the origin and destination of a data message and the date and time when it was sent or received.
2. An obligation to retain documents, records or information in accordance with paragraph (1) does not extend to any information the sole purpose of which is to enable the message to be sent or received.
3. A person may satisfy the requirement referred to in paragraph (1) by using the services of any other person, provided that the conditions set forth in subparagraphs (a), (b) and (c) of paragraph (1) are met.

Chapter III. Communication of Data Messages

Article 11. Formation and validity of contracts

1. In the context of contract formation, unless otherwise agreed by the parties, an offer and the acceptance of an offer may be expressed by means of data messages. Where a data message is used in the formation of a contract, that contract shall not be denied validity or enforceability on the sole ground that a data message was used for that purpose.
2. The provisions of this article do not apply to the following: [...].

Article 12. Recognition by parties of data messages

1. As between the originator and the addressee of a data message, a declaration of will or other statement shall not be denied legal effect, validity or enforceability solely on the grounds that it is in the form of a data message.
2. The provisions of this article do not apply to the following: [...].

Article 13. Attribution of data messages

1. A data message is that of the originator if it was sent by the originator itself.
2. As between the originator and the addressee, a data message is deemed to be that of the originator if it was sent:
   (a) By a person who had the authority to act on behalf of the originator in respect of that data message; or
   (b) By an information system programmed by, or on behalf of, the originator to operate automatically.
3. As between the originator and the addressee, an addressee is entitled to regard a data message as being that of the originator, and to act on that assumption, if:
   (a) In order to ascertain whether the data message was that of the originator, the addressee properly applied a procedure previously agreed to by the originator for that purpose; or
   (b) The data message as received by the addressee resulted from the actions of a person whose relationship with the originator or with any agent of the originator enabled that person to gain access to a method used by the originator to identify data messages as its own.
4. Paragraph (3) does not apply:
   (a) As of the time when the addressee has both received notice from the originator that the data message is not that of the originator, and had reasonable time to act accordingly; or
   (b) In a case within paragraph (3)*(b)*, at any time when the addressee knew or should have known, had it exercised reasonable care or used any agreed procedure, that the data message was not that of the originator.
5. Where a data message is that of the originator or is deemed to be that of the originator, or the addressee is entitled to act on that assumption, then, as between the originator and the addressee, the addressee is entitled to regard the data message as received as being what the originator intended to send, and to act on that assumption. The addressee is not so entitled when it knew or should have known, had it exercised reasonable care or used any agreed procedure, that the transmission resulted in any error in the data message as received.
6. The addressee is entitled to regard each data message received as a separate data message and to act on that assumption, except to the extent that it duplicates another data message and the addressee knew or should have known, had it exercised reasonable care or used any agreed procedure, that the data message was a duplicate.

EXHIBIT 7   197

Article 14. Acknowledgement of receipt

1. Paragraphs (2) to (4) of this article apply where, on or before sending a data message, or by means of that data message, the originator has requested or has agreed with the addressee that receipt of the data message be acknowledged.

2. Where the originator has not agreed with the addressee that the acknowledgement be given in a particular form or by a particular method, an acknowledgement may be given by
   (a) Any communication by the addressee, automated or otherwise, or
   (b) Any conduct of the addressee sufficient to indicate to the originator that the data message has been received.

3. Where the originator has stated that the data message is conditional on receipt of the acknowledgement, the data message is treated as though it has never been sent, until the acknowledgement is received.

4. Where the originator has not stated that the data message is conditional on receipt of the acknowledgement, and the acknowledgement has not been received by the originator within the time specified or agreed or, if no time has been specified or agreed, within a reasonable time, the originator:
   (a) May give notice to the addressee stating that no acknowledgement has been received and specifying a reasonable time by which the acknowledgement must be received; and
   (b) If the acknowledgement is not received within the time specified in subparagraph (a), may, upon notice to the addressee, treat the data message as though it had never been sent, or exercise any other rights it may have.

5. Where the originator receives the addressee's acknowledgement of receipt, it is presumed that the related data message was received by the addressee. That presumption does not imply that the data message corresponds to the message received.

6. Where the received acknowledgement states that the related data message met technical requirements, either agreed upon or set forth in applicable standards, it is presumed that those requirements have been met.

7. Except in so far as it relates to the sending or receipt of the data message, this article is not intended to deal with the legal consequences that may flow either from that data message or from the acknowledgement of its receipt.

Article 15. Time and place of dispatch and receipt of data messages

1. Unless otherwise agreed between the originator and the addressee, the dispatch of a data message occurs when it enters an information

system outside the control of the originator or of the person who sent the data message on behalf of the originator.

2. Unless otherwise agreed between the originator and the addressee, the time of receipt of a data message is determined as follows:

   (a) If the addressee has designated an information system for the purpose of receiving data messages, receipt occurs:

       (i) At the time when the data message enters the designated information system; or

       (ii) If the data message is sent to an information system of the addressee that is not the designated information system, at the time when the data message is retrieved by the addressee;

   (b) If the addressee has not designated an information system, receipt occurs when the data message enters an information system of the addressee.

3. Paragraph (2) applies notwithstanding that the place where the information system is located may be different from the place where the data message is deemed to be received under paragraph (4).

4. Unless otherwise agreed between the originator and the addressee, a data message is deemed to be dispatched at the place where the originator has its place of business, and is deemed to be received at the place where the addressee has its place of business. For the purposes of this paragraph:

   (a) If the originator or the addressee has more than one place of business, the place of business is that which has the closest relationship to the underlying transaction or, where there is no underlying transaction, the principal place of business;

   (b) If the originator or the addressee does not have a place of business, reference is to be made to its habitual residence.

5. The provisions of this article do not apply to the following: [...].

PART TWO—ELECTRONIC COMMERCE IN SPECIFIC AREAS

Chapter I. Carriage of Goods

Article 16. Actions related to contracts of carriage of goods

Without derogating from the provisions of part one of this Law, this chapter applies to any action in connection with, or in pursuance of, a contract of carriage of goods, including but not limited to:

   (a) 1. Furnishing the marks, number, quantity or weight of goods;
       2. Stating or declaring the nature or value of goods;

EXHIBIT 7   **199**

    3.   Issuing a receipt for goods;

    4.   Confirming that goods have been loaded;

(b) 1.   Notifying a person of terms and conditions of the contract;

    2.   Giving instructions to a carrier;

(c) 1.   Claiming delivery of goods;

    2.   Authorizing release of goods;

    3.   Giving notice of loss of, or damage to, goods;

(d) Giving any other notice or statement in connection with the performance of the contract;

(e) Undertaking to deliver goods to a named person or a person authorized to claim delivery;

(f) Granting, acquiring, renouncing, surrendering, transferring or negotiating rights in goods;

(g) Acquiring or transferring rights and obligations under the contract.

Article 17. Transport documents

1. Subject to paragraph (3), where the law requires that any action referred to in article 16 be carried out in writing or by using a paper document, that requirement is met if the action is carried out by using one or more data messages.

2. Paragraph (1) applies whether the requirement therein is in the form of an obligation or whether the law simply provides consequences for failing either to carry out the action in writing or to use a paper document.

3. If a right is to be granted to, or an obligation is to be acquired by, one person and no other person, and if the law requires that, in order to effect this, the right or obligation must be conveyed to that person by the transfer, or use of, a paper document, that requirement is met if the right or obligation is conveyed by using one or more data messages, provided that a reliable method is used to render such data message or messages unique.

4. For the purposes of paragraph (3), the standard of reliability required shall be assessed in the light of the purpose for which the right or obligation was conveyed and in the light of all the circumstances, including any relevant agreement.

5. Where one or more data messages are used to effect any action in subparagraphs (f) and (g) of article 16, no paper document used to effect any such action is valid unless the use of data messages has been terminated and replaced by the use of paper documents. A paper document issued in these circumstances shall contain a statement of such termination. The replacement of data messages by paper documents shall not affect the rights or obligations of the parties involved.

6. If a rule of law is compulsorily applicable to a contract of carriage of goods which is in, or is evidenced by, a paper document, that rule shall not be inapplicable to such a contract of carriage of goods which is evidenced by one or more data messages by reason of the fact that the contract is evidenced by such data message or messages instead of by a paper document.

7. The provisions of this article do not apply to the following: [...]

EXHIBIT 8

COUNTRIES THAT HAVE LEGISLATIONS ADOPTING PROVISIONS OF MODEL LAW ON ELECTRONIC COMMERCE

Legislation implementing provisions of the Model Law has been adopted in:
Singapore (1998), Australia (1999), Colombia★ (1999), Republic of Korea (1999), Bermuda (1999), the United States (Uniform Electronic Transactions Act, adopted in 1999 by the National Conference of Commissioners on Uniform State Law), Canada (Uniform Electronic Commerce Act, adopted in 1999 by the Uniform Law Conference of Canada), France (2000), India★ (2000), Ireland (2000), Mauritius (2000), Mexico (2000), Philippines (2000), Slovenia (2000), the Bailiwick of Guernsey (2000), the Bailiwick of Jersey (2000) and the Isle of Man (2000), all Crown dependencies of the United Kingdom of Great Britain and Northern Ireland, namely Cayman Islands (2000), and the Turks and Caicos Islands (2000), overseas territories of the United Kingdom of Great Britain and Northern Ireland; and in the Hong Kong Special Administrative Region of China (2000), Jordan (2001), Panama★ (2001), Venezuela (2001), the Province of Quebec (2001), Dominican Republic★ (2002), Ecuador★ (2002), New Zealand (2002), Pakistan (2002), South Africa★ (2002), Thailand (2002), China (2004), Vietnam (2005), and Sri Lanka (2006)

★ Adopted except for the provisions on certification and electronic signatures

EXHIBIT 9

STRUCTURE AND KEY CONDITIONS OF UCP 500, URC 522 AND ISP98

UCP 500

The latest revision of the Uniform Customs and Practices (UCP) for Documentary Credit has 49 Articles under the following sections:

- A. General provisions and definitions (Articles 1–5)
- B. Form and notification of credits (Articles 6–10)
- C. Liabilities and responsibilities (Articles 13–19)
- D. Documents (Articles 20–38)
- E. Miscellaneous provisions (Articles 39–47)
- F. Transferable credit (Article 48)
- G. Assignment of proceeds (Article 49)

Section A defines the scope of operations and liabilities for the LC issuing banks. It specifies that under an LC all parties concerned deal with documents and not with goods, services and/or other performances to which the documents may relate. It also specifies that LCs are separate transactions from sales or other contract(s) on which they may be based and banks are in no way concerned with or bound by such contract(s), even if any reference whatsoever to such contract(s) is included in the credit.

Section B outlines the types of letters of credit—revocable and irrevocable. Revocable credits can be cancelled without prior notice or consent of the beneficiary. In trade practice most LCs issued are irrevocable. The section also talks about the responsibility of the 'advising bank' to verify the authenticity of the LC issuing bank before advising the LC to the beneficiary. The section also discusses the role of the 'confirming bank'. In international trade the country from where the LC has been issued could be conceived to give rise to payment risk if sufficient foreign exchange reserves are not available with the country for payment of the goods. Having the LC confirmed by a bank in the developed country can cover such risks. The LC confirming bank thus steps into the shoes of the LC issuing bank for making payment under the LC and in turn is covered by the LC issuing bank.

Section C states that banks must examine all documents stipulated in the credit with reasonable care and the issuing bank, the confirming bank, if any, or a nominated bank acting on their behalf, shall each have a reasonable time—not to exceed seven banking days following the day of receipt of the documents—to examine the documents and determine whether to take up or refuse the documents and to inform the party. The banks do not assume

EXHIBIT 9   **203**

liability in case of delay, loss or damage to documents when their agents such as, couriers handle the documents. Similarly, the bank is not liable for delay or loss of transmission messages.

Section D is the most important section for LC operations and it defines the documents that are presented under the LC. The section states that when documents other than transport documents, insurance documents and commercial invoices are called for, the credit should stipulate by whom such documents are to be issued and their wording or data content. Where original documents are required, for e.g. bill of lading, banks will accept as an original documents like computerized statements, carbon copies, etc. provided that the document is marked as original and, where necessary, appears to be signed in some way. The section then goes on to define the specifications for the following documents:

- Ocean bill of lading
- Non-negotiable Seaway bill
- Charter party bill of lading
- Multi-modal transport document
- Air transport document
- Road, rail or inland waterway transport documents
- Courier and postal receipts
- Transport documents issued by freight forwarders
- Insurance documents
- Commercial invoices

Section D also describes acceptance of the freight payable/freight pre-paid documents. The section further specifies that if ambiguous terminologies such as, "first class," "well-known," "qualified," etc. are used, banks will accept the relative document(s) as presented, provided that it appears on its face to be in compliance with the other terms and conditions of the LC.

Section E covers the treatment of amount and quantity covered under the LC. If the words 'approx', 'about', etc. have been used along with the amount of the LC, a tolerance of +/- 10% will be allowed on the amount or the quantity or the unit price to which they refer. Further, partial drawings and/or shipments are allowed, unless the credit stipulates otherwise; i.e. the seller can present documents more than once under the LC and claim money as per the terms of the LC.

Section E also specifies that all credits must stipulate an expiry date and a place for presentation of documents for payment. It goes on to add that the banks must specify a period after the expiry date during which the documents as per the LC must be presented to the bank and that if this period is not specified it will be deemed to be 21 days after the shipment. The section also defines how holidays should be handled.

Sections F and G discuss the transferability of a LC. This situation is required where the seller wishes for example, to outsource the production to another party. So, instead of issuing a new LC, the same LC that has been received by the seller is transferred to the third party in their favor so that they become the beneficiaries of the LC.

URC 522

The Uniform Rules for Collections (URC 522) has the following 6 sections:
A. General provision
B. Form and structure of collections
C. Form of presentation
D. Liabilities and responsibilities
E. Payment
F. Interest charges and expenses
G. Other provisions

Section A defines that provisions of URC are applied on collections defined as handling of documents by banks in order to:
1. Obtain payment and/or acceptance, or
2. Deliver documents against payment and/or against acceptance, or
3. Deliver documents on other terms and conditions

Article 3 defines the parties to the collection process as under:
1. The 'Principal' or the seller who gives documents for collection
2. The 'Remitting bank' or the seller bank
3. The 'Collecting bank' or an intermediary bank
4. The 'Presenting bank' or the buyer bank
5. The 'Drawee' or the buyer

Section B defines that all collections must be accompanied with instructions to the bank and the banks will not examine the documents to obtain instructions. The collection instruction must contain amongst other things:
- The name and postal address of the drawee
- The amount to be collected
- List of documents included
- Details of the conditions for payment or acceptance
- Exact period of time in which the action must be taken by the drawee
- Charges to be collected
- Instructions in case of non-payment or non-acceptance

Section C covers the presentation process and the care that the presenting bank should exercise while presenting the documents and accepting payments or acceptance from the drawee.

EXHIBIT 9
205

Section D covers the liabilities and highlights the fact that the banks have no obligation to take any action in respect of the goods to which a documentary collection relates, including storage and insurance of the goods, even when specific instructions are given to do so. Banks will only take such action if, when, and to the extent to which they agree to do so in each case. The bank does not take liability for delay, loss or damage of documents in transit and so too for electronic messages.

Section E covers payments under the collections and specifies that partial payment should not be accepted for release of the documents unless allowed by the collection instructions. In case of receipt of payments in currency other than that specified in the collection order, the bank will verify the convertibility of the currency before accepting such payment as consideration for release of the documents.

Section F covers handling of interest and charges where, if the collection instruction specifies that interest be charged, then the presenting bank should not release the documents without the collection of interest charges. Similarly, where the collection instruction specifies that the collection or other charges are to be paid by the drawee, the presenting bank must ensure that these are collected before releasing the documents.

Section G states that the presenting bank is responsible for seeing that the form of the acceptance of a bill of exchange appears to be complete and correct, but is not responsible for the genuineness of any signature or for the authority of any signatory to sign the acceptance. The presenting bank must promptly advise the collecting bank/remitting bank of the payment, acceptance or non-payment and non-acceptance. The remitting bank is supposed to revert immediately with instructions in case of non-acceptance and if it does not do so within 60 days, the presenting bank may return the documents.

ISP 98

The International Standby Practices (ISP) is covered under the following sections:

Rule 1   General provisions
Rule 2   Obligations
Rule 3   Presentations
Rule 4   Examination
Rule 5   Notice, preclusion, and disposition of documents
Rule 6   Transfer, assignment, and transfer by operation of law
Rule 7   Cancellation
Rule 8   Reimbursement obligations
Rule 9   Timing
Rule 10 Syndication/participation

Under the general provisions, the standby is defined as an irrevocable, independent, documentary and binding undertaking. As the standby is independent, the enforceability of the issuer's obligation is not affected in any way through any provision in the underlying transaction or any other issue. Since a standby is documentary, an issuer's obligations depend only on the presentation of documents and an examination of required documents on their face. The general provisions also facilitate the SBLC to be operated electronically by presentation of documents through an electronic medium.

Rule 2 specifies the obligations of the issuer of the standby as having to pay or accept on complying presentation. A standby may nominate a person or agency to advise, receive a presentation, effect a transfer, confirm, pay, negotiate, incur a deferred payment obligation, or accept a draft, on their behalf. Any amendment to the standby should have the consent of the beneficiary. The advising bank has the responsibility to ensure the authenticity of the bank issuing the standby.

Rule 3 states that the standby should indicate the time, place and location within that place, person to whom, and medium in which presentation should be made. The receipt of a document or an electronic message (say from SWIFT) required by and presented under a standby constitutes a presentation. It must identify the standby under which the presentation is made. A presentation is timely if made at any time after issuance and before expiry of the expiration date. The presentation is deemed to be valid if the beneficiary makes a non-complying presentation and subsequently substitutes this or makes another complying presentation.

The beneficiary can make multiple presentations under the standby unless expressly stated otherwise. If words like "about" or "approx." are used to specify the amount, it would imply a variation of +/- 10% versus the amount mentioned in the standby. If the beneficiary makes a claim demanding the standby to be extended or to be paid otherwise, if it is not being paid then the beneficiary can treat this as a consent for extension of the standby. The rule also details how a presentation should be handled on holidays.

Rule 4 discusses examination of the demand document presented under the standby. The demand document must be issued in the same language as the standby; it should not be post-dated and, should be issued by the beneficiary. However, the bank does not need to do any signature verifications for the beneficiary. The text of the demand can be flexible unless some text has been specifically defined in the standby for inclusion in the demand. If the standby requires that the demand document must be counter-signed by the applicant or some other agency then this should be witnessed on the demand document.

Rule 5 outlines that the bank must give notice of dishonor of a demand to the beneficiary within 3 working days of receipt of a demand. If the issuer of

EXHIBIT 9 **207**

the standby believes that the demand is discrepant, then he may at his own discretion, seek waiver of the discrepancy from the applicant.

Rule 6 states that a standby is not transferable unless otherwise stated. The transfer can be effected by the issuer or the advising bank on receipt of a valid request from the beneficiary along with payment of any fee as required. The transferee can then make a claim under the standby, like a regular beneficiary.

Rule 7 regarding cancellation states, that the standby can be cancelled only with the consent of the beneficiary in writing and after obtaining the original standby.

Rule 8 states that where the issuer of the standby has made payment under a demand as per the terms of the standby, he is entitled to a reimbursement of the amount paid, from the applicant along with any fees and charges incurred by him.

Rule 9 states that the standby must have an expiry date. If no time for expiry is mentioned it is presumed to be the standard closing business hour at the place of presentation.

Rule 10 states that unless otherwise mentioned, the issuer can sell participation in the standby to other banks. This however, would not affect the rights of the beneficiary.

EXHIBIT 10

KEY CONSIDERATIONS OF e-UCP

The e-UCP is a supplement to the UCP covering electronic presentation of documents. It includes rules regarding such matters as the format for such documents, how they are to be presented, and what happens if they are corrupted. The International Chamber of Commerce emphasizes that the e-UCP is "an update rather than a full revision of the rules. It represents a bridge between current UCP500 and the processing of the electronic equivalent of paper-based documents and it is to be used in tandem with, *not* as a replacement of UCP500." As a supplement, the e-UCP does not alter the existing articles of UCP500. When documents are all to be presented in paper form, it has no effect.

For a letter of credit to be made subject to e-UCP it must specifically specify this. The e-UCP cannot stand on its own, and therefore incorporates the UCP. However, conversely a UCP based letter of credit does not incorporate e-UCP.

The e-UCP deals only with electronic presentation of documents and not with electronic creation or delivery of letters of credit. For example, since many years letters of credit have been issued electronically using SWIFT. These are typically, advised to the beneficiary by sending them by mail or courier. Some banks now also provide for electronic delivery of letters of credit through the portal or by mail.

By receiving the e-UCP based LC on paper, through mail or courier does not limit the beneficiary's ability to create and present documents electronically.

Even if a letter of credit is subject to the e-UCP, the letter of credit may stipulate that the beneficiary present some or all of the documents on paper. It is also possible for the applicant to give the beneficiary the option to present specified documents either on paper or electronically. This gives him the option to (a) present only paper documents that are subject to the provision of UCP or (b) present electronic documents as well, which are subject to the provision of e-UCP. This is addressed in e-UCP Articles e1 and e2.

The e-UCP anticipates that there will be "mixed presentations" of paper and electronic documents. Furthermore, it anticipates that presentation of electronic documents will happen individually rather than all the documents in a batch at the same time. In order to provide the banks with a mechanism for assembling these individual documents, the rules require that each presentation of documents include the relevant LC number and that the

EXHIBIT 10 **209**

beneficiary present a "notice of completeness" when all the documents have been presented.

Even a letter of credit that calls entirely for paper documents may be made subject to the e–UCP. The only change will be that the LC must specify acceptable formats for each document. There is no harm in making the LCs that call only for paper documents subject to the eUCP as long as this additional information is included. If the format specified for all documents is paper, none of the rest of the e–UCP applies—the LC is effectively the same as any LC issued subject to simply the UCP.

Just as letters of credit specify mailing addresses, LCs calling for electronic presentation will specify electronic addresses where documents have to be presented.

Like UCP, the eUCP does not specify any specific document formats. It is left to the parties to decide this bi-laterally. Practically, the format chosen must be one that the beneficiary or other originating party can create and that certainly the nominated bank, but probably also the issuing bank and the applicant, can read. The logical choices for documents would be as follows.

(a) If human readable documents are to be presented—Windows versions of Microsoft Word (*.doc), ASCII text (*.txt), and Adobe Acrobat 5.0 (*.pdf). Possibilities for scanned images include graphic image format (*.gif) and bitmaps (*.bmp). However some legal jurisdictions or companies may not accept some documents in scanned form, e.g. documents such as bill of lading or bill of negotiation.

(b) If computer readable documents are to be presented—XML based file formats as are being discussed by various standards and other agencies. Also possibly ASCII text (*.txt) file formats. However, in such a case it would be difficult to specify the format as a text of the LC unless a standard message format is being referred to.

Whether or not documents are presented as e-mail attachments, as in the case of formats, the parties must agree to the means of presentation. If e-mail is to be used as the means of presentation, concerns may arise about security.

Faxes fall within the e–UCP definition of electronic records. Nonetheless, they are not automatically acceptable. All e–UCP credits must specify the format, means of presentation and means of authentication for each document. The applicant will have to specify fax as an acceptable format and the bank nominated to receive presentation by fax, is expected to provide a fax number for the beneficiary to use. The means of authentication will also have to be specified and can be complex.

Further, the e–UCP requires that all electronic documents follow the standard security norms that address:

- Authenticity
- Integrity
- Non-repudiation
- Confidentiality

Unless otherwise instructed, the nominated bank is responsible for verifying not just the identity of the beneficiary who is presenting the documents, but also whether the document is complete and unaltered. It is recommended that the applicant specify means of authentication desired so that the nominated bank knows exactly what to do.

Article e5(f) covers this directly. It says, "an electronic record that cannot be authenticated is deemed, not to have been presented." This will result in a discrepancy that can possibly be corrected by the beneficiary or waived by the applicant as per regular UCP provisions.

Article e11 indicates that the bank receiving the corrupted file can require re-presentation without refusing the documents. It goes on to explain what happens to the deadlines for examination and presentation. Article e11 does not define what constitutes corruption of data. It is left to the courts/national law to interpret the meaning of corruption of an electronic record.

All this explains why the e-UCP implementation has been so difficult. Attempting to get all parties on standard message formats, standard mediums and at the same time, for successful conclusion of the transaction is a huge task. It is not simple to start using electronic documents, at least yet. Before a letter of credit is issued calling for electronic documents, the capabilities of all the parties to generate and process electronic documents will need to be assessed. Some of these are outlined as follows:

(a) The ability of the parties involved to create, send, receive and process electronic documents (systems capabilities, means of presentation, means of authentication, etc.)

(b) The data format for each e-document would have to be standardized. It is unimaginable to believe that each LC will specify the bits and bytes as document formats

(c) The medium of presentation and exchange of documents will have to be standardized and agreed upon and conditions of non-receipt of electronic documents will have to be managed by the systems and also as processes

(d) The ability of third party issuers, like carriers and insurance providers, to issue electronic documents

(e) The willingness of governmental authorities (e.g., customs and port authorities, the Ministry of Finance, exchange control boards) to accept electronic documents or even printed copies of electronic documents

EXHIBIT 10 **211**

(f) The legal framework in countries with respect to the legal status of electronic documents and electronic signatures—for example, in some countries electronic signatures are not inherently recognized as valid and binding; in other countries, like Singapore and the United States, electronic signatures are generally acceptable and valid, but not on bills of exchange, acceptability of electronic bill of lading etc.

The e-UCP is just a beginning and just highlights the complications of digitizing the traditional trade business of banks.

EXHIBIT 11

TABLE OF CONTENT—OBTAINING ELECTRONIC EVIDENCE IN CRIMINAL INVESTIGATIONS

TABLE OF CONTENTS

EXHIBIT 11   **213**

- II. SEARCHING AND SEIZING COMPUTERS
  WITH A WARRANT
  - ❏ A. Introduction
  - ❏ B. Planning the search
    1. Basic strategies for executing computer searches
       (a) When hardware is itself contraband, evidence, or an instrumentality or fruit of crime
       (b) When hardware is merely a storage device for evidence of crime
    2. The Privacy Protection Act
       (a) A brief history of the Privacy Protection Act
       (b) The terms of the Privacy Protection Act
       (c) Application of the PPA to computer searches and seizures
    3. Civil liability under the Electronic Communications Privacy Act
    4. Considering the need for multiple warrants in network searches
    5. No-knock warrants
    6. Sneak-and-peek warrants
    7. Privileged documents
       (a) The Attorney General's regulations relating to searches of disinterested lawyers, physicians and clergymen
       (b) Strategies for reviewing privileged computer files
  - ❏ C. Drafting the warrant and affidavit
    Step 1: Accurately and particularly describe the property to be seized in the warrant and/or attachments to the warrant
    Step 2: Establish probable cause in the affidavit
    Step 3: In the affidavit supporting the warrant, include an explanation of the search strategy (such as the need to conduct an off-site search) as well as the practical and legal considerations that will govern the execution of the search
  - ❏ D. Post-seizure issues
    1. Searching computers already in law enforcement custody
    2. The permissible time period for examining seized computers
    3. Rule 41(e) motions for return of property
- III. THE ELECTRONIC COMMUNICATIONS PRIVACY ACT
  - ❏ A. Introduction
  - ❏ B. Providers of electronic communication service vs. remote computing service
  - ❏ C. Classifying types of information held by service providers
    1. Basic subscriber information listed in 18 U.S.C. § 2703(c)(2)
    2. Records or other information pertaining to a customer or subscriber
    3. Contents

❑ D. Compelled disclosure under ECPA
   1. Subpoena
   2. Subpoena with prior notice to the subscriber or customer
   3. Section 2703(d) Order
   4. § 2703(d) Order with prior notice to the subscriber or customer
   5. Search warrant
❑ E. Voluntary disclosure
❑ F. Quick reference guide
❑ G. Working with network providers: preservation of evidence, preventing disclosure to subjects, and Cable Act issues
   1. Preservation of evidence under 18 U.S.C. § 2703(f)
   2. Orders not to disclose the existence of a warrant, subpoena, or court order
   3. The Cable Act, 47 U.S.C. § 551
❑ H. Remedies
   1. Suppression
   2. Civil actions and disclosures

• IV. ELECTRONIC SURVEILLANCE IN COMMUNICATIONS NETWORKS
❑ A. Introduction
❑ B. Content vs. addressing information
❑ C. The Pen/Trap Statute, 18 U.S.C. §§ 3121-3127
❑ D. The Wiretap Statute ("Title III"), 18 U.S.C. §§ 2510-2522
   1. Introduction: The general prohibition
   2. Key phrases
   3. Exceptions to Title III
      (a) Interception authorized by a Title III Order, 18 U.S.C. § 2518
      (b) Consent of a party to the communication, 18 U.S.C. § 2511(2)(c)-(d)
      (c) The Provider Exception, 18 U.S.C. § 2511(2)(a)(i)
      (d) The Computer Trespasser Exception, 18 U.S.C. § 2511(2)(i)
      (e) The Extension Telephone Exception, 18 U.S.C. § 2510(5)(a)
      (f) The 'Inadvertently Obtained Criminal Evidence' Exception, 18 U.S.C. § 2511(3)(b)(iv)
      (g) The 'Accessible to the Public' Exception, 18 U.S.C. § 2511(2)(g)(i)
❑ E. Remedies for violations of Title III and the Pen/Trap Statute
   1. Suppression remedies
      (a) Statutory suppression remedies
      (b) Constitutional suppression remedies

EXHIBIT 11   **215**

2. Defenses to civil and criminal actions
    (a) Good-faith defense
    (b) Qualified immunity
- V. EVIDENCE
  - ❑ A. Introduction
  - ❑ B. Authentication
    1. Authenticity and the alteration of computer records
    2. Establishing the reliability of computer programs
    3. Identifying the author of computer stored records
  - ❑ C. Hearsay
    1. Inapplicability of the Hearsay Rules to computer generated records
    2. Applicability of the Hearsay Rules to computer stored records
  - ❑ D. Other issues
    1. The Best Evidence Rule
    2. Computer printouts as "summaries"
- **End notes**
- APPENDIX A: Sample network banner language
- APPENDIX B: Sample 18 U.S.C. § 2703(d) application and order
- APPENDIX C: Sample language for preservation request letters under 18 U.S.C. § 2703(f)
- APPENDIX D:
  - ❑ 1. Model form for IP trap and trace on a web-based e-mail account
  - ❑ 2. Model form for pen register/trap and trace
  - ❑ 3. Model form for IP pen register/trap and trace on a computer network intruder
- APPENDIX E: Sample subpoena language
- APPENDIX F: Sample language for search warrants and accompanying affidavits to search and seize computers
- APPENDIX G: Sample letter for provider monitoring
- APPENDIX H: Sample authorization for monitoring of computer trespasser activity

REFERENCES

1. www.abnamro.com
2. www.avolent.com
3. www.bolero.net
4. www.bottomline.com.
5. www.cash-tech.com
6. www.chase.com
7. www.CheckFree.com
8. www.citicorp.com
9. www.db.com
10. www.dhl.com
11. www.emergis.com
12. http://en.wikipedia.org
13. http://www.exeter.ac.uk/~RDavies/arian/amser/chrono.html—Davies Glyn, & Davies Roy, A *History of Money from Ancient Times to the Present Day*
14. www.harborpayments.com
15. www.hsbcnet.com
16. www.iccwbo.org
17. www.ifxforum.org
18. www.iso20022.org
19. www.mastercard.com
20. www.mddl.org
21. www.metavante.com
22. www.oasis-open.org
23. www.openapplications.org
24. www.oracle.com
25. www.rosettanet.org
26. www.sap.com
27. www.swift.com
28. www.TradeBeam.com
29. www.TradeCard.com
30. www.twiststandards.org
31. www.uncitral.org
32. www.ups.com
33. www.usbank.com/cgi_w/cfm/commercial_business/products_ and_services/corp_payment/powertrack.cfm

34. www.usdoj.gov/criminal/cybercrime/cccases.html
35. www.visa.com
36. www.xign.com
37. Lawson John, *History of Banking*
38. Christopher Martin, *Logistics and Supply Chain Management*
39. UCP 500
40. URC 522
41. ISP 98

Index